Iterate

Iterate

Ten Lessons in Design and Failure

John Sharp and Colleen Macklin
illustrations by Steven Davis with Yu Jen Chen
diagrams by Tuba Ozkan and Carla Molins Pitarch

The MIT Press
Cambridge, Massachusetts
London, England

This book was set in ITC Stone Sans Std and ITC Stone Serif Std by Toppan Best-set Premedia Limited. Printed and bound in the United States of America.

Library of Congress Cataloging-in-Publication Data

Names: Sharp, John, 1967- author. | Macklin, Colleen, author.
Title: Iterate : ten lessons in design and failure / John Sharp and Colleen Macklin ; illustrated by Steven Davis and Yu Jen Chen ; drawings by Tuba Ozkan and Carla Molins Pitarch.
Description: Cambridge, MA : The MIT Press, 2019. | Includes bibliographical references and index.
Identifiers: LCCN 2018028590 | ISBN 9780262039635 (hardcover : alk. paper)
Subjects: LCSH: Design--Psychological aspects. | Design--Technique. | Failure (Psychology)
Classification: LCC NK1520 .S47 2019 | DDC 745.4--dc23 LC record available at https://lccn.loc.gov/2018028590

10 9 8 7 6 5 4 3 2 1

Contents

Acknowledgments

This project couldn't have happened without a bewilderingly large group of people. For starters, we must thank the subjects of our case studies in the book and in our video series: Jad Abumrad and Robert Krulwich, Amelia Brodka, Wylie Dufresne, Cas Holman, Miranda July, Alexis Lloyd, Matthew Maloney, Andy Milne, Nathalie Pozzi and Eric Zimmerman, Allison Tauziet, and Baratunde Thurston. We'll be a little cheesy and admit we've been inspired by all of you.

Over the last five years, we had the pleasure of working with a group of research assistants from the MFA Design and Technology program at Parsons School of Design at The New School. Gabrielle Patacsil served as producer for the initial case study interviews and the related video series. Shuangshuang Huo shot and edited most of the videos, with the remainder shot and edited by Kabeer. Angelica Jang created the imagery and animations used on the website and in the videos. Miyeon Kim created animations for one of our videos, and helped us brainstorm approaches to the diagrams and illustrations for the book. Aakanksha Aggarwal, Ryan Best, Yu Jen Chen, Connie Chu, Clare Churchouse, Mario Dcunha, Barsha Maharjan, Jim Pinkenberg, Carla Molins Pitarch, Aucher Serr, Yanbin Song, and Nicolas Stark participated in a "diagram jam" to help us think through visualizing creative practice. Steven Davis created the illustrations with the input of Yu Jen Chen, while Tuba Ozkan and Carla Molins Pitarch developed and produced the diagrams included in the book.

The involvement of these great people, as well as travel funding, came courtesy of support from The New School Provost's Office Faculty Research Fund; the Parsons Dean of Faculty Research Assistant program; and the Parsons School of Art, Media, and Technology Research, Scholarship and Creative Practice Fund.

Of course there are all the people that helped turn our ideas and research into this book: Doug Sery, who ushered us through the process of becoming MIT Press authors; Noah J. Springer, who kept us on track throughout the writing process; and Matthew Abbate and Paula Woolley, whose careful attention during the editing process cleaned our manuscript up quite nicely.

Last, but never least, we must thank Renee and Nancy, our respective partners in crime, fun, and love.

Colleen and John
Brooklyn, Spring 2018

Preface

If you've ever played a game, it is likely that you've experienced failure. Lots of it. That's how games work—we fail our way toward understanding through play. At some point, likely after a few failed attempts, we learn that the shiny red stuff is lava, those mushroom creatures should be jumped over (or on), and the upper pinball flippers are indeed useful in avoiding the dreaded central gutter. Games are an alternate universe where failure is simply part of the fun.

In our capacity as game designers, we—Colleen and John, the authors of this book—think about failure a lot, in no small part because game design is often about making failure fun. Perhaps because this failure inversion involves a kind of alchemy, game design is *hard*, and filled with all sorts of failures itself: crises of creativity, false starts in finding a path to fun, tensions between design goals and player expectations. Our main tool for working with all this failure? Iteration, or the cyclical process of conceptualizing, prototyping, playtesting, and evaluating a game's design.

As you might have already guessed from the title of this book, we're big fans of iteration.

≈

Though we are currently both game designers, our creative practices have been diverse. Over the years, one or both of us have also worked in graphic design, web design and development, photography, DJing, VJing, advertising, and printmaking. Throughout it all, we've been fortunate to learn from each of the communities of practice we've worked within. And in our own work and in others', we have seen again and again how the cyclical nature of iteration is used to make sense of, learn from, and overcome the inevitable presence of failure.

We are also educators. Collectively, we've taught for over 40 years in university art and design programs (currently we both teach at Parsons School of Design in New York City). As we teach, there are two ever-present challenges we face: assisting students in the development of an effective creative process, and helping students learn to accept failure as an inevitable, even welcome aspect of creative practice. Really, these are one and the same—failure is ever-present in creative practice, so any useful approach to making things has to account for failure. We help our students learn how to conceptualize the things they want to create; how to develop and employ craft skills to give form to their ideas; how to use research to expand and bring rigor to their ideas; how to receive (and give) constructive criticism on their work and process; and finally, how to understand themselves and others better through everything they see, feel, and learn as they work.

In other words: We teach creativity.

≈

In looking at the broad domain of creativity, we draw as much on our experiences as art school professors as on our own creative practice and the practices of our friends and colleagues. Over the years, we've collected practice-based examples from the arts, design, science, and any other field that we could use in our classrooms and in our own work. It was a short step from there to decide we wanted to share what we've learned with others. And thus this book, and our accompanying video series, found at http://www.iterateproject.com.

A Focus on Failure

Looking through research journals like *Design Studies* and *Creativity Research Journal*, we can find innumerable approaches to understanding creativity. Some are qualitative in nature, others quantitative. Many bring to bear scientific methods that strive to capture the essence of something ineffable—creativity. Shifting over to popular media, we can find an endless supply of breathless examples of how a practitioner created a particular work of art, wrote a critically lauded musical, or "disrupted" an entire industry. Invariably, these stories boil down to humble-brag variations on "my muse showed me the way," or "my genius flowed out of me (shrug emoji)." Ultimately all of these approaches end up making creativity feel out of reach to mere mortals like ourselves. Most of these discussions of creativity, particularly in the fields of design and engineering, focus on two goals: problem solving and innovation. Both are closely associated with invention and the commercial instrumentalization of creativity. In creative practice, both lead to particular intentions and desires, and often boil down to institutionalized processes that leave little space for other motivations and outcomes. And ultimately, they privilege success over anything else.

We decided early in our research on creative practice that instead of looking at success or problem solving, we would focus on failure and its relationship to iteration. This decision comes from our own experience as game designers and educators, where failure is a present and often productive partner in the creative process. But more generally, we want to understand how iteration transforms failure in creative practice. We imagine creativity as an engine that takes its practitioner to many different "places," whether it's different intentions they bring to their practice, the processes they develop, or the outcomes that result. The reason we iterate is to incorporate failure into the process and use it to the advantage of the end result, learning from it and seeing things that we might not have found without trying and testing our ideas. More than a setback, failure is the fuel to keep the iteration engine running. In the words of game designer Nick Fortugno, "Prototyping is experimentation, and experiments don't fail when they have results—the experiment works even when it proves your theory wrong."[1] The bottom line within iterative processes: Failure is success. It's not always the kind of success we like to celebrate, but nonetheless failure is the likely outcome of almost any experiment, and therefore a positive outcome.

How This Book Works

This book is divided into three sections: Creativity, Failure, and Iteration; Ten Perspectives; and Failing Better.

Section I: Creativity, Failure, and Iteration attempts to synthesize the research on each of these three subjects through our perspective on creative practice framed by the relationships between creativity, failure, and iteration. The culmination of this section is our identification of the four components of creative practice: intention, outcome, process, and evaluation.

Chapter 1, Creativity, establishes our definition of creativity: the process by which an individual or group intentionally produces an outcome that is appropriate, aesthetic, and authentic to its context and community.

The second chapter, Failure, looks closely at this often maligned phenomenon to help us understand the reasons we fail, and why we don't always want to admit to it; the relationships between being wrong, making mistakes, and failure; the processes used to analyze and learn from failure; and ultimately, how to "fail better."

Chapter 3, Iteration, establishes a baseline understanding of the iterative process: Given a particular intention, iteration is a cyclical process used to reach a desired outcome through a series of successive attempts. The chapter also identifies four components of iterative practice: The process begins with an intention from which emerges a process that leads to an outcome. This outcome is evaluated, providing the necessary information to begin another loop of the cycle. This cycle repeats until the intention and outcome match as closely as they can (or until time or resources run out).

The fourth and final chapter in this section, Ten Perspectives on Iteration, explores one of the primary findings in our interviews and research: No two iterative processes look alike. We present a framework in which we consider five different points of emphasis within iterative creative practice, each of which we present as a continuum—context, intentions, processes, evaluation, and outcomes. To emphasize that there's no single way to iterate, we introduce two perspectives on each of the five continua: material and reflective contexts, targeted and exploratory intentions, methodological and improvisational processes, internal and external evaluation, and convergent and divergent outcomes.

The first section is fairly dense, contains quite a bit of secondary research, and is, for lack of a better word, academic. To keep things grounded, we employ plenty of illustrations, examples, and anecdotes about cupcakes, yard sale posters, and attempts to draw cows.

Section II: Ten Perspectives is the heart of this book: ten case studies featuring a wide array of creative practices organized around and elucidating the framework developed in chapter 4. We cast a wide net in the selection of our case studies: a winemaker, a stop-motion animator, radio journalists, a chef, an architect, a game design duo, a jazz musician, a professional skateboarder, a comedian, a toymaker, and an artist. Our hope with these examples is to show how a variety of creative practitioners confront, create, celebrate, overcome, and otherwise learn from failure, each in their own, very different way. Each practitioner begins with different intentions; employs different processes; uses different methods for evaluating their work; seeks different outcomes from their efforts; and works with different tools, timescales, collaborators, and contexts. However, despite their differences, they all have something in common: They all iterate.

Section III: Failing Better returns to the start. We look at some of the skills and considerations necessary to embrace failure in creativity, revisiting ideas about creativity, failure, and how we become reflective practitioners who can work with, not against, failure.

Finally, in the postscript, we reflect on the intentions, process, outcomes, and evaluation of this project, including the failures we encountered along the way. Consider this the afterword to the years we have spent on this book and its companion interview series.

≈

If our experiences as designers and educators have taught us anything, it's that there's no silver bullet methodology for creative practice. To that end, this book strives to go beyond surface understandings and perceptions about creativity and its relationship to failure by looking closely at a variety of iterative practices. At the same time, we're cautious about reductive "scientism,"[2] or what design scholar Nigel Cross might call "design science,"[3] in which creativity is distilled to a rote process, and failure is just a puzzle solved if you know the correct answer. Ultimately, creative practitioners find their way through years of trial and error—landing on a process that works for them. Each of the methods described in the case studies is different, and certainly each works for the practitioners employing it.

In the research and writing of this book, we've drawn on a wide range of disciplines—psychology, design research, creativity studies, anthropology, business management, art and design theory, philosophy, art and design practices, literature, education theory, literary criticism, and engineering, among others. We've combined our experiences and research with existing studies into creative practice to create something closer to an anthropological study than a how-to manual, and more design ethnography than design science. As we interviewed different practitioners over the years, we developed our own theories about the relationship between creativity, failure, and the iterative process, in an effort to help you, the reader, turn them into something useful for your own practice, whatever it might be.

In looking across diverse fields to find the ways creative practitioners iterate, we are not assuming that by adapting a skateboarder's process someone will be able to skate well; or by understanding the ways a chef approaches menu development, a novice cook will be able to invent delicious and unique recipes with ease (let alone successfully run a restaurant). Instead, we hope to broaden the ways we think about creativity and failure and the role iteration plays in creative practice. Plus, it's just nice to step outside of our practice-based bubbles sometimes and see how others do things.

While this book is written from the perspective of two designers and art school professors, it's not meant to be a book only for other designers or for art school students and faculty. Instead, we're looking at how the iterative process serves as a useful tool for confronting, embracing, and learning from failure—useful skills for everyone. We focus on creative practitioners in this book, but you needn't be a creative practitioner to benefit from the ideas explored here. Iteration is a tried-and-true way to mitigate failure across a variety of different problem sets and pursuits. We hope this book provides a more human-scale measure of failure and success; and however you use this book, from whatever field or set of problems you are looking to tackle, we hope that you find the approaches to iteration helpful in developing a more productive relationship with failure.

In other words, fail better.

Section I Creativity, Failure, and Iteration

Ever tried. Ever failed. No matter. Try Again. Fail again. Fail better.[1]

Samuel Beckett reminds us that creative practice is a sequence of attempts that more often than not result in one failure after another. At first glance, this may seem nihilistic—Why try at all if you know you're going to fail? To our eyes, Beckett suggests an iterative way of looking at the world—cycles of trying, failing, trying and failing again, over and over, each time hopefully emerging a little wiser than the last. Beckett offers an honest, healthy perspective: We're going to get it wrong (a lot), but no matter, don't give up, just try to do a little better next time.

Most creative projects emerge from film scraps on the cutting room floor, waste baskets overflowing with crumpled paper, and abandoned prototypes. Even though these failed experiments are swept out of view once the work is complete, creative practitioners all know they exist, and that they were an integral part of the process. That's because you can't separate creativity from failure. Even across a career, each finished work provides lessons for the next, so long as one approaches their practice with an iterative mindset. This is the focus of this first section of the book: exploring the synergistic relationship between creativity, failure, and iteration.

1 Creativity

Looking Closer at Creativity

"Creativity" is a fancy-sounding word with a pretty simple meaning: the act of creating. However, in the West, prior to the Renaissance, creation—or *creatio*, to use the contemporary Latin term—was a strictly divine act, not one for mere mortals. In fact, in the Middle Ages, it would have been blasphemous to say that one was creative—that was God's domain. These days, to be creative is to be human—from the creation of a work of fine art to the invention of a new cupcake flavor, and from Danger Mouse's *Gray Album* (a mash-up of the Beatles' White Album and Jay-Z's *Black Album*) to a well-timed joke lightening up a tense moment. Creativity happens at all scales.

Psychologist James C. Kaufman organizes creativity into what he calls the "four C's": big-C creativity, little-C creativity, mini-C creativity, and pro-C creativity.[1] **Big-C creativity** describes the work of people like the writer Mary Shelley, the boxer Muhammad Ali, the artist Pablo Picasso, and the singer Beyoncé. They are masters of their craft, and set a very high bar that few can reach. **Little-C creativity** is the everyday, run-of-the-mill creativity we all perform, recognizing the minor triumphs of life that emerge from creative thinking and problem solving, but that don't rise to the level of something necessarily applause-worthy—improvising on a recipe when you are short an ingredient or two; creating a quick napkin sketch to help a friend understand an elusive concept; tying your shoes in the dark while your dog nips at the laces or managing to arrive at work on time despite cascading delays and obstacles along the way. The third category, **mini-C creativity**, relates to the progress and insights made within learning contexts—picking up a new technique in sight drawing; connecting the dots between a chemistry lesson and the tingle of a sip of soda; a child telling a fantastic tale of the goings-on in their pillow fort. Finally, there is **pro-C creativity**, the category for professional or otherwise skilled creative practitioners who have not reached the ranks of the big-C immortals.

The big-C creatives are outliers, providing us with models about as useful as the *South Park* formula for a successful business: "Phase one: underpants. Phase two: ??. Phase three: profit!!!"[2] Little-C and mini-C creativity are important parts of creative practice; they are the basic building blocks of creativity, and where a lot of the details of big-C and pro-C creative practice happen. Pro-C creativity is where the creative rubber hits the road, so to speak, and where we focus our attention in this book.

A lot of people gather under the pro-C banner; to barely scratch the surface: painters, poets, graphic designers, architects, actors, athletes, musicians, novelists, filmmakers, furniture designers, chefs, comedians, and cartoonists. Clearly, there are a lot of activities, creations, and intentions grouped under the broad category of creativity. But what does it mean to be creative? Rather than making value judgments about whether someone is creative or not, we'd rather home in on how creativity happens.

Creative vs. … Not Creative?

The modern study of creativity began in 1950 with Joy Paul Guilford's opening remarks at the annual American Psychological Association convention. He challenged attendees to pay more attention to creativity, a subject ripe for exploration given the challenges of post-World War II recovery, the Cold War, and the space race. Creativity was "in."[3]

In his talk, Guilford identified four characteristics found in creative people: fluency, flexibility, originality, and elaboration.[4] **Fluency** is a facility and capacity for developing ideas appropriate to a context or problem, while **flexibility** indicates breadth in the kinds of ideas an individual could generate for a wide range of situations. **Originality** highlights the capability to come up with unexpected and new ideas, and **elaboration** is the skill to act upon and develop those ideas into something material and meaningful.

To put these four characteristics in context, let's consider a graphic designer tasked with creating a business card for their own design firm. This being a pretty basic communication design challenge, we can presume this

designer has **fluency**—they have the basic typography and layout skills, they've seen a lot of business cards, they know the basics of the form, they know that each industry has different expectations for how information is presented, and more than likely, they have created business cards before. Our graphic designer should also have the **flexibility** necessary to sketch out four or five ideas that explore different styles, professional tones, and information hierarchies. These sketches represent some real **originality**—a few follow the traditional horizontal layout, some try out a less conventional arrangement of the expected elements, some closely follow the company's visual branding, and some push on these boundaries. After feedback from everyone in the company, our designer has the ability to **elaborate** on the initial sketches, and after a couple more rounds of mock-ups, lands upon a design everyone is excited about.

Our business card designer is within the boundaries of most conceptions of creativity. But what about someone working outside of the confines of recognized creative contexts?

Consider someone designing a poster for a yard sale. In preparation for the project, they spend some time looking at yard sale signs around the neighborhood, and taking mental notes on the typical information included. Back at home, they grab a piece of paper and doodle a quick layout for the poster based on the examples they saw. They then open up software on their computer, and proceed to create the poster. Once it is complete, they print it out, make sure there aren't any obvious mistakes, and then run off copies to put up around the neighborhood.

Was this a creative act? Or just someone making a yard sale poster? Kaufman, whose four "C's" of creativity we discussed earlier, helps answer

this question by providing a two-part definition of creativity (emphasis ours): "First, creativity must represent something different, new, or **innovative**. … It isn't enough to just be different—creativity must also be **appropriate** to the task at hand."[5]

Our graphic designer and their business cards likely fit this definition, but unless our designer of the yard sale poster happened to bring an unexpected flair to the project, they would not meet Kaufman's criteria for innovation, even if the poster was appropriate for the task.

Let's look more closely at these two aspects of creativity, appropriateness and innovation. A creative act is **appropriate** if it is deemed valuable by its community—the person to whom the witty phrase was spoken, the people enjoying the well-made meal, the community of fans appreciative of the expansion of a favorite character's role in a television series. In other words, appropriate creative acts result in things that make sense for their time, place, and community. Similar ideas show up in other appraisals of creativity. Engineer David Cropley and educational psychologist Arthur Cropley suggest relevance and effectiveness are important criteria,[6] both of which correspond with being appropriate. Interaction designer Christoph Bartneck suggests that design seeks effectiveness, reliability, and efficiency[7]—all also related to appropriateness. Two thousand years earlier, Vitruvius's *firmitas*, *utilitas*, *venustas* (well-made, useful, and beautiful) encapsulate and expand upon both Bartneck's and the Cropleys' criteria, giving us a well-rounded conception of Kaufman's appropriate creative practice. Appropriateness makes a lot of sense as a criterion for appraising creativity. According to this measure, our business card designer and our yard sale poster designer both remain in the creative camp.

Then there is Kaufman's other term, **innovative**. We expect the fruits of creativity—the things creative practitioners make—to be new and unfamiliar, and therefore to open up new potentials—experiential, economic, intellectual, and otherwise. From a financial perspective, innovation points toward new markets and new consumer demand, both of which lead to new revenue streams. While these are relevant, they are not the be-all and end-all values for creativity. If we were to really scrutinize our enterprising business card designer from this vantage, we'd realize they aren't much more innovative than the yard sale poster designer. Maybe there were a few nice touches, but isn't a business card still just a business card? Innovation sets a really high bar, one most of us seldom make it over.

Cognitive psychologist Robert W. Weisberg provides a helpful term in untying the knot we've gotten ourselves into through our collective focus on innovation: intention.[8] What did the creative practitioner set out to do? What goals did they set for themselves? For Weisberg, **intention** is an important factor in the context of innovation: If the creator hadn't set out to produce the novel aspects of the work, should they be viewed as creative in all the ways we've already discussed? Intention helps us ground innovation in the context of appropriate: Was the innovative aspect of the work within the practitioner's intentions? And did that lead to something appropriate for the context and community?

Psychologist and poet Anatoliy V. Kharkhurin's "four-criterion construct of creativity" expands upon the intentional and the appropriate by adding the qualities of aesthetic and authentic.[9] The **aesthetic** criterion evaluates the intentions of a work, and the ways in which those intentions are made material in the work itself. What was the creative practitioner trying to do? What were their goals for the work? How did these connect to the decisions and choices made in creating the work? Kharkhurin uses the artist Joseph Beuys as an example. Beuys explored the symbolic and expressive potential of unexpected artistic materials, including felt, fat, newsprint, and other atypical objects. Beuys created a visual and material language that combined to create an idiosyncratic form of beauty, and to convey an essential truth.

Essential truths come into play with Kharkhurin's criterion of **authenticity**: There should be an honesty to the creative process and the things it produces. In other words, the means by which people create and the things that they produce should be authentic to who they are, to their goals, to the contexts in which they are produced and used, and to the people who come in contact with and use them. As Kharkhurin conceives of authenticity, a creative practitioner develops their voice, and finds their truth over time by practicing their craft. We embrace Kharkhurin's more open evaluative system for creativity, as it acknowledges values beyond innovation and newness, and opens up creative practice to have more abstract, immaterial, and inward-facing criteria that allow for intentions beyond problem solving and usefulness.

Our business card designer has aesthetic intentions (as well as professional and financial ones, among others) to produce an authentic business card template that would stand out among the din of business cards.

Our yard sale poster designer, on the other hand, has more utilitarian intentions—getting people to show up at their yard sale and spend money, with little to no consideration of other values. To fulfill their task, the business card designer needed to create a product that mixed innovation and utility, while the yard sale poster designer only needed to make a sign with the appropriate text.

Intention, aesthetic, and authenticity provide some insight into the motivations of both designers, but the question of whether both processes are creative is still not fully resolved. Psychologist Teresa Amabile provides a helpful litmus test: determining whether the process for creating something is algorithmic or heuristic.[10] To explain these terms, Amabile uses baking as an example: Someone baking a cake from a recipe is conducting an **algorithmic** task, or following well-known steps to achieve an outcome. Someone trying to invent a new kind of cake is performing a **heuristic** task by using prior knowledge and experience as tools for addressing the task in

ALGORITHMIC   HEURISTIC

the absence of a step-by-step process. The difference here is the degree to which the process is not just rote, well-established, and well-known (algorithmic) but leads to learning something new or creating something unexpected (heuristic).

A good analogy for understanding the differences between algorithmic and heuristic acts is to think of connect-the-dots drawing versus freehand drawing. Two people stand before a cow in a field. Both decide the cow is worth commemorating in a drawing. One person pulls out a pad and sketches the cow using sight-drawing methods. The other happens to have a connect-the-dots book of farm animals, and so flips to the page of the cow, and starts carefully creating lines from dot to dot. The dot connector executes an algorithmic task, while the freehand illustrator carries out a heuristic task.

Finally, we have a point of distinction we can draw between our business card designer and our yard sale poster designer. Though both put time and energy into their work, the poster designer was more or less carrying out an algorithmic task. And our business card designer? Even if designing a business card is as close to a "garden-variety"[11] task as a professional communication designer can get, they treated the assignment as a heuristic task, as they had to juggle a number of considerations, not the least of which was coming up with a design that would represent their company proudly. The business card designer had the intention to create an aesthetically innovative yet relatable design that was authentic to their design firm, and also to their industry peers, their clients, and their prospective clients.

We can now propose our definition of creativity:

Creativity is the process by which an individual or group intentionally produces an outcome that is appropriate, aesthetic, and authentic to its context and community.

Let's consider our business card designer. As a graphic designer, they used a process recognized by their field to produce good work. The output of this process was a business card design that operates within the conventions of the business card form—appropriate to the task at hand, in other words. At the same time, the business card design contributes to the field of communication design by innovating within the form—perhaps the business card design places emphasis on the email address and Instagram account instead of the traditional emphasis on the person's name and phone number, an innovation to keep business cards relevant in the age of social media. The choice of paper, typeface, color, and composition bring aesthetic properties of the business card form into play in a way that is authentic to the designer, the firm for which they work, and the communities within which the firm does business. From this vantage, creativity doesn't have to be groundbreaking, it just has to meet the needs of the task and fit the expectations of the community.

On the other hand, we have our yard sale poster designer. They followed a process—one that was driven more by efficiency than by anything else. Instead of having their own authentic aesthetic goals, they sought to emulate the form of yard sale posters they had seen before. And while the output was appropriate, it was not necessarily authentic or aesthetic, nor did it contribute to the larger field of yard sale poster design. This is not to say that our yard sale poster designer failed at their goal. Perhaps they succeeded in drawing people's attention and bringing buyers to the sale, but, compared with our business card designer, the process they used isn't one we could call creative.

It's a Process

At the start of her influential book *The Social Psychology of Creativity*, Teresa Amabile raises a basic but still very important question: "How is creative performance different from ordinary performance?"[12] The opposing terms— "creative" and "ordinary"—are adjectives of a shared noun: "performance." Amabile views creativity not as a capacity or innate characteristic, but as a process performed within a given context. This is more comfortable territory, as it moves away from value judgments on the person and the things they make, and toward the methods they employ and the ways their work is appropriate to its context. In this book, we see creativity as a process, not a characteristic or a capacity—an idea reflected in the beginning of our definition, "creativity is the *process* ..."

Once we shift to a performance/process model of creativity, the question shifts from "What is creative?" to "How does creative performance happen?" Psychologist John B. Watson frames the questions well: "How do we ever get new verbal creations such as a poem or a brilliant essay? The answer is that we get them by manipulating words, shifting them about until a new pattern is hit upon."[13] Watson makes clear that

creativity is a transformative process that takes effort, and is not borne of innate genius.

More than two decades before Guilford's 1950 provocation to the American Psychological Association, the social psychologist Graham Wallas proposed a four-stage process for creativity: preparation, incubation, illumination, and verification.[14] During the **preparation** phase, the practitioner considers their intentions for the creative act. This might be tackling a thorny engineering problem, trying to theorize about the origins of the universe, capturing a particular emotion in a painting, or writing a eulogy for a recently departed friend. This leads to the **incubation** phase, where the practitioner gestates on the task. Incubation produces **illumination**— the path forward, the way (or ways) to accomplish the task. It is during this phase that the thing is produced. Finally, **verification** evaluates and reflects on the work, allowing the creative practitioner to loop back through the process until they finish the project. For Wallas, the movement through these phases is fluid, and often overlapping:

In the daily stream of thought these four different stages constantly overlap each other as we explore different problems. An economist reading a Blue Book, a physiologist watching an experiment, or a business man going through his morning's letters, may at the same time be "incubating" on a problem which he proposed to himself a few days ago, be accumulating knowledge in "preparation" for a second problem, and be "verifying" his conclusions on a third problem. Even in exploring the same problem, the mind may be unconsciously incubating on one aspect of it, while it is consciously employed in preparing for or verifying another aspect.[15]

What makes our business card designer creative, then, is not that they have a job title denoting creativity, but that they use a process recognized by graphic designers to generate successful results. Our yard sale poster designer likewise followed a process, though they ended their process before they arrived at a creative outcome. They failed to do the extra work to hit upon a new pattern, as Watson describes.

As we will see, there is no one single process, just as there is no single motivation for creativity. And within a given field, there is seldom a single accepted path—even for those with very structured processes. Creativity doesn't happen in a vacuum—it happens within shifting contexts, and practitioners change too. As they gain experience, they learn more, and become increasingly aware of their own process.

Becoming a Reflective Practitioner

We now have basic principles for identifying creativity as a process instead of a capacity or characteristic. The term "creative practitioner" starts to make more sense in this light—creative practitioners are people who practice creativity. But how do people become creative practitioners? The short answer is that they learn to develop a clear sense of their creative goals, of the process and craft skills needed to achieve those goals, and an awareness of their creative limitations and strengths. In other words, they become **reflective practitioners**.

Let's unpack the idea of reflective practitioner starting with the "practitioner" half of the phrase. As you've likely noticed, we use the term "creative practice" a lot. The phrase is derived from a couple of sources: Pierre Bourdieu's practice theory, but also a general conception of creativity as a field and domain—graphic design, contemporary art, game design, and so on.[16] Bourdieu's **practice theory** is composed of five elements developed over the course of twenty years: capital, habitus, agents, the field, and field works. **Capital** are the economic, social, cultural, and prestige (what Bourdieu called "symbolic") resources that allow someone to participate in a practice. **Habitus** speaks to the "muscles" or skills someone develops to help them carry out their practice. **Agents** are the people who interact with the practitioner and, in the process, empower or thwart the practitioner's work. The **field** is the community of practice within which one works.

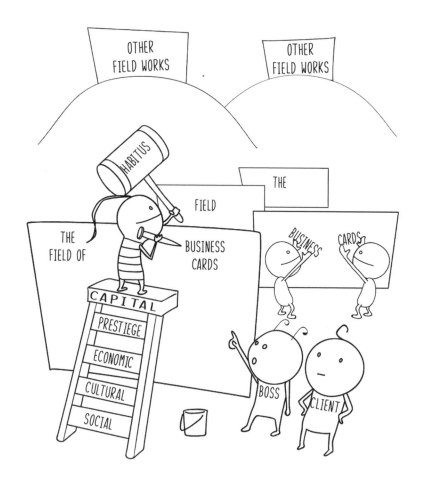

Finally, the **field works** are the end results created by the field that establish the standard and expectations for what that field creates.

Our business card designer clearly operates within Bourdieu's conception of a practice: They work within the field of communication design, and with a group of fellow agents at their design firm. The firm has the capital to operate, in no small part based on the prestige and cultural capital that emerges from their visual identity—including those business cards they designed for the company. The designer has the habitus to do the job, including the base knowledge of the field from which they can derive inspiration as well as lessons of what to do and what not to do. In other words: Our business card designer is indeed conducting a practice—in this case, a creative practice—that is enabled by their reflective approach to design.

And the term "reflective"? This is where the philosopher and urban planner Donald Schön comes into the picture. Schön wanted to better understand what enabled high-performing professionals to excel.[17] Through his study, as presented in *The Reflective Practitioner*, he identified **reflection** as a critical component of creative practice. By this, Schön meant the process by which people considered what they were doing by seeking patterns in prior experience and knowledge, and applying these to the task at hand. More importantly, reflection allows for a constructively critical assessment of one's performance and ideas. And so to become an effective creative practitioner, one first has to become a reflective practitioner.

Schön identified two key forms of reflection: reflection-in-action, and reflection-on-action. **Reflection-in-action** is aptly named, as it connects to the process by which practitioners consider and learn from their work as it is happening. This is the stream-of-consciousness consideration and decision making that happens while someone is conducting a task; more colloquially, this is "thinking on your feet." Reflection-in-action is informed by **knowledge-in-action**, or the application of prior knowledge to inform a decision. The key to knowledge-in-action is that the practitioner has internalized the knowledge to the point that it becomes almost instinctual, and is therefore easily accessed and acted upon.

Schön's other term, **reflection-on-action**, refers to the analysis or consideration that happens after the creative act. This is a form of evaluation in which the practitioner looks back on the goals they had hoped to accomplish, the means by which they went about it, and the outcome that was produced. Together, reflection-in-action, knowledge-in-action,

and reflection-on-action are essential skills for creative practitioners. These skills allow us to grow, and to feel progress in the mastery of our craft.

Consider the skateboarder in the illustration above. They want to learn a new trick, maybe a kickflip. To start learning the trick, they gather knowledge about how it is done, probably from watching others perform it in person and in videos and photos. Using this baseline knowledge, they start trying to perform the trick themselves. The more they try the trick, the more knowledge they gain (so long as they are reflecting on all the above). They are now building knowledge-in-action, which allows them to apply their knowledge-in-action to make adjustments mid-trick via reflection-in-action. After trying the trick a few times, and achieving varying levels of success, they think about their technique, consult other skaters, or watch skating videos—in other words, reflection-on-action.

The ability to produce creative works is dependent on the experience of having done so before. This, of course, creates an interminable chicken-and-egg problem for creative practice—one cannot be a true reflective practitioner until one has already been in the practice of creating. One of the better explanations of how to become a reflective practitioner comes from Scott McCloud's *Understanding Comics*, a treatise on comic books delivered in comic book form. The chapter called "The Six Steps" insightfully breaks down the path creative practitioners follow to master their crafts.[18] Ultimately, to fully realize a novel, useful, aesthetic, and authentic creative practice, people must have something to say—or, as McCloud puts it, have an **idea** or **purpose** they hope to convey. This is done by intimately knowing the **form**—whether it be comics, games, poetry, or cooking—in which they want to express this idea. Mastering a particular **idiom**, or a style or language within that form, is necessary to realize their vision. And to really know the ins and outs of an idiom, practitioners need to know the **structure** of their medium. Without **craft**, or a knowledge of making, practitioners are left with nothing but unrealized ideas. And finally, mastery of the **surface** of the form is essential, as this is the point of contact with the audience, and the means by which the audience interacts with and ultimately experiences the ideas the practitioners hope to convey.

McCloud theorizes the process by which our business card designer came to master their medium to the point where they could express ideas fluently within it. It begins at the surface and ends at the purpose. The surface is where audiences come in contact with things. For example, someone reads comic books by focusing on the visuals; someone watches films by looking at sequenced images and listening to dialogue, environmental sounds, and a musical score. The more interested our designer became in their medium, the more they started looking under the hood at the craft required to create business cards. From there, our designer began to see patterns in how works in the medium were organized. They started to see subtle differences in the ways business card designers express themselves in the medium. They started to understand why a particular typeface or composition was chosen to express or deliver the things the creator wanted to share. And finally, our business card designer understood how to convey specific messages through their medium. At last, our business card designer became a reflective practitioner.

It Takes a Community of Practice

McCloud's six steps, presented in reverse above, provide a path to a fully realized creative practitioner, but they don't really include a map to get from point A (surface) to point B (purpose). So how does one advance from fan to reflective practitioner?

Despite our culture's love of the myth of the lone genius, few creative practitioners operate in total isolation. Consider our business card designer again: They weren't working in a vacuum—they had co-workers whose opinions informed the design, they had their design training and mentoring that shaped their craft skills but also their ideas about excellence in business card design, they used tools created by others that enabled their design. So, yes, our business card designer did much of the work, but they were not alone. They were part of a **community of practice**. Participation in a community of practice is one of the primary ways we learn the craft of a medium; it's where we learn process, and where we come to understand what is and is not valued in the creative output of our field.

The term "community of practice" originates with anthropologist Jean Lave and educational theorist Etienne Wenger's explorations of how learning happens within communities organized around particular crafts and professions.[19] Lave and Wenger coined the term to refer to the configurations of people connected through a particular field of work, or a practice. A community of practice is made up of people with varying levels of expertise and experience, from masters to newbies just entering the field. Communities of practice are locations for **situated learning**, or learning that happens in the same place where it is put into practice. Among the things Lave and Wenger came to realize about communities of practice was that learning is seldom a top-down affair. Instead, it often emerges in lateral peer-to-peer situations, from individual efforts later evaluated by other community members, and through many other informal channels outside traditional understandings of knowledge sharing and acquisition.

Wenger later expanded on the concept of communities of practice by categorizing three ways in which community members engage with one another: mutual engagement, joint enterprise, and shared enterprise.[20] **Mutual engagement** describes how practitioners within the community talk to one another, when and where they interact, what they do alone, and what they do in groups. **Joint enterprise** is what everyone in the community understands to be their common purpose and goals. In other words, joint enterprise is the value-based glue that holds everyone together, establishing what the community values about their craft, the artifacts they create, and even what they value about the community itself. Finally, a **shared repertoire** is the set of resources produced and enjoyed by members of the community that help it and its members sustain the group and prosper. This repertoire can include things like the shared use of tools, spaces, and research materials; the ways the community approaches and encourages peer learning; and even the symbolic benefits of community membership in society at large.

Coming back to our business card and yard sale poster designers, we can again tease out some of the things that separate the two. For one, the business card designer is operating within a community of practice through the joint enterprise of their design firm. The designers in the firm engage with

one another within the confines of their office, but also through the cultural standards they have developed—everyone works from ten until seven, seated at shared work tables using laptops, and they use a shared process for moving from ideas to sketches to prototypes to finished projects. And the joint enterprise of the firm—designing awe-inspiring business cards—establishes a shared repertoire, creating clear expectations of the quality required, the processes by which the company creates, critiques, and ultimately completes projects. Part of this shared repertoire is a robust library of business card samples, design books, type specimen books, and an in-house typeface design team.

And our yard sale poster designer? They were largely operating alone, doing something out of the ordinary of their typical day, without what we would consider a community of practice to provide support.

We now have all the pieces needed to become a reflective practitioner. Creative practitioners become reflective practitioners by learning about their community's joint enterprise and participating in their shared repertoire, both of which are given form by the structures of their mutual engagement.

It Ain't Easy

As education scholar and philosopher Gloria Dall'Alba notes, reflective practices are developed by negotiating the ambiguities creative practitioners encounter along the way. These encounters allow the development of knowledge that is put into practice, which in turn expands, refutes, and otherwise informs existing knowledge.[21] It's not always a smooth journey; as Dall'Alba and her collaborators make clear, "The process of becoming professionals is always open-ended and incomplete."[22] In essence, we are always in the process of becoming more reflective practitioners. Or, as Samuel Beckett sees it, we are, at best, failing better. The author, educator, and social activist bell hooks provides a thoughtful grounding for this continual act of becoming:

The vital link between critical thinking and practical wisdom is the insistence on the interdependent nature of theory and fact coupled with the awareness that knowledge cannot be separated from experience. And ultimately there is the awareness that knowledge rooted in experience shapes what we value and as a consequence how we know what we know as well as how we use what we know.[23]

hooks suggests the key to becoming a reflective practitioner is to learn through our experiences, and to continue learning from and reflecting on our practice regardless of how long we have been doing it or how well-recognized we become. Developing our critical thinking and practical wisdom is a process, just as creativity is a process. And that process involves something that many avoid acknowledging, even when it is omnipresent in creative practice: failure.

2 Failure

Failure Is Not the Opposite of Success

Too often, we see creativity as a binary—either someone succeeds, or they fail. An artist is well known, or they struggle in the shadows of obscurity. A designer's work is genius, or it is mediocre. Even though we know there is more to creativity than these stark extremes, this is how the story has been told for at least five hundred years—from the earliest western art histories regaling the genius of Michelangelo to today's *New York Times Magazine* profiles on the creatively rich and famous. With our expectations based on the likes of painter Georgia O'Keeffe, basketball star Michael Jordan, the Beatles, and architect Zaha Hadid, it is no wonder we're scared of failure—the bar for creative success is set so high, we can't make sense of how to reach it.

Then there are those phoenixes rising from the ashes of failure captured in the mythologies of Edison's ten thousand attempts at the lightbulb and Steve Jobs dropping out of college to found Apple. In these modern fables, failure is the monster conquered on the hero's journey to the pinnacle of creativity. But these stories are part of the problem, as they tell us failure should only be recognized when it leads to the greatest successes, and otherwise should be swept under the rug. To rein in our expectations around success and failure, we return to our definition of creativity from the previous chapter:

Creativity is the process by which an individual or group intentionally produces an outcome that is appropriate, aesthetic, and authentic to its context and community.

Instead of pegging creativity to impossible standards, we suggest more realistic, and ultimately, more useful expectations: making something appropriate (meaning it is useful, in the broadest sense), aesthetic (as guided by individual or community expectations), and authentic (taking into account the wants, needs, and interests of a given community). And if we fail to achieve these more modest intentions? Well, we'll more than likely have generated knowledge, in itself a valuable contribution for our reflective practice. Because failure, when carefully and honestly examined, is how we learn.

Failure as a Strategy

As game designers, we, the authors of this book, spend a lot of time thinking about failure. It should be no surprise, then, that game design has its own literature about failure, most notably Jesper Juul's *The Art of Failure*. One of the more important ideas Juul explores is being able to identify the cause of the failure—understanding why, for instance, the player lost a life, failed to solve a puzzle, or was sent back to the beginning of the level. Was it because the player lacked the skills? Or did the designer make the level too hard? Or was it because something distracted the player's attention? Drawing on attribution theory from social psychology, Juul discusses the three kinds of **failure attribution**: a person, an entity, and the circumstances around the situation. Juul's example is a student receiving a poor grade on a test: "we can decide that this was due to (1) person—personal disposition such as lack of skill, (2) entity—an unfair test, or (3) circumstance—having slept badly, having not studied enough."[1]

Juul created several small games to test how players reacted to failure. He discovered that in gameplay, the best kind of failure—the kind that felt "right" to players—is the failure that we can attribute to our own mistake or lack of skill. This might seem like a paradox, as typically we don't want to take the blame for something that went wrong. But in a game, we learn to be okay with our failures because they give us the opportunity to improve. These are failures that we "own," and that we can do something about next time around. The same holds for creative practice and the process of becoming a reflective practitioner: The best failures are ownable failures— the ones we had agency in bringing about, and therefore can learn from.

Juul also observed that the act of failing forced players to try new strategies, revealing new possibilities, and even aspects of the game world that

they might not have otherwise noticed. Let's say a player is new to poker. They have learned the basic rules—that a full house beats a pair (and all the other hierarchies of hand values), and that they must either ante up or fold when it is their turn. However, as they play, they begin to notice that their chips are diminishing, and that they aren't doing as well as the other players. They play conservatively to stay in the game, and fold with a decent hand—three of a kind. Imagine their surprise when the winner takes the pot with just a pair of threes! The sting of the loss—and their failure— leads to a revelation: They can pretend to have a great hand and if they're the last to fold, they can win. The failure has revealed a new strategy: bluffing.

Failure can also be liberating, allowing us to fly under the radar of expectations and break through into new terrain. This is the discovery that artist Richard DeDomenici made during a fateful attempt to dial a phone with a piano.[2] DeDomenici noticed that when dialing a phone, each number press triggered a corresponding tone. When combined as a sequence of tones, that phone number was called. He wondered if it was possible to dial a phone using other devices to generate tones, and discovered that in some cases, particularly with an electric piano, it was indeed possible. DeDomenici decided to do a stage performance of this parlor trick. Despite his successful tests ahead of the show, he failed to make the phone dial by using the piano during his performance. Much to his surprise, the audience seemed fascinated by his persistence and dogged confidence that such a ridiculous plan could work. This discovery opened a whole new world for his art practice—failure wasn't always bad, and in some cases, provided new ways to perceive the world, and to express oneself.

Queer theory has its own embrace of failure, as explored in *The Queer Art of Failure*, by Judith (also known as Jack) Halberstam. Halberstam articulates how queerness adopts failure as a response to social norms:

Failure allows us to escape the punishing norms that discipline behavior and manage human development with the goal of delivering us from unruly childhoods to orderly and predictable adulthoods. Failure preserves some of the wondrous anarchy of childhood and disturbs the supposedly clean boundaries between adults and children, winners and losers.[3]

In Halberstam's view, failure is an antidote to society's obsession with success, and is a liberating alternative to a formulaic life. Like the failure Juul observes in games and like DeDomenici's revelation, the queer art of failure generates new strategies—taking it a step further by defining new goals that change where we look for success and how we measure it.

Many scholars now believe that such failures have historically been obscured by optimistic slogans and so-called positive thinking, neither of which, according to the report, has had a verifiable effect: Americans' overall failure rate went up nearly 2,350 percent over the past decade, with 1,435,643 instances of failure reported last Sunday alone.

This important breakthrough in creativity research appeared in a very unexpected place: the satirical news site *The Onion*, in an article title

"Failure Now an Option."[4] Despite its facetious intentions, it hit a chord with almost anyone who has ever made something. Failure is more than an option: It is an honest, inevitable, and necessary part of life. It isn't an end, it is a clue. When something fails, it not only tells us what doesn't work, but potentially reveals new paths to "make it work," to borrow Tim Gunn's *Project Runway* mantra. Henry Petroski, the elder statesman of failure studies, puts it well:

Every failure is a revelation of ignorance, an accidental experiment, a found set of data that contains clues that point back to causes and further back to mistakes that might have been made in design, manufacture, and use. Not to follow the trail to its source is to abandon an opportunity to understand better the nature of the technology and our interaction with it.[5]

From this vantage point, failure—so long as it hasn't led to great loss, death, and hardship—is an essential ingredient in learning from doing. It's the quality of failure, and the impetus and persistence to try again, that often determines whether something—whatever it is—will find a place in the world. Indeed, much of culture—from the Mona Lisa to Levi's 501 jeans to the U.S. Constitution—wouldn't have been possible without plenty of failure along the way.

What We Mean When We Talk about Failure

Okay, failure is great and all, but what is it, exactly? In 2001, the artists and writers Tim Etchells and Matthew Goulish created the art project Institute of Failure, a think-tank dedicated to the study and celebration of failure. They generated a list of twenty-three types of failure: accident, mistake, weakness, inability, incorrect method, uselessness, incompatibility, embarrassment, confusion, redundancy, obsolescence, incoherence, unrecognizability, absurdity, invisibility, impermanence, decay, instability, forgettability, tardiness, disappearance, catastrophe, and uncertainty.[6] This unwieldy list makes clear the great range and depth of failure in our world.

We can organize the Institute of Failure's extensive list into three key groups: being wrong, making a mistake, and failing. As journalist Kathryn Schulz explores, **being wrong** stems from holding beliefs that turn out to be false. To be wrong is to come to incorrect conclusions—misinterpreting facts or a situation that leads to the assumption that we're right when we aren't.[7] Examples include providing an incorrect answer to a math problem

because one misremembers a mathematical principle (an error of process), thinking a drive will take fifteen minutes when it will take thirty (an error in estimation), or believing the earth is flat (an error of belief).

Mistakes, on the other hand, are things we make or do. **Making mistakes** can result from being wrong—undertipping because of misremembering how to calculate percentages, for example. Mistakes can also arise from inattention, or a lack of action—letting cupcakes burn because of inattention—and from deviation—speeding up the bake time by increasing the temperature, resulting in burnt cupcakes. Mistakes can also emerge from a lack of information, not knowing how to do something, or a lack of ability—trying to assemble an Ikea couch without the instructions, which results in more of a deconstructed chaise lounge than a sofa.

Being wrong is an error of assumption, information, or belief, while a mistake is an enacted error caused by misinformation, inattention, or deviation. And failure? **Failure** is the consequence of being wrong and/or making a mistake. We failed to arrive on time because we were wrong about the travel time, we ruined dinner because we weren't paying attention, we crashed our model rocket because we were deeply confused about the shape of the earth. We might be wrong about something (assuming the oven is Fahrenheit when it is Celsius), which leads to a mistake (overcooking our cupcakes), which results in a failure (a burnt batch of cupcakes).

So now we have a better sense of how being wrong and making mistakes can lead to failures. But what is failure, exactly, besides a burnt batch of cupcakes? A good place to start making sense of failure is with economist and business leadership expert Amy C. Edmondson's nine types of failure, organized in a continuum from "blameworthy" to "praiseworthy":[8]

Deviance: Someone decides to purposefully deviate from the regular processes that were designed to avoid or at least mitigate failure—trying to speed up the baking of a cake by increasing the temperature; purposely ignoring the empty warning light on the gas gauge while driving a long distance.

Inattention: Someone knows how to avoid failure, but their attention to a situation inadvertently lapses, thereby enabling failure—wandering off while soup warms up, being distracted by one's phone while crossing the street and walking in front of a moving car.

Lack of ability: Someone is focused on the task, but doesn't have the skills or experience to mitigate failure—the classic I Love Lucy scene of Lucy and Ethel bumbling on the candy assembly line, or someone trying to bake a cake without knowing how to measure ingredients.

Process inadequacy: Someone has the necessary skills and experience, but uses a process that doesn't allow for acknowledging or addressing failure—asking someone to use an Ikea assembly guide for the wrong piece of furniture, seasoning soup made from scratch without tasting it as you go.

Task challenge: Someone has the skills and experience, and is applying a process known to mitigate failure, but is confronted with an extraordinarily difficult task: raking leaves in a windstorm, or the proverbial herding of cats.

Process complexity: Someone has the skills and has the process, but unpredictable complexities lead to unforeseen situations beyond their control—flying a plane when an unanticipated windstorm hits, or showing up to babysit the neighbor's two kids only to discover a Girl Scout troop awaiting your leadership.

Uncertainty: A situation that obscures unknown factors that will likely lead to failure—choosing between a bowl of salt and a bowl of sugar without being able to taste it, or making calculations for a rocket launch without important information on weather conditions.

Hypothesis testing: A controlled context designed to tease out the unknowns in order to mitigate failure—trying out a new recipe a few days before a big dinner party, or planning a museum heist using a scale model.

Exploratory testing: A controlled context open to inquiries into unknown and unexplored spaces where there are no right and wrong answers—sketching ideas for a new dress design, or freestyle rapping as a way to generate ideas for a new song.

Edmondson arranges these nine kinds of failure on a continuum, with blameworthy failures at one end, and praiseworthy failures at the other. She further segments them into three categories of failure: preventable, complexity-related, and intelligent.[9] As the name suggests, **preventable failures** are at the blameworthy end of the spectrum. They relate to deviations from failure-mitigating practices, lapses in attention, and lack of necessary preparation or skill. Many of the errors encountered in cooking fit into this category—trying to speed up the baking time by increasing the oven temperature (deviation from a failure-mitigating process) for cupcakes

PREVENTABLE FAILURES

DEVIATION

LACK OF ABILITY

INATTENTION

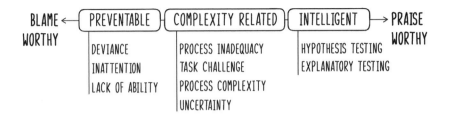

COMPLEXITY RELATED FAILURES

that leads to them burning (lack of attention); not knowing how to measure ingredients by volume instead of weight (lack of ability).

Complexity-related failures stem from the middle of the continuum, and relate mostly to processual and knowledge-based failures—the task at hand is beyond the skills of the individual or the process they employ; the task is of such complexity that preparation or mitigation was impossible. Continuing with our baking example, our baker tries to use a baguette

INTELLIGENT FAILURES

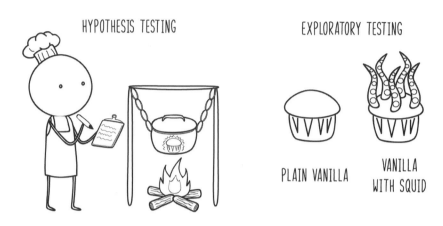

HYPOTHESIS TESTING

EXPLORATORY TESTING

PLAIN VANILLA

VANILLA WITH SQUID

recipe to make cupcakes (process inadequacy); they are asked to bake a thousand cupcakes in an industrial kitchen when their prior experience was limited to baking a dozen in their own home (task challenge); they are unsure if their ingredients are fresh and up to the challenge (uncertainty); or they are asked to bake cupcakes over an open fire in an unpredictable climate (process complexity).

Finally, at the praiseworthy end of Edmondson's spectrum, we find **intelligent failures**. These are hypothesis tests and exploratory tests that open up potentials, and treat failure as an opportunity to learn rather than something to be avoided. We'll wrap up our cupcakes-over-an-open-fire example: doing a test bake of a single cupcake in a Dutch oven to figure out timing and distance from the fire (hypothesis test). Or instead, an intrepid baker takes a basic vanilla cupcake recipe and sees what happens when cardamom is added (exploratory test).

Some failures aren't really failures at all. Hypothesis tests build upon existing knowledge, while exploratory tests help discover new potentials for understanding. In both cases, failure is activated and turned into a feature, something to be sought and learned from. In other words, they are purposeful failures. The more we can approach failure with a sense of purpose and anticipation, the more we turn failure into a tool for learning, and less of a thing to be avoided and feared.

Learning to Fail

In the field of educational sciences, failure is understood to be a healthy part of learning. Mark Cannon and Amy C. Edmondson have identified three necessary activities relating to failure inside organizations: detection, analysis, and experimentation.[10] **Detection** of failure seems like a clear first step, but as Cannon and Edmondson note, there is a tendency to avoid acknowledgment of failure either by not noticing its presence, ignoring its presence, or hiding its existence. Once failure is detected, it should be **analyzed**—what caused it? What impact did it cause? What can be learned from it? Failure is much more likely to be detected and analyzed inside a culture of **experimentation**. An individual or organization that builds failure into its values, intentions, and processes are far more likely to be receptive to failure, and in turn, are more likely to learn something new.

Let's use as an example someone burning a dozen cupcakes intended for a party later that evening. Our humble baker **detects** the problem when they notice the smell in the house turns from "mmm, cupcakes" to "uh oh, something's burning." One response that **acknowledges** the problem would be to throw out the burnt cupcakes, jump in the car, and buy a dozen on the way to the party. This response detects and acknowledges failure, but otherwise sweeps the whole situation under the rug. If our baker is to really learn from the situation, they will also **analyze** what happened to understand why the cupcakes burned. The more the baker is open to experimentation, the more likely they are to roll up their sleeves and bake another batch after taking care to check the oven temperature and setting a timer.

The more ambiguity around an instance of failure, the less likely anyone will be able to sort out why it happened. Attribution theory (which Juul used in the game example) is referenced again by Christopher Myers, Bradley Staats, and Francesca Gino to make sense of how businesses learn from failure. As they have noted, acknowledgment is ultimately the most important step in learning from failure. If there isn't an **attribution of responsibility**, to use their term, it is very unlikely anyone will learn from the failure.[11]

Despite the advantages in acknowledging failure, some individuals have a difficult time doing so. Psychologist Carol Dweck has identified two dispositions that directly affect how receptive someone is to learning from

FAILURE ANALYSIS

failure: the fixed mindset and the incremental mindset.[12] The **fixed mind-set** has a difficult time accepting failure as a part of the learning process, as these individuals see their capabilities and intelligence as inherent traits that can't be changed. The **incremental or growth mindset** is based on the idea that knowledge is developed over time, and that learning emerges from failure. A person with a fixed mindset can shut down when faced with difficulty or failure—"I just don't have a knack for baking" or "I can't figure

FIXED MINDSET

INCREMENTAL MINDSET

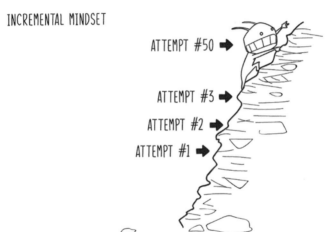

out how to put this couch together." But when someone with an incremental mindset fails in their first attempt to bake cupcakes, they view it as a necessary step to eventually getting them right. We might hear the incremental learner say something like "now I think I know what I did wrong, and I can get it right the next time." The willingness of our cupcake baker to detect and acknowledge the problem, analyze its causes, decide that they can do better, and then try again demonstrates that they approach things with an incremental mindset.

There are other reasons beyond a fixed mindset that people avoid acknowledging failure. Cannon and Edmondson note that resistance to admitting failure often emerges from social and technical barriers.[13] **Social barriers** result from psychological anxieties like a fear of others' reactions, damage to one's self-esteem, harm to one's status or reputation, and the consequences caused by the failure. These psychological barriers too often lead to process breakdowns where individuals and groups are unable or unwilling to make themselves open to failure—disagreements about whether or not there was failure, political maneuvering around the failure event, external pressures to not put the time and energy into analysis of the situation. If a community of practice is resistant to failure, then its community members will in turn struggle to acknowledge and address its presence.

Technical barriers also prevent us from acknowledging and understanding failure. Technical barriers often include processes and practices that do not allow for the likelihood of failure, as well as those that don't provide time and resources for analyzing failures when they occur—again, often an issue emerging from the practices of the community.

Our humble cupcake baker illustrates these ideas well. Perhaps instead of trying to bake the cupcakes again, they decided to run to the store and pick up a dozen cupcakes for the party. A lack of confidence in their pastry skills and a desire not to embarrass themselves by showing up empty-handed created social barriers that kept them from really facing up to the issue. And technical barriers were in their way too: There was a lack of time before the party, and their uncertainty about the inner workings of their oven prevented them from getting to the bottom of their culinary mishap. Combined, these barriers led our cupcake baker to altogether avoid identifying the root of the problem. And this leaves them with nothing but a dozen small, blackened cakes, and no real path for learning from the situation.

Social and technical barriers together prevent the creation of a culture of experimentation that understands failure as an acceptable—even welcome—part of the process. Creative practice necessitates not only an openness to failure, but also the ability to acknowledge, analyze, and respond to its presence. It may seem strange to say, but vulnerability is an essential ingredient for failure. This vulnerability is not one of being unaware or unprepared, but instead an intentional vulnerability that transforms failure from something to fear to something to respectfully acknowledge, consider, and integrate into one's practice. In the case of our cupcake baker, knowing that they might fail at their first batch because they've never made cupcakes before is an admission of their vulnerability in the face of a new baking

BARRIERS TO ACKNOWLEDGING FAILURE

SOCIAL BARRIERS

TECHNICAL BARRIERS

challenge. To reckon with this, they wake up early to provide ample time in case they need to bake a few more batches to get them just right.

In this light, one additional barrier should be mentioned: the **resource barrier**. American poetry scholar Matthew Sandler points out that the value of reflecting on failure dates back to the nineteenth century in self-help books like Wilbur Crafts's *Successful Men of Today and What They Say of Success* and Samuel Smiles's genre-defining *Self-Help*. Sandler quotes a passage from Smiles that epitomizes the valor in embracing failure: "Failure is the best discipline of the true worker, by stimulating him to renewed efforts, evoking his best powers, and carrying him onward in self-culture, self-control and growth in knowledge and wisdom."[14]

This assertion assumes an incredible amount about the circumstances, the wherewithal of the person, and the resources at their disposal to act upon the failure. In too many of the hagiographies of failure, those who serve as models are those with the social, economic, and cultural privilege to do so. Sandler puts it well:

Smiles casts failure as a helpful god, dispensing fortune and education at turns, a programmatic claim that undergirds his compendium of sketch biographies of successful men. Such optimism, however, assumes both that this "true worker" has the resources to "carry onward" after failing and that he is capable of perceiving the paradoxical "discipline" of failure.[15]

The ability to recognize and respond to failure asks a good deal of us, and shouldn't be treated as a given. Sandler notes that the burden of recognizing failure was equally challenging for those with privilege in the presence of resource barriers.[16] People might lack financial, material, temporal, or contextual resources to fully rebound from failure. Someone may not have the emotional capacities to continue. So yes, failure requires a vulnerability and openness, but we should not assume we all have the resources to face failure head on.

Anticipating and Analyzing Failure

Learning from failure is the key to Beckett's "fail better." However, the process of learning from failure is never cut and dry, as it isn't always easy to sort out its causes. Even when the causes of failure are understood, the path forward isn't always obvious. Still, there are some basic steps we can take to understand why we have failed. In fact, there is an entire engineering discipline devoted to this: failure analysis, or in its more formal name, failure modes and effects analysis (FMEA). Detailing the steps involved in FMEA would take an entire book, so suffice it to say that engineering's methods for recognizing and addressing failure are comprehensive. The multistep methodology begins with analyzing all the possible root causes underlying the failure, followed by the identification of corrective actions. After testing the effectiveness and feasibility of the actions, engineers choose the actions they will take. And finally, they identify actions to take in order to mitigate future failures. In the design of airplanes, bridges, and buildings, it's clearly important to be as meticulous as possible in mitigating failure. Similar to game designers who obsess over the crafting of fun failure, engineers are equally obsessive about finding and fixing dangerous failure.

FAILURE ANALYSIS PROCESS

Though engineers use exceedingly comprehensive processes to analyze failures as diverse as airplane crashes, network outages, and water leaks, we can borrow from this process to learn from creative failures as well. In this spirit, we propose a simplified failure analysis process for creative practice: establish, analyze, diagnose, plan, and enact. First, **establish** the goals, the intended outcomes, and the resources available for the effort. With these in place, **analyze** the available information from the instance of failure under consideration—in many cases, this involves talking to stakeholders and others who can provide valuable critique. Once as much as is necessary or reasonable is learned, **diagnose** the cause of the failure. With a working theory in hand, revisit the goals, outcomes, and resources to make sure the **plan** will help you reach a meaningful conclusion. And once the plan is in place, **enact** the response to the failure.

Let's return to that burnt batch of cupcakes to see our failure analysis process in action. First, we establish the parameters of our analysis. We want to understand why we burnt the cupcakes in the first place—a task to which we're willing to devote an afternoon. We analyze our recipe to see if there was an obvious error in it, and we try to retrace our steps by making another batch using the recipe. This batch also burns. After consulting the friend who gave us the recipe, we then realize that our new oven is set to Celsius, not Fahrenheit! This leads to our diagnosis—we had set the oven to a much higher temperature than we should have. We have a working theory in hand, and so we try again using an appropriate Celsius oven temperature. This turns out to be the problem—the oven was way too hot, which confirms our suspicions about why we charred the first batch of cupcakes. And so we enact a plan: going forward, make sure to convert recipes from Fahrenheit to Celsius.

Making Sense of Failure

Our cupcake baker made a mistake, and after some trial and error, they were able to resolve it themselves. But it isn't always easy to understand why or how we fail. When it comes to understanding creative failures, at times the root causes and corrective actions aren't as cut and dry—they are often subjective. This is where the analysis step of our failure benefits from multiple perspectives—from **critique**. To seek critique is to gain clarity from as many subjective interpretations as possible. The practice of critique is so "critical" to creative practice that it is the heart of most art and design school curriculum. Because we never know what we're going to hear or see, critique requires an openness and a vulnerability to hearing painful truths—as well as accepting compliments on and criticisms about what works.

Learning to provide and receive critique is a skill, one that begins with an openness to failure. If we revisit our cupcake baker once more, we find them happily presenting a perfectly baked batch of homemade vanilla cupcakes to the friend who is hosting the party. They watch expectantly as their friend takes a bite. "Hmm," their friend says, "could use a pinch of salt to balance the sweetness, but overall, it's a pretty good cupcake. *Love* the sprinkles." Yet another person may excitedly pick up a cupcake, peel off the liner, take a bite, and suddenly make a horrifying face, quickly turning away. They haven't spoken a word, but they've said volumes through their reaction. The lesson our baker takes away from these unsolicited critiques is that, indeed, everyone's taste in cupcakes is different. The responses also suggest that not everyone is going to get what you are up to—maybe adding salt could be worth a try, maybe not; perhaps vanilla isn't to everyone's taste. Critique is an important part of creative practice, as it provides additional perspectives, and provides more brain power for failure analysis.

Sense making is the operative skill in failure analysis, whether it be engineering's more complex version, our simplified version for creative practice, or the ability to receive and interpret critique. What is the failure, exactly? What caused it? Are we understanding the situation correctly? Do we know enough about the context of the failure? Are we taking into account enough variables to avoid oversimplification? In his book *Drift into Failure: From Hunting Broken Components to Understanding Complex Systems*, human factors and safety expert Sidney Dekker notes that the reductionist underpinning of modern science is always at risk of oversimplification:

The belief that, by applying the right method or the best method, we can approximate the true story of what happened is Newtonian too: it assumes that there is a final, most accurate description of the world. And underneath all of this, of course, is a reproduction of the strongest Newtonian commitment of all: reductionism.[17]

This reductionism can result in missed interpretation, and poor solutions for addressing and learning from the causes of failure. We should take from Dekker's warning the lesson that we should remain honest and humble in the face of our failures, and be realistic about the truth of our practices.

Making something is likely going to lead to failure. There's just no way around it. It is part of the creative process. Knowing how to accept failure without giving up is essential to all forms of creative practice. For many, this is really scary. But given the ubiquity of failure, this fear is akin to being afraid of breathing, or of the daily cycles of the sun and the moon. Our jobs as creative practitioners require a certain degree of deprogramming of our attitudes about failure. Instead of seeing failure as either a source of shame or a badge of honor, we try to see it as something to learn from and a natural part of the creative process.

Some processes leverage failure better than others. What is the best tool for addressing failure? In our opinion, it's iteration.

3   Iteration

The Craft of Failure

Iteration, in its most basic form, is a pretty straightforward idea: It's a cyclical process used to reach a desired outcome. The underlying presumption of iteration is that creative practitioners most likely won't hit their goals on the first try, and so they need a cyclical process that treats failure as a productive step rather than a conclusive end.

The field of game design is a great example (and also happens to be the one we practice). It is really hard to get a game's design right on the first try. It's impossible to predict what players will do in a game, how they will interpret the game's goals, and what they will consider "fun." This is because game designers do not directly create play experiences. Instead, they design rules that generate play. For example, to create a game that's funny, the designer can't simply tell a joke; they must create rules and a context that will generate funny situations. This is a second-order design problem.[1] Second-order design is a concept derived from mathematics and logic involving the introduction of variables into an equation. With second-order design and games, those variables are the players, and how they engage with a game. When do they play? Why do they play? How do they interpret the rules and generate strategies? What do they feel while playing?

A game designer can't fully see their game until it is played; even then, different players may play it in unexpected ways that break the game, or at least diverge from the designer's intentions. All this indirection and uncertainty leads to a lot of game design failures. But instead of giving up, game designers use failure as a fuel to make their games better. This is the power of iteration—it allows creative practitioners to find their way through the thicket of uncertainty and failure that is creativity.

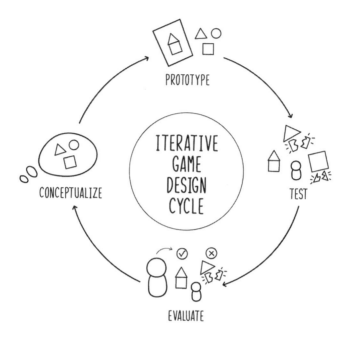

PROTOTYPE

ITERATIVE
GAME
DESIGN
CYCLE

CONCEPTUALIZE

TEST

EVALUATE

Game designers conceptualize, prototype, playtest, and evaluate their games in repeating cycles in order to "find the fun."[2] The process begins with a **concept**: make a puzzle game out of tetrominoes, create a conversation engine for socializing, develop a competitive structure within which players can compare their cooking skills. **Prototypes** are then created to give form to aspects of the concept. **Playtests** of the prototype let the designer see what kind of play the game actually produces, which they can measure against the play they hoped to produce. This is often where failure most clearly emerges, as players struggle to interpret rules or devise winning strategies, or simply fail to have fun. With the results in hand, the game designer then **evaluates** the playtest, the prototype, and their concept to see how to best move closer to their goals in the next cycle of iteration.

Iterating on Iteration

These four steps—conceptualize, prototype, playtest, and evaluate—date back to mid-twentieth-century software development. Though the term "iterative" wasn't commonplace at the time, software engineers spoke of "incremental development," in which small portions of the software were designed, programmed, and tested. It was already obvious to engineers that the traditional "waterfall" approach—where a thing was conceived of, planned, built, then put into use—was "rather stupid" for creating something of even minimal complexity.[3] Though the paths through the iterative process vary greatly, the approaches used in the early years of software development have stuck, and led to a shared understanding of the value of iterative processes.

The iterative methodologies of computer science in turn build on the more general scientific method of posing a question, developing a hypothesis, testing the hypothesis, analyzing the results, and finally drawing a conclusion on that initial question. The physicist Richard Feynman described the practice of science using the analogy of learning to play chess:

What do we mean by "understanding" something? We can imagine that this complicated array of moving things which constitutes "the world" is something like a great chess game being played by the gods, and we are observers of the game. We do not know what the rules of the game are; all we are allowed to do is to watch the playing.[4]

As Feynman describes, science observes a phenomenon—hopefully multiple times—in order to learn the underlying rules. Repetition is a key aspect of science as well—it often takes multiple attempts to figure out the right questions and experiments to generate answers. Cycles of observation are required, sometimes with intentional changes made to validate theories about what is happening, why it is happening, and how it is happening. And then? Other scientists repeat experiments to test the validity of each other's work. In other words, science is an iterative process of theorizing, prototyping, testing, and analyzing.

We can also look to business practices for examples of iteration. The concept of "kaizen," employed most famously in Toyota's car manufacturing methods, embodies incremental innovation through successive iterations over time within the context of an organization. The Japanese word *kaizen* means "continuous improvement"—or, in our word, iteration. There are two aspects of kaizen that stand out in the context of a business. First, kaizen manifests as a value of making small improvements over time with an eye to incremental changes that will make things better for everyone. Second, in a company like Toyota, everyone, from CEO to floor sweeper, can make suggestions about how to improve. Kaizen, then, is at once an acceptance of the present *and* a quest to make things better, emerging from a supportive culture of critique. It is an honest, open acceptance of things as they are, but with an eye to doing better next time.

The field of interaction design practices a more deliberately evaluative form of iteration. Stephanie Houde and Charles Hill's "What Do Prototypes Prototype?"[5] approaches iteration as a valuable tool for thinking by making:

what the thing does (role), how it impacts the senses of those who use or interact with it (look and feel), and how to create it (implementation). Take as an example a team tasked with designing an office chair. To help them sort through their task, they consider the potential **roles** for an office chair by doing some quick experiential prototypes of sitting in different kinds of chairs. This leads to their initial **look and feel prototypes** to see what the experience is like doing typical office tasks while seated in prototype chairs they have created. These inform the team's understanding of the chair's usability, or the balance between its comfort and its appropriateness for the task. And once they start honing in on a design solution to their office chair, they conduct a series of **implementation prototypes** that help them assess the viability of materials, and the means by which the chair can be fabricated most efficiently, sustainably, and cost-effectively.

As valuable as Houde and Hill's conception of iteration is, their focus remains firmly within the problem-solution conception of iteration. More exploratory approaches can be found in Buddhist sand mandalas and Oulipo writing exercises—iterative practices in form if not in name. Buddhist sand mandalas are symbolic representations of the universe. In this centuries-old ritual, a group of monks draws a schematic representation of the Buddhist universe and then spends a week or more carefully rendering the scene with colored sands using specially designed metal tubes. Once the sand painting is complete, a brief ceremony takes place that concludes with the destruction of the painting, followed by the dumping of the sand into a nearby body of water. The ritualized creation and destruction of sand mandalas captures the Buddhist conception of life as ephemeral. Each time the ritualized sand paintings are created, another iterative cycle unfolds.

Oulipo (an abbreviation of the French Ouvroir de Littérature Potentielle, or the workshop for potential literature) was founded by writer Raymond Queneau and mathematician François Le Lionnais in 1960 as a loosely organized group seeking to explore and expand literature. The primary Oulipo tool is the constraint—a set of rules that govern a writing exercise. Famous examples are N+7, in which a piece of writing is transformed by substituting all nouns with the word that appears seven words later in the dictionary; and Snowball, in which the first word in a poem is one letter, the second two letters, the third three letters, and so on. Sometimes the outputs of Oulipo constraints were published (like Georges Perec's novel *La Disparition*, which does not use the letter E), but more often than not, the resulting texts were treated as something between exploratory research and writing calisthenics. Oulipo constraints are iterative writing algorithms that help us see literary potentials we might otherwise overlook.

What connects game design, the scientific method, kaizen, Houde and Hill's prototyping categories, Buddhist sand mandalas, and Oulipo? They are all iterative processes, even if they don't use that term. Game design embraces the uncertainty of second-order design through incremental, iterative design cycles; the scientific method recognizes the importance of process and reproducibility in the creation of knowledge; kaizen blends the iterative mindset with a focus on the here and now; Houde and Hill's prototyping uses iterative making as a form of researching through making. And in our later examples, Buddhist sand mandalas are born from religious practice and the lessons of patience and humility; and Oulipo's iterative exercises use writing and mathematics in the pursuit of new possibilities.

The Six Components of Iterative Practice

Let's return to our earlier definition of "iteration": Given a particular intention, it is a cyclical process used to reach a desired outcome. This definition dovetails with our conception of creativity explored in chapter 1: Creativity is the process by which an individual or group intentionally produces an outcome that is appropriate, aesthetic, and authentic to its context and community. It's incredibly challenging to hit all these points—appropriate, aesthetic, and authentic—and thus failure is always present during the creative process. Iteration allows us to turn those failures, big and small, into catalysts for failing better. In other words, iterative practices are particularly adept at helping creative practitioners learn from failure.

We see iteration as composed of six key components: intention, process, outcome, evaluation, context, and actors. A project begins with an **intention**, from which emerges a **cyclical process** designed to reach a particular **outcome**. An **evaluation** must take place to assess the outcome of the process and whether or not the results meet the creative practitioner's intentions. All of this occurs within a place and time, or **context**, and by and for **actors**—or, in simpler terms, people. Because the desired outcome more than likely wasn't achieved the first time through the cycle, the process is repeated—in successive loops as many times as necessary to meet the intentions for the project. In essence, each component is revisited iteratively.

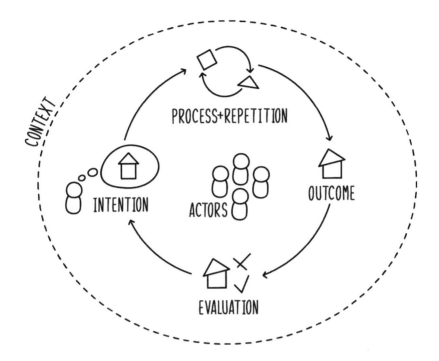

An **intention** can be many things, but it generally connects to what they hope to create, and why someone would use iterative processes in the first place. Are they attempting to validate a theory? Or are they iterating as a generative process of discovery? Are they following through on an idea? Or are they seeking the best means of achieving a goal?

The intentions shape the iterative **process**, as it will dictate the best means of meeting the goals. We've already talked about a few of these—the iterative cycle of game design, the research-as-making of Houde and Hill, the ritual of Buddhist sand paintings. Process emerges from intention in subtle and substantive ways. If the intention is to generate something new, then a process that enables unexpected results will be best. If the intention is to verify a shared experience, then the process should be designed to provide those results.

A key characteristic of iterative process is that it is **cyclical**. The iterative game design process, for example, is often described as a four-step loop loosely composed of concept, prototype, test, and evaluation—which then leads to revisiting the concept, making a new prototype, testing that prototype, evaluating it, and on and on until the desired outcome is reached.

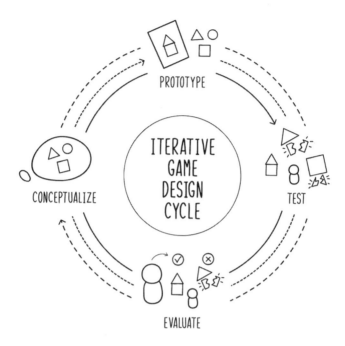

Depending on how each loop unfolds, each cycle through the process may bring about revisions to the intention, the outcome, and even the process itself. The cycles through the iterative process aren't necessarily identical; depending upon what happened and what was learned in previous loops, changes—subtle and pronounced—are inevitable as the creative practitioner works toward their intended outcome. A cyclical process is also present in the idea of practice—musicians practicing their instruments through chord progressions, or martial artists practicing their forms, teaching their muscles to memorize each movement. Each time, they are evaluating their own per-formance, and getting closer to their goal though mind-body training.

Each cycle through the iterative process results in an **outcome**, hope-fully one in alignment with the intentions that catalyzed the process in the first place. Sometimes, the outcome of one cycle is a small step forward, sometimes a step backward on the path to reach the intended goal. When the project is over, the hope is that the outcome substantially moves toward or even reaches the intended goal. So if the intention was creative explora-tion, then the outcome will be hard to predict, but will hopefully have the desired, unexpected results. If the intention was to validate a theory, the outcome will be more predictable: The theory was proved or the theory was disproved. Intent, process, and outcome are the three primary elements driving all iterative processes. Put more simply, intent provides the why, process the how, and outcome the what.

But how does a practitioner know what the outcome should be at the end of a cycle through their iterative process? Most of the processes we've found through the case studies in this book involve some form of **evaluation**—understanding how close one is to the intended outcome. This evaluation can take many forms—an assessment by the practitioner (or practitioners) working on the project, a critique from people outside the team, feedback from testers, client notes, and so on. The evaluation phase is really a version of the failure analysis discussed in chapter 2: Establish a goal for and parameters of the analysis, analyze the available information, diagnose the cause of the problems, plan a response for the next cycle, and put that plan into action. Of course, not everyone evaluates their results in the same way, as not all practitioners conceptualize, prototype, or test in the same way. Still, without evaluation, we would never know whether we were getting closer to or further from our goal.

We've identified the why (intention), how (process), and what (outcome and evaluation) of iteration. There are two additional important things to recognize when looking at creative practice: where and when the iteration happens, and who is involved. This cyclical process doesn't happen in a vacuum; iteration takes place within a context and is carried out by actors, or the people participating in the creative act.

Iteration happens within a place and time: in other words, a **context**. This includes the location where creative practitioners work, but also the resources (time, financial, material, intellectual, and so on) at their disposal, and the larger communities and organizations within which they operate. Context constrains process in both subtle and obvious ways. If someone is working on a new game project in their spare time, they are going to approach iteration in a very different way than someone conducting practice-based research at a large university. A person conducting iterative processes within the R&D lab of a large-scale baked goods firm[6] is going to tackle projects in a different way than someone at home making a batch of cupcakes for a party. The process of an artist exploring new conceptual territory will undoubtedly differ from that of an ice skater developing a routine. Context can also modify intention and outcomes—an improv performance has a constantly shifting context that changes how actors respond to and resolve the situation, often with the audience participating and thereby creating context as well.

Context leads to the final part of our iteration system: the **actors**—not actors as in theater, per se, but those who enact and interact with the creation. These are the people directly and indirectly involved in the iterative process—not only the creative practitioner(s), but also the people working with them. In addition to the team directly involved, there can also be other stakeholders who get a say—company executives, people holding the purse strings, the intended audience for the thing being made, or participants in an experience.

These are the six **components** of iteration—intentions, process, outcomes, evaluation, context, and actors. We call them components because each one is emphasized differently depending on the practitioner(s), and they provide for a wide range of iterative methodologies, beyond the limited perspective of problem solving and innovation.

Tools for Failing Better

We now have the six components of iteration—intention, process, outcome, evaluation, along with the context in which iteration takes place and the actors who participate in the process. But what allows a creative person to develop this practice? One of John's students once asked him how he was able to predict problems in a game prototype before playtesting it. What was his secret? The answer, of course, was simple: experience, making the "practice" derivation of "practitioner" the operative concept.

One of the key tools for developing an iterative mindset is conceptual foresight, a term coined by Joy Paul Guilford, the father of modern creativity research.[7] **Conceptual foresight** is a form of knowledge, built up through experience, that allows practitioners to predict the implications of decisions and actions. In other words, conceptual foresight is the ability to develop insights from past experiences that help the practitioner make sense of their current challenges. As psychologist and creativity researcher Michael Mumford points out, this skill is both evaluative and generative; the practitioner can both assess a given situation and generate ideas for how to act upon it. For iterative processes, this is an essential skill—what we call evaluation—because, more often than not, the results of an iterative

CONCEPTUAL FORESIGHT

PENETRATION

cycle stray from expectations. Being able to evaluate what happened and to then come up with a plan for moving forward is a critical part of iteration in all its forms.

Guilford and colleagues developed two closely related concepts that expand upon the importance of conceptual foresight: penetration and redefinition.[8] **Penetration** is the ability to see meaning in a situation that others lacking prior experience might not notice—in other words, to penetrate the surface-level details visible to everyone. A more experienced furniture designer will have insights into the construction of a chair back that someone less experienced would struggle to see.

Redefinition, on the other hand, is the ability to reimagine the use of an object, concept, or situation to fit a given context or set of constraints.[9] In iterative processes, penetration and redefinition clearly build on conceptual

foresight, enabling a practitioner to identify useful information, discard impertinent information (penetration), and abstract this information from a given context to imagine possible next steps (redefinition). These skills really are the key to effective iterative practices, as the often-unexpected outcomes that happen along the way can be bewilderingly confusing without the ability to see through the noise to the insights hidden inside failure. Following through with our furniture designer, experience provides the ability to reimagine the possibilities of rocking chairs, seeing a whole new model of chair for spritely rockers.

One final concept from Guilford's work rounds out this set of iterative skills: problem sensitivity. **Problem sensitivity** is the awareness of and focus on the overarching goal of a task (or, in our language, the **intentions** of the task).[10] Without problem sensitivity, there is no overarching direction to guide conceptual foresight, penetration, and redefinition. Without problem sensitivity, a furniture design team may lose focus on the intention—create a chair that encourages focus and productivity—and

instead veer off into lounge chair territory. Only after lots of trial and error do we develop conceptual foresight, learn the ability to penetrate the surface with more sophisticated understanding, and redefine the creative potential of things around us. And problem sensitivity, the ability to stay focused on the goals at hand, is critical to making the most of the other three skills.

It is this group of four concepts—conceptual foresight, penetration, redefinition, and problem sensitivity—that support the intention, process, repetition, and outcome components of iteration. For our purposes, these four skills are essential for understanding failure as a frequently visited waypoint in the creative process, and not as a conclusion. While these are the skills necessary to develop an iterative mindset, the practice of iteration is the first step. And that practice has several components that are shared across a variety of creative disciplines.

Creativity, Failure, and Iteration

Creativity, failure, and iteration are forever intertwined, even if we don't always associate the three concepts. Anyone who has tried to make something knows that creativity more often than not results in failure. Not

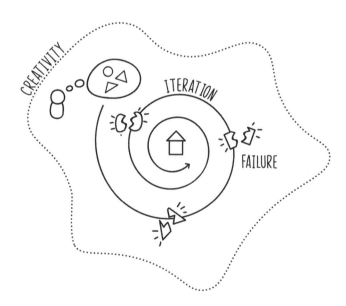

necessarily giant, embarrassing, or damaging failures, but still, something less than or different from what was hoped or intended.

Whenever we try something new, or when we're learning something for the first time, we run the risk of failing. This leads to two options: give up (which means accepting failure), or try again. When Samuel Beckett writes, "Ever tried. Ever failed, no matter," he's sharing a secret: Even though he's considered one of the most influential playwrights of the twentieth century, failure was as familiar to him as it is to someone trying to create for the first time. And when he asks us to "try again, fail again, fail better," he's encouraging us to continue on—to iterate, and through that process, come up with something else, arriving at a better failure we'll strive to improve upon the next time.

That space between failure and the desired outcome is seldom narrow. Education activist Parker Palmer has a term for the distance between success and failure: the tragic gap.[11] Palmer uses the phrase in a discussion of the hard challenges of making the world a better place, but this idea also applies to smaller-scale efforts to create something. Iteration is a tool we can use to close that tragic gap, one iterative cycle at a time. When approached from an iterative perspective, the tragic gap seems insurmountable only if we are unwilling to incrementally progress across the expanse.

The iterative cycle provides opportunities to convert weakness into strength by using the knowledge derived from failure to shorten the gap between practitioners and their goals. Iteration allows us to move more carefully through the creative process, but it also allows us to take risks: to explore the possibilities of our ideas, to find better solutions, to do things we didn't think we were capable of.

Creative practice is a practice of failure as much as it is a practice of creating—we're often failing far more than we're succeeding, after all. From this perspective, iteration is the art of intentional failure, or what anthropologist and designer Jamer Hunt calls "predicted failure."[12] This isn't to say iterative practices produce fruitless outcomes. Think of failure as a flashlight; it illuminates the things that don't work and also, when we look closely, shines light on the path ahead toward the next version of an idea, and ultimately, the realization of a thing in the world. This iterative process of coming up with an idea, making a version of it, testing it, and refining the idea takes many forms as well. It might be fast or slow, continuous or in spurts; it may focus on one goal or many outcomes, and may end only to be picked up again in a completely new context. However it is done, across our own experiences and in talking to many other practitioners, we have found that iteration—in whatever form it takes—is a tried and true method for dealing with and learning from failure. Through our research for this book and our own experiences, we have seen the rewards that come from embracing an iterative mindset: the willingness to accept failure as a creative partner. And as we will see, this mindset can take many forms.

4 Ten Perspectives on Iteration

Creativity as a System

As we looked closely into the practices of the people we interviewed for this book, we couldn't help trying to make sense of the relationships between creativity, failure, and iteration in their work. Thinking of creativity as an iterative engine, with failure as its fuel, we imagined how it might actually work. We drew diagrams with lots of dotted lines and arrows between our six components (intention, process, outcome, evaluation, contexts, and actors) to try to understand the dynamics of creativity. We looked at each case study and tried to identify the "moving parts" in their practices.

In other words, to make sense of it all, we took a systems approach. We borrow this methodology from Donella Meadows's book *Thinking in Systems: A Primer*. Meadows's systems thinking emerges from the larger field of systems dynamics. It provides tools to better understand large, complex phenomena: the migration of predatory animals and their impact on other flora and fauna; the flow of material and capital through supply chains; the multifaceted social infrastructures that support (or not) populations in large cities. We use these methods and the basic conception of systems thinking throughout this book to help us analyze and understand the creative practices of the artists, designers, athletes, performers, and craftspeople we have studied.

In its most basic form, a system is composed of three things: elements, interconnections, and a purpose or function. **Elements**, each of which have unique attributes, are the things in a system. In the system that is the human body, our organs are all elements, as are our bones, muscles, nerves, and so on. These elements have **interconnections**—our bones are connected to our muscles by tendons, which enable us to move around; our lungs and our digestive and endocrine systems provide the fuel. The elements and their interconnections within a system have **purpose** or **function**—the various systems in our bodies sustain our lives, allow us to move around, do things, think and feel, and so on.

We're particularly attuned to systems because games are systems, too. Take the classic game of Rock-Paper-Scissors. It's fairly easy to map the system of this game: Rock beats scissors, scissors beats paper, and paper beats rock. However, despite its simplicity, Rock-Paper-Scissors is a surprisingly strategic game. There's a good deal of nuance inside it, but suffice it to say that the game is a system: The possible moves are the elements of the system with specific interconnections, which players put into action through the dynamics of psychology and strategy.

An important thing to keep in mind about systems thinking: There is always a purpose or function to the system, but also to the use of systems mapping, and the analysis it supports. The purpose of the analysis shapes the way the phenomenon is thought about, what is deemed important, and what is not. In our Rock-Paper-Scissors analysis, we could have brought any number of goals and focuses to our analysis. We could have focused on the social systems of the game and explored the ways people interact with one another, the kinds of human relationships the game creates, and so on. We could have focused on the cultural systems from which the game emerged, and the game's many variations across a wide swath of cultures and communities. But we didn't. We focused on gameplay to help us illustrate how we can break down a phenomenon using systems thinking. The point? The goal of a systems analysis will shape how the underlying phenomenon is understood.

What, then, is the purpose of our systems analysis of iteration within creative practices? We have two primary goals. First, we want to see beyond the typical approaches to iteration as being solely the realm of problem solving and innovation. Systems thinking lets us carefully consider the "moving parts" of creativity and more fully see the range of intentions, processes, and outcomes of creative practice—thus our identification of intention, process, outcome, evaluation, context, and actors as the component parts of iterative practice. Second, we want to understand how iteration mitigates failure in creative practice. Systems thinking affords the opportunity to better understand the relationships between creative practice and failure, and to see the ways iteration interacts with them.

As we drew dotted lines on the whiteboard trying to make sense of it all, we were interviewing creative people to see whether and how they used failure and iteration in their practices. The first thing we discovered was that yes, indeed, everyone iterates (even if they didn't call it that, or even do so consciously). The second thing we quickly realized is that no two iterative processes looked alike. If one practitioner worked in a very methodological way, we found another out there who improvised. If one worked in a very material and physical context, another worked in a reflective, ideas-based one. So rather than identify one unified field theory for iterative practice, we came up with the idea of the continuum—a sliding scale of iterative processes—each considered from the vantage of one of the six components of iteration.

The Five Continua

Through our interviews we've discovered a variety of different approaches to iteration, motivated by different intentions, repeating in different ways in varying time frames, and resulting in a radically different set of outcomes. As described in the previous chapter, the six components of iteration are intention, process, outcome, evaluation, context, and actors. If we consider each of these as variables within a system of iteration, each practitioner fills them with different values, in both meanings of the word: as a quantity, and in terms of what's important. With these six components, we can see a variety of possibilities for iterative practice.

With this in mind, we set out to identify some of the varied ways in which practitioners use iteration. One practitioner may put more emphasis on the intentions leading into their process, whereas someone else may see the particulars of their process as the most important. Still another practitioner may find the evaluation phase of iteration as the most critical, and therefore central to their iterative practice. Others may allow their iterative practice to be guided by the outcomes they seek. And finally, the most basic piece of the puzzle: the context within which a practitioner enacts their iterative practice in the first place. ("Wait!" you might ask, what about the sixth component of iterative practice, actors? The fact is, all of these practitioners emphasize the people involved in the creative process, as well as their community of practice, their stakeholders and audiences. So actors are referred to implicitly across all the case studies.)

To that end, our five pairs: **Material and reflective contexts** consider the environment surrounding the iterative process, and what it's made of, from ideas to actual things in the world; **targeted and exploratory intentions** establish the desired outcomes; **methodological and improvisational processes** determine the kind of process used in the pursuit of the intentions and outcomes; **internal and external evaluation** speaks to how and who evaluates progress toward the intended outcomes; and **convergent and divergent outcomes** indicate the expectations placed on the results of iterative creative practice.

For each continuum, we include a small diagram distilling the particulars of each pole. Hopefully these provide some sense of the differences between the points on each continuum, and how each iterative practice is a system, a tiny constellation within a star field of multiple possibilities.

Continuum I: Material and Reflective Contexts

Iterative practice, above all, presumes active creation. However, what is being created is so fundamental that most people don't even think of it as a decision: Are they iterating with materials or on ideas? Is iteration in service of learning the physical properties of things or the conceptual aspects of things? This first continuum looks at the surrounding forces encountered during the creative act: Does the creative practitioner encounter material constraints and realities requiring them to respond accordingly, or do the constraints emerge from the practitioner themselves, creating a context that supports their intentions? In both cases, the creative practitioner establishes their intentions for the project, which by default establishes the hoped-for outcome. Where these differ is the context within which

the project takes place, and the mechanisms by which the challenges confronted along the way are addressed.

Material contexts represent the expected "hands-on" approach of iterative practice. We work with the material to try to shape it into an outcome—but as we do so, we learn more about that material, and about other external forces that shape the possible creative outcomes. The classic example of the sculptor finding the form within a chunk of marble fits here. Material iteration connects to Donald Schön's "reflection-in-action" (discussed in chapter 1), or the act of thinking about one's practice during the creative act. Here, the iterative practice is about thinking through making, and pursuing one's goals by working with material constraints and within a given context. Material contexts also draw heavily on Schön's concept of "knowledge-in-action" (also discussed in chapter 1), in which past experiences help one respond to an unexpected situation: designing a toothbrush for astronauts to use in zero gravity, for instance.

To get closer to material context as the anchoring value in an iterative practice, let's look at the process of an experienced toothbrush designer. Over their years of practice, our senior toothbrush designer might have arrived at an approach to iteration that focused on the material aspects of the toothbrush. Perhaps they work on the handle, sculpting different forms and playing with materials (in this case, molded plastic). Or maybe they experiment with different shapes for the brush's head. In both cases, the toothbrush designer operates within a material context in which iterative practices guide them through their design tasks.

Reflective contexts, on the other hand, emerge from intentions to learn from and consider ideas and other works as thoughtful influence on one's own creation. Our use of the term "reflective" draws upon Schön's "reflection-on-action," in which one critically evaluates one's work either after reaching a logical stopping point or upon completion of the work. We expand this form of reflection to include other works outside of one's repertoire that might inspire creative practice. This usually involves watching, listening, playing—however one engages with the thing under consideration. The intention for the reflection begins with one goal or more—to find inspiration, to learn something new, to consider a work in a new way, etc.

MATERIAL CONTEXTS

Maybe our toothbrush designer has a reflective practice in which they draw inspiration for their brush designs by looking at the history of toothbrushes and dental hygiene. They might examine the brushes made by others by taking careful measurements or even using them to brush their own teeth. Repetition is an important component of reflective contexts, as it can often take more than one listening to a song, reading of a novel, viewing of a film, or playing of a game to pinpoint the specific aspect from which one draws inspiration.

The presence of failure in material and reflective contexts differs in form. In material contexts we take a tinkerer's approach to understanding the materials we are working with, and failure is certainly embedded in this, as materials break, fail, and push against our creative will. In reflective contexts, we explore how another work was created in order to discover solutions to problems or failures and unknowns in our own work.

REFLECTIVE CONTEXTS

Our case studies for material and reflective contexts couldn't be more different. First is the winemaker Allison Tauziet, whose material practice integrates her senses, seasonal change, the unpredictability of Mother Nature, the natural properties of her vineyard, and her experiences from previous years to create award-winning wines. She mitigates failure by using her senses to guide her each step of the way, because, as Allison says, "you can only pick the grapes once."[1]

For reflective contexts, we look to the animator Matthew Maloney. He constantly watches films, reads books, plays games, and listens to music as part of his creative process. He uses reflective iteration in a number of ways: as a form of mental conditioning, as a tool to help him home in on a solution to a particular intention, as a shortcut to get him back into a specific creative headspace, as a divining rod for creative expression, and as a measuring stick for assessing his progress as a filmmaker.

Continuum II: Targeted and Exploratory Intentions

The second continuum considers the overall goals of iteration. Put most simply, targeted intentions ask how to achieve a specific goal, while exploratory intentions have no specific end result in mind. These approaches have a relationship similar to that of applied and basic scientific research. Applied research attempts to solve a concrete, specific problem: creating a more humane mousetrap, developing economic policy to close the gap between rich and poor, producing a more energy-efficient air conditioner. Basic research, on the other hand, begins with hypotheses and questions in order to expand our understanding: exploring the depths of the planet, tinkering with the chemical properties of food, seeking new possibilities for machine learning.

Architect, designer, and MIT professor Neri Oxman describes this dichotomy between basic and applied research through the four different disciplines of science and engineering, art and design, referencing the "Bermuda Quadrilateral," John Maeda's four-point square matrix where art, design, science, and engineering occupy their own corners.[2] Oxman explains the different roles of each: "The role of Science is to explain and predict the world around us; it 'converts' information into knowledge. The role of Engineering is to apply scientific knowledge to the development of solutions for empirical problems; it 'converts' knowledge into utility."[3] Art and design are seen in similar dichotomies: "The role of Design is to produce embodiments of solutions that maximize function and augment human experience; it 'converts' utility into behavior. The role of Art is to question human behavior and create awareness of the world around us; it 'converts' behavior into new perceptions of information."[4] In terms of our continuum, targeted intentions result in utilitarian outcomes (the design and engineering roles described by Oxman). Targeted intentions hope to convert knowledge into something that can be acted upon; they translate

TARGETED & EXPLORATORY INTENTIONS

what we know into something accessible and understandable. Targeted intentions seek to answer "how?" questions, like "How might we build a better mousetrap?" On the other hand, exploratory intentions result in outcomes adding to general knowledge (art and science), without an initial presumption of what that knowledge might be. Exploratory intentions set out to answer "why?" questions, like "Why do the planets revolve around the sun?"

Before we get carried away by partisanship between these two sides, it's important to note that they feed into each other; design utilizes materials science, engineering often builds on forms found in sculpture—and the relationships travel in all directions. In fact, Oxman's meditation on these disciplines turns this territorial map into a space of exploration and transformation, one where creative practitioners might cycle through different roles, science to design, for instance. She says, "How can we re-occupy the four corners of the 'Bermuda Quadrilateral' as transitory embodiments of creativity and innovation? Better yet, how can we travel them, or even co-exist within them, in a way that is at once meaningful and productive? Can operating within one domain generate a kind of 'creative energy' that enables the easy transition to another?"[5] This is the point of any of our continua, that each position exists on a sliding scale, one transforming into the other rather than occupying discrete locations. However, for the sake of explanation between the extremes of targeted and exploratory intention, let us look at these approaches a little more closely, using our toothbrush designers as examples.

Perhaps our toothbrush designer dreams of making a perfectly balanced brush that sits in the hand so comfortably that brushing is a pleasure—a **targeted intention** for their practice if ever there was one. Targeted intentions for the creative act focus on addressing known problems or issues using the shared tools, techniques, and knowledge at the practitioner's disposal. It is akin to closing gaps, to use Lars Hallnäs's phrase[6]—finding a way from where we are to where we need to be in order to address a particular goal. In this case, our toothbrush designer's targeted intention to improve toothbrushes might begin by asking: How might I design a more ergonomic toothbrush?

Exploratory intentions, on the other hand, lead our toothbrush designer to "why" questions: Why do we view brushing our teeth as a chore, rather than an opportunity to focus on our inner selves? Another toothbrush

TARGETED INTENTIONS

designer's intention might be to reimagine the ritual of toothbrushing as a meditative activity, in the process questioning why toothbrushing is often considered a chore instead of a pleasure. In other words, targeted intentions use existing knowledge to address a known issue (the fit of a toothbrush), while exploratory intentions seek to develop new knowledge (how to shift cultural assumptions about brushing our teeth).

Exploratory intentions anticipate more open-ended outcomes. Instead of having a particular problem to solve, exploratory iterative practices look to open up possibilities and understanding. Exploratory intentions for the creative act expand the possibility space of a medium, a tool, a style, or any other aspect of creative practice.

How is failure leveraged in targeted and exploratory intentions? It takes different forms: Targeted intentions recognize failure as their originating source, seeking to "build a better mousetrap" and, in the words of Beckett, "fail better." Failure is an impetus for the redesign of something, or for making an improvement in the world. Exploratory intentions start with

EXPLORATORY INTENTIONS

a fundamental question approached through incremental experiments, without knowing whether an answer is possible or not. On the exploratory end of the continuum, failure is anticipated and even welcome. Not every new theory or proposition is going to be accurate or on point. Because they provide an opportunity to learn, the failure of exploratory intentions aren't really failures at all.

Our two case studies for this continuum may seem unexpected, but they point to the breadth of exploratory and targeted intentions within an iterative mindset. We look at Jad Abumrad and Robert Krulwich's targeted iterative process to create long-form journalistic radio. Jad, the founder and co-host of *Radiolab*, and Robert, his long-time co-host, have spent years experimenting with radio as a storytelling medium integrating voice, music, and sound design. The immersive soundscapes we've come to expect from the program are the product of years of constant creation in service of a particular intention punctuated by lots of failure.

We also look at the exploratory iterative practice of chef Wylie Dufresne and his inquiries into how and why we cook the way we do. His restaurants are veritable laboratories for pushing our expectations about food. As Wylie puts it, his teams take the familiar and serve it in an unfamiliar way, and take the unfamiliar and serve it in a familiar way, in the process expanding our understanding of cooking and eating.

Continuum III: Methodological and Improvisational Processes
The third continuum continues the focus on the iterative process itself: Is a tried-and-true methodology always used, regardless of all other factors? Or is the iterative process a dynamic response to the moment, changing as the unfolding process necessitates? When iterative practices are more prescribed and use a step-by-step process, the presumption is that the methodology is designed to achieve the intended goals. With improvisational processes, the presumption is that the process will reveal itself through engagement with the context leading to a satisfactory outcome.

In her book *Plans and Situated Actions: The Problem of Human-Machine Communication*, Lucy A. Suchman compares the navigational practices of European explorers and the Trukese, a Micronesian culture.[7] The Europeans would always plan out the exact route to reach their destination, and once on the journey, would focus their navigational energies on staying on that preplanned route. The Trukese, on the other hand, would set their destination, and then begin their journey, with their navigational attention placed on movement toward the desired location rather than on a predetermined route. Suchman uses this comparison to establish the fundamental difference between what she calls **planned action** and **situated action**. Planned action assumes the predefined plan will reach its goal, and so trust is placed in the process. On the other hand, situated actions place trust in each step of the process, and evaluating the outcome of that step to determine the next step on the path toward the goal.

 METHODOLOGICAL & IMPROVISATIONAL PROCESSES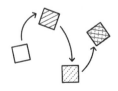

Our conception of methodological process is similar to Suchman's planned action. Methodological processes establish a plan for execution believed to accomplish the given goal. But this doesn't mean all methodology-based creative acts are as set as the routes of those European navigators. Instead, more often than not, methodologically based creative processes use trusted steps in a process that will get the practitioner to the desired outcome. For example, we might have a toothbrush designer who trusts their process, each and every step, as it always leads them in interesting directions and produces top-notch toothbrush designs. Perhaps they studied a little game design at the toothbrush academy, and so adopted playtesting as brush testing, focusing on how brushers experience their prototypes. The iterative process is trusted to navigate the toothbrush designer to a well-designed toothbrush based on their observation of the brushing process.

On the other hand, there are improvisational processes, which more closely align with those of the Trukese navigators. Instead of relying on a predefined plan, improvisational processes rely on intuition and on-the-fly decisions to find the way to the intended outcome. Imagine there is a toothbrush designer who is a big fan of improvisational comedy. Their methodology incorporates "yes … and" scenarios for toothbrushing, leading them to imagine a wide array of contexts and situations. In the absence of a set process and material, improv comedians rely on basic techniques, like "yes … and"—taking what came before, and building upon it, instead of changing directions or being critical. They also employ "active listening"—staying focused on what is happening in the moment rather than planning their next action.

Improvisational iteration leverages one's faith in one's own perceptions to guide the process, incorporating conjecture, instinct, and context as dynamic guides—with failure interpreted through intuition, under the surface. In improvisational iterative processes, failure provides a shifting context to respond to in the moment. Failure might also be difficult to call or see as "failure," as it simply provides a new state to respond to. To use the navigational metaphor, a Trukese sailor doesn't veer off course because the course is not known—navigation is a moment-to-moment process.

METHODOLOGICAL PROCESS

Methodological processes anticipate failure, employing a plan that rec-ognizes failure as an important state which we can account for through pro-cess. Failures are more visible and identifiable in a methodological process. Because a plan exists, it is easy to see when there is a departure from it. In the case of the European explorers' navigational strategy, failure to stay on course is responded to through a course correction—so that the plan can proceed.

When the iterative approach is anchored by process, intentions will be reshaped based on where the process leads. Evaluation can be central to a process-based approach, but still, it is only one of the steps, or perhaps just an input to be considered, in the flow of improvisation. And the outcomes of a process-focused iterative approach will always be accepted as truth, as they were the result of the tried-and-true methodology.

IMPROVISATIONAL PROCESS

Our case studies for methodological and improvisational processes are the collaboration of architect Nathalie Pozzi and game designer Eric Zimmerman, and the musician and composer Andy Milne. The design of games is one of the more open-ended forms of creation, particularly if the designer relies on playtesting. A strong methodology is important for guiding a game through this process. For a look at **methodological processes**, we study how architect Nathalie Pozzi and game designer Eric Zimmerman employ a rigorous prototype-and-playtest process to design their playfulinstallations.

A very different perspective is explored through the work of Andy Milne, a jazz musician, educator, and composer. Andy's process is improvisational. His views on **improvisational process** focus on the in-the-moment nature of jazz improvisation, with an emphasis on recognizing the current melodic situation, and responding to it with confidence and style. This process is employed in both live performance and composition—both improvisational in nature, but with varying timescales (composition, as Andy describes it, is live improvisation slowed down).

Continuum IV: Internal and External Evaluation

The fourth continuum focuses on how the iterative process is evaluated, and by which actors: Is the critical evaluation focused inward, on the practitioner(s) and other involved stakeholders, or is it externalized, consulting others outside the stakeholder group? The traditional view of iteration is that ideas are turned into prototypes that are tested, and the results of those tests are then evaluated to see what can be learned about the initial concept. In most cases, the presumption is that the testing of the prototype involves people other than the individual or team. But beyond this, the kind of feedback solicited from the external testers can vary. Is the hope simply to determine whether the prototype is meeting the intended goals? Or is it to gain inspiration, or even to engage the testers in the design process?

Evaluation is the pivotal phase in iterative processes—this is when the work done thus far is reviewed and critiqued, and plans are laid for what needs to happen next. Maybe it requires a decision about how to most efficiently prototype around a new insight, or it might be at the end of a full iterative loop and decisions need to be made about how to proceed. The quality and impact of subsequent decisions and actions— whether a simple choice needs to be made about a material or a bigger decision made about the next iterative cycle—depends on insightful evaluation. And who participates in this evaluation process is an important consideration.

Donald Schön's ideas about reflective practices come into play again here, in the form of his concept of "reflection-on-action," or an evaluation of processes and work already complete. This moment of reflection doesn't mean that a project is complete, but rather that the work is in a state that

 INTERNAL & EXTERNAL EVALUATION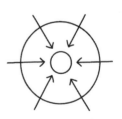

can generate constructive feedback—and the process is at a place where pausing to reflect and evaluate is both feasible and worthwhile.

The usefulness of the evaluation, whether internal or external, is dependent on the critical appraisal skills of the evaluator(s). What prior experiences are brought to bear? What expertise does the evaluator have in terms of the medium, the work's use, or whatever other values are guiding the work's creation? Another industrious toothbrush designer may have an evaluation-based approach to their iterative practice that is **internal**, using their own insights as a guide. Here, they might focus on an engineering-based approach, using computer physics simulations to test the flexibility and strength of their toothbrush designs.

On the other hand, with external evaluation, a different toothbrush designer might desire different critical appraisal skills—those of toothbrush users—in order to see if the brush is going to provide the desired qualities. In this case, surveying the toothbrushing public for their opinions could help determine whether or not a particular design would be successful.

External evaluation reveals the fallibilities of communication and the gap between our subjective experiences. It uses failures between the author and the audience (or the user, or the player, or communities) to adjust the form to be more communicative or evocative of the maker's goal. Internal evaluation takes a more assured subjectivity, where the outcomes the author intends are left open to interpretation. In this case, failure is more personal, as it stems from the practitioner's inability to see or respond to the issues raised in the course of iteration.

External evaluation, in the way we explore it in this book, is not always dependent on having additional people involved in the evaluation. With enough distance—whether through time, space, or medium—one can evaluate one's own work from an external vantage. Examples of external evaluation done by the creator of the work are found when painters take a step back from their painting, when writers print out a draft to see how it reads on the page, or physicists return to a problem after a period of time away to bring new experiences to bear on it. In addition, both forms of evaluation described here involve a process of internalizing feedback—being able to learn through others' subjectivity and evaluate one's own behavior in response.

INTERNAL EVALUATION

An evaluation-based iterative process is going to always put the critical evaluation of each cycle at the forefront. Here, intentions will likely shift due to the decisions made based on the evaluation. And if the process isn't allowing for usable feedback, then changes will likely be made to strengthen the quality of the evaluations. And the outcome of an evaluation-based iterative process plays an important role, as it is often the thing under evaluative consideration. When evaluation anchors an iterative approach, everything else focuses on making sure there is an opportunity to learn from each cycle.

Internal evaluation and external evaluation can nest inside one another. In the flow of work on a new poem, a poet continuously considers word choice, thinks through its theme, explores new metaphors for expression, and so on. These on-the-fly internal evaluations happen during the creative act. Given the fluid nature of these decisions—what Schön called "reflection-in-action"—they don't lend themselves to external evaluation. But once the poet gets the poem to a place that seems stable—something that happens after many microscale evaluations—then external evaluation

EXTERNAL EVALUATION

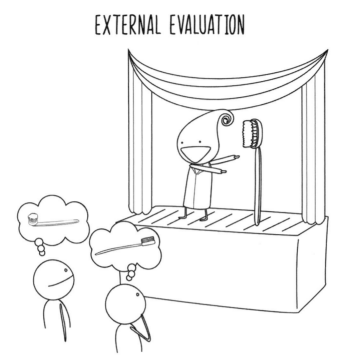

in front of an audience, or what Schön would call "reflection-on-action," may make sense.

Our case studies for internal and external evaluation are the professional skateboarder Amelia Brodka and the comedian Baratunde Thurston. For an example of **internal evaluation**, we look at Amelia Brodka's approach to skateboarding. Like other professional skateboarders, Amelia develops tricks through a process of trial and error and a heavy dose of repetition. What emerges out the other side are tricks that she and others in the skateboarding community use in competitions. Skateboarding tricks require a fine-tuned internal evaluation system, enabling skaters to push themselves to master new tricks and to improve upon those they already know.

For **external evaluation**, we study the comedian Baratunde Thurston, who uses humor as a tool to critique race, economics, and politics. Baratunde is also a media maker and technologist, creating new outlets for comedy and politics. Like many comedians, Baratunde tunes his material through a process of writing and performing to determine what works, what doesn't, and how to get across his ideas in the best possible form.

Taking into account the response of others to evaluate the success and failures of a project is at the center of this consideration.

Continuum V: Convergent and Divergent Outcomes

The fifth and final continuum considers the outcomes of iteration: Does the iterative process converge on a particular solution in a particular medium, or does the process divergently explore multiple possibilities? We borrow these concepts from the psychologist Joy Paul Guilford,[8] who used them to better understand decision making and problem solving. Guilford's foundational research into human creativity surfaced the ideas of convergent thinking and divergent thinking.[9] One type of thinker tends to converge on the best possible answer to a given goal, while another group tends to follow seemingly divergent paths to seek out multiple answers to a given goal. Guilford believed that the optimal process was to use divergent methods in the early stages of a project, and once a suitable solution was reached, shift to convergent strategies. This, of course, isn't a one-size-fits-all solution for creative practice—some creative practitioners follow convergent strategies all the way through, while others remain divergent throughout the process.

Some creative practitioners draw upon existing knowledge and experiences in order to converge on an outcome. Another graduate of our toothbrush academy developed an approach to iteration focused on the outcomes of their process. Sometimes they try to converge on a particular outcome, using each cycle through the process to get them closer to their ultimate goal: eliminating the need for toothpaste once and for all. Other times, they use a divergent approach, which remains open to a variety of solutions. In this case, they strive to develop new potentials for the craft of toothbrush design by generating a variety of different toothbrushes for the market.

CONVERGENT & DIVERGENT OUTCOMES

CONVERGENT OUTCOME

DIVERGENT OUTCOMES

These two examples point out the important role of knowledge for creative practitioners. Guilford broke the act of thinking into three types of actions: **cognition** (the ability to understand and discover), **production** (the ability to produce solutions), and **evaluation** (the ability to assess one's cognition and production).[10] Without working knowledge, these three skill sets are nearly impossible—How would someone know where to start? How would they know how to create within their craft? How would they be able to evaluate their output?

In most cases, knowledge is a good thing—it means having the craft skills to create a work, knowing the methods that tend toward satisfactory outcomes, having encountered certain problems before and knowing how to address them. But knowledge within the creative act can also be limiting. In her book *The Storm of Creativity*, architect Kyna Leski considers the importance of unlearning during the creative act.[11] As Leski puts it, "Unlearning is about questioning what you thought you know."[12] Part of what Leski wants to draw our attention to is the way prior knowledge can limit our thinking. She uses Alex Faickney Osborn's brainstorming techniques as an example[13]—most times, brainstorming exercises draw out the most obvious and already known ideas, techniques, and solutions. This is because the basic process of brainstorming puts emphasis on the ability of the participant to rapidly draw upon existing stores of knowledge at the expense of valuing the time it takes to more broadly consider the problem space and potential solutions. Within Guilford's framework, this existing knowledge provides the framework and context for cognition, the processes and procedures for production, and the insights necessary for evaluation. But from the perspective of Leski's unlearning, this prior knowledge can create boundaries that constrain creative exploration, limiting the practitioner to only solutions already known and understood.

Leski frames the problem well: "If your starting point is to name and identify solutions before unlearning, it is unlikely to lead to anything creative or outside what you already know."[14] In the context of convergent and divergent outcomes, convergent outcomes are more often borne from working within one's knowledge—whether that be material, processual, technical, or otherwise. And divergent outcomes more fully embrace Leski's idea of unlearning.

All that being said, convergence gets a bad rap. As Arthur Cropley has argued, this is the case if for no other reason than that convergent thinking has been described as maintaining the status quo, and therefore falls short of the "innovative" and "novel" expectations demanded of creativity.[15] Indeed, divergent thinking plays into the mythology of creative genius, whereby someone creates an unimaginable thing by virtue of their genius. As Cropley makes clear, convergent thinking is a critical part of the creative process, even in those cases where divergent outcomes were desired, or divergent processes were employed. Cropley points out the paradox of the convergent/divergent dichotomy: Without knowledge of some sort— craft skill, knowledge of materials, an understanding of the context, and so on—how can one really make anything effective, let alone innovative?

Iterative processes guided by convergent outcomes, when they work well, inch away from failure one step at a time. At the same time, if there are faulty assumptions guiding the process, or a lack of critical evaluation along the way, convergent processes can easily lead to failure. Divergent outcomes, on the other hand, seek to explore, without regard to whether failure is along the path. In both cases, failure becomes a source of learning for future practice.

Our case studies for convergent and divergent outcomes are the toy and play designer Cas Holman and the artist Miranda July. Practitioners aiming for **convergent outcomes** know where the iterative process should end up—even if the goal is elusive. As an example, we look at Cas Holman, who designs play: playgrounds, toys, learning activities, and everything in between. Her work is both playful and inspiring to players and educators alike in its pursuit of "empowering play," using constructivist learning principles and explorations of identity.

Where convergent methods often begin with a "how can we ..." question, **divergent outcomes** more likely begin with a "what if we ..." question. Divergent methods follow a line of inquiry to see where it might lead, to see what new knowledge it can produce, even if that means realizing that the question needs to change. Divergent outcomes can arise from questioning the medium for delivering a story, exploring the scale at which something should be done, or investigating the affective potential of an idea. We look at the artistic polymath Miranda July: writer, filmmaker, visual artist, performance artist, and media artist. Across her career, she has explored the beauty of the mundane, vulnerability, and self-destructive behavior. What connects her work is her ideas, each ending up somewhere different through explorations of medium and technique.

Different Practices and Different Perspectives

Though we introduce them here as discrete concepts, these five continua aren't mutually exclusive. All of the continua engage all of the components of iteration, but each has its own emphasis or approach. Some emphasize context (material and reflective), some intent (targeted and exploratory), others outcomes (convergent and divergent); some focus on the evaluation of creative works (internal and external evaluation), while some are more attentive to process (methodological, improvisational). And all five continua directly engage with the actors involved in the creative act.

While we aren't claiming that these continua are the only considerations for iterative creative practice, we do see them as useful concepts for teasing out the nuances of iteration, and for seeing iteration as a part of a diverse set of practices beyond simply being a tool for problem solving. It was important to us to create a model of iterative creative practice that faithfully models the complex, messy realities of creativity, while at the same time trying to make sense of the many creative approaches one can take. We can't help but see the iterative cycles in the creative practitioners we are studying, perhaps because we rely on iteration in our own practice, and teach it to our students to inform theirs. That said, the perspectives we found are incredibly diverse, and we're sure that if we were to extend our research to twenty case studies, we would find even more ways to think about iteration. So, while these are not the only ways one can approach iteration, they provide some exciting insights for a range of creative practices.

Section II   Ten Perspectives

Learning to fail better is easier said than done. It requires an openness to the unknown, an intentional vulnerability to expose oneself to challenges and uncertainty, and a thoughtful, constructively critical eye to appraise and make sense of failure. An uncommon set of attributes, certainly, but these are the characteristics we found in the practitioners we interviewed for the case studies in this section.

Section II of the book, comprised of ten case studies presented in five pairs, show the breadth of iterative creative practices: Material and reflective contexts consider whether the iterative mindset is formed through material or more ephemeral conditions; targeted and exploratory intentions establish the desired outcomes; methodological and improvisational processes determine the kind of process used in the pursuit of the intentions and outcomes; internal and external evaluation speaks to who evaluates progress toward the intended outcomes and how; and convergent and divergent outcomes indicate the expectations placed on the results of iterative creative practice.

Our intention with the ten case studies that follow is to look closely at a variety of practices to help us see the complexity of creativity and its relationship to failure, but also to see the possibilities for iteration when viewed more closely. The case studies are paired up based on a shared aspect of creative practice emphasized in their work, to form five continua. Within these continua, the case studies explore different facets of context, intention, process, evaluation, and outcome.

Think of the case studies as being somewhat akin to medicine's morbidity and mortality conferences (those discussions of patient injury or death seen in TV shows like *Grey's Anatomy* and *E.R.*). But instead of wanting to learn how to avoid failure, as morbidity and mortality conferences do, we want to learn how failure operates as an honest, frequent part of the creative process. By looking closely at the iterative practices of individuals working in a wide array of creative disciplines, we have seen how different each approach truly is and that there is not just one effective methodology.

As we worked on this project, something became quite clear: no two fields, and no two communities of practice within a field, talk about, think about, and assess their intentions, process, and output in quite the same way. Every community of practice has its own language for communicating about what it does, and why. Each has its own process for how it goes about practicing its craft and practical methods for making sense of and working through failure.

But while each of these practitioners do things differently, they all, in one way or another, iterate.

5 Material Contexts: Allison Tauziet, Winemaker

Allison Tauziet makes wine. Not just any kind of wine. Incredible, award-winning, you've-never-tasted-anything-like-this wine. Colgin Cellars, where Allison is winemaker, sits perched on the side of a mountain in Napa, California, with sweeping views of the valley below. If you haven't heard of Colgin, it's likely because their wines are pretty hard to get. They produce cabernet sauvignon and Bordeaux-style blends in relatively small quantities, only available in select restaurants and to a limited list of lucky clients.[1] The high demand for their wines is understandable—fourteen of their wines have received perfect 100-point ratings from the influential wine critic Robert Parker, placing Colgin among only a handful of rare producers who have received such accolades. Allison was responsible for twelve of these

Allison Tauziet. Photography credit: Kabeer.

perfect scores, making her the only woman winemaker in the world who has received that many 100-point ratings.

Sounds like success, right? It is, especially when your collaborator is the unpredictable and capricious Mother Nature. For thousands of years people have managed to plant, cultivate, and harvest grapes, and then use natural fermentation processes to create wine.[2] But to pull this off as successfully as Allison has involves a dedication to these time-honored processes, as well as a keen sense of what nature might throw at her, year after year.

Vineyards dot the landscape along the valleys and hills of Napa Valley, the epicenter of California wine country, and during the harvest the ripe grape smells from the "crush" infuse the air. It's here that Allison was first introduced to the art of winemaking at a young age, literally breathing it in on weekends spent there with her father. So it only makes sense that when Allison began attending nearby University of California, Davis, she took an elective course called Introduction to Winemaking. It was during a slideshow on the first day of class that Allison saw an image she knew had to be her future: a woman in rubber boots knee-deep in the materials of winemaking: grapes, juice, gigantic steel drums, hoses ... When Allison saw that image, she thought to herself: "That's what I want to do."[3]

And that's exactly what twenty-year-old Allison did. That same year, she drove up to Domaine Chandon vineyard, famous for their Moët & Chandon sparkling wines, and asked to see the winemaker for an internship. Of course, the winemaker, sparkling wine legend Dawnine Dyer, was busy, as famous winemakers tend to be. So Allison left her résumé, and then followed up with a call. And another call. She called once a day until one day Dyer called her back. Allison thinks that a combination of her persistence and the fact that, like herself, Dyer also began her career in her twenties led to the returned call and her first opportunity in the industry. There was a kinship—one woman in boots to another. She was hired.

Allison's work at Domaine Chandon perfectly replicated that image of the woman-in-boots that she'd held in her mind. Her first job was to measure the sugar and acidity in grape samples to assess their maturity. This involved getting covered in sticky juice, surrounded by bees while hand-crushing fifty buckets of grapes a day. She loved it. Inspired by her experience at Domaine Chandon, Allison ended up double-majoring in fermentation science and French at UC Davis. Being in the winery combined a lifelong love of science with the pleasure of working with her hands, her senses, and the physicality of winemaking. After graduating and completing her internship at Chandon, Allison spent a year interning at the Conseil Interprofessionnel du Vin de Bordeaux in France. When she returned to Napa, she worked in the cellar at Far Niente, where she continued learning her craft under the mentorship of some of Napa's best winemakers.

In 2005, Allison arrived at Colgin Cellars as assistant winemaker/estate manager, and was soon thereafter promoted to winemaker. The promotion also led to a shift in context. The pre-Colgin phase involved spending most of her time in the winery, working with the grapes, the chemistry of fermentation, and the art of blending. At Colgin, Allison's territory expanded to include not just the winery, but also the surrounding fields of the vineyard. Now, the materials she needed to learn to work with encompassed acres and acres of land: the vines, the soil, the weather, and an entire ecosystem. Her world expanded, as did the **material context** of her practice. The boots, however, remained the same.

Nature Doesn't Fail

It's just plants. It's just a huge garden.
—Allison Tauziet

Nature is both the context and constraint for the winemaking process. A winemaker's collaboration with nature turns three simple things (a suitable site, fruit, and the process of fermentation) into outcomes that are varied, complex, and delicious. But of these three inputs, one is cited by winemakers as the most influential to a wine's character: the "terroir," winespeak for the environment of the vineyard. All of the raw materials of Allison's practice emerge from the terroir—the vineyard's orientation to the sun and fog, its soil, and the surrounding flora and fauna. The untrained eye would certainly say that Colgin's IX Estate is awe-inspiring. The grapevines ascend a gentle slope on a secluded mountaintop overlooking Lake Hennessey and St. Helena in the valley below. To an expert, however, there's even more to love. The hillside faces east, bathing the fields in a gentle morning light, something grapes particularly like. The soil is rocky and volcanic, which allows for ample drainage and gives a concentrated mineral quality to the fruit. And the fruits grown on these hills produce powerful, inky-black red wines. Wine connoisseur and critic Robert Parker has said that the IX Estate is "as close to a viticultural nirvana as I've ever seen."[4]

Allison's role as winemaker is "to take all of that and harness it into something that is really elegant and beautiful." Harnessing the power of such a great site often results in incredible wines, but working with nature can also be unpredictable, inconsistent, and downright risky. There are no do-overs for a bad harvest, and the cycles of iteration that define the craft of making wine are measured in years, each representing a full annual cycle through the winemaking season. Working with the whims of nature to mitigate failure requires patience and a Zen-like sense of going with, not against, the flow. And when that flow takes unpredictable turns, a winemaker, like a whitewater rafter, needs to be ready to react to whatever sudden shift nature throws at her.

Nature is also, by nature, impossible to replicate, control, or rewind—no matter how hard humans try. In winemaking, as in whitewater rafting, there's no turning back—there's only forward motion and reacting to the flow of water to keep from capsizing. Humans can help guide natural processes to amplify or diminish their effects, but they can't change nature's course. With every year that passes, the vines get older and more deeply rooted. At the same time, climate change creates more volatility in seasonal patterns. However, despite the constant flux, Allison has developed a harmonious view of nature over the years—working with it, not against it. She says, "Nature does not fail. Everything happens for a reason and it's a kind of beautiful reason. Always. Be it a flood after a drought, or vice versa, there's always a balance there, and so there's no fault to that."

Balancing nature's extremes while at the same time amplifying the unique qualities of each year's harvest involves an intimate knowledge of the material conditions provided by nature, learned by making wine, year after year—in other words, iteration through making. Allison's practice takes place in a material context. She works with the same materials every year (the site, grapes, and the processes of fermentation), but each year nature provides a slightly (or substantially) different timetable, set of challenges, and fruit qualities. To help her mitigate these changes and their impact on the centuries-old winemaking process, Allison and her team use iteration, over the course of seasons and years, to reach an outcome that best expresses both her intentions and nature's unique contribution.

Making Sense of the Details

Nature plays the starring role in winemaking, with humans simply tending to the process and intervening to enhance what nature does already, like training vines that naturally want to climb along a wire, or pruning the vines to help concentrate the plant's energy into the fruit. Allison's view of the process emphasizes paying careful attention to her natural collaborators:

What we can do as humans in the process is pay attention to all the little things that can help bring out and accentuate the beauty from that site. So I start by paying a lot of attention in the vineyard and the agricultural side of it. That's when I am a farmer, asking: What can you do to make really great fruit? I then transition—paying a lot of attention when it comes to making the wine. So from beginning to end, it's a really harmonious experience, and that translates into the wine.

Walking in the vineyards, Allison seems to notice everything, as if her senses were specially tuned to nature's frequencies. She is attentive to the tiniest of details—both in the vines and, beyond them, in other plants and natural phenomena, like the hourly fog levels, the moment surrounding trees begin to bloom, temperature fluctuations, and the changing direction of the wind. This attention to detail is how Allison works with, not against, the material constraints of nature. Allison's approach to working

Colgin IX Estate Vineyard. Photography credit: Kabeer.

with nature echoes the farmer-philosopher Masanobu Fukuoka, who advo-
cated that farmers observe nature more thoughtfully in order to labor less
thoughtlessly.[5] Allison's approach to making the best fruit she can embodies this ideal—she observes the details in her natural context in order to
make wine, thoughtfully.

However, the details are always changing. Allison says, "I don't think
you can ever completely know it; you just continue to learn about it,
because it's changing always." The materials of Allison's practice (the vines,
the weather, the qualities of the fruit) are alive and in constant flux. To find
harmony with this, Allison's practice is also constantly changing.

"Vintage" is a sophisticated-sounding term that simply refers to the year
in which a wine is made. Each vintage tells a unique story, which makes
a lot of sense when you think about it—there are a million details in the

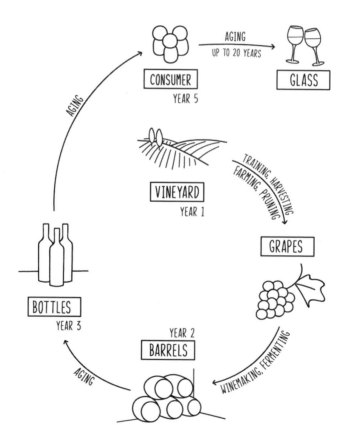

winemaking process, large and small, and they're different every year. The drama unfolds first with the site, then with how the vines are planted, how they're trained and pruned, what's planted around and among the vines, the weather patterns, the decision of when to harvest, the method used to crush the grapes, the fermentation process, and the blending of grapes. But there's still no wine until it's time: While the winemaking cycle marked by the vintage is one year, the resulting wine takes about three or more years to reach a glass.

If the vintage tells a story, then the harvest is the story's climax. This is the most exciting—and risky—time of the year. As Allison notes, "You can only pick the grapes once. We've proven you can't put it back on the vine." Acre by acre, there's one chance a year to get it right. With such a long yet fixed timeline, how does one learn to avoid picking the grapes at the wrong time, or making another mistake in the process? The answer is, with patience, attention to detail, and years of iterative experience to draw from.

Because winemaking is such an extended process within a constantly changing context, remembering what happened a year ago becomes essential. For Allison, this involves careful observation of all the material

A page from Allison's calendar. Image: Allison Tauziet.

qualities of nature, a strong sense memory, and a lot of note taking. She keeps a daily calendar—the one most people use to jot down appointments and schedules—to write down what's happening out in the fields: the angle of the sun, the wind, the fog patterns, and the flora beyond the vines, from the fall when the buckeyes defoliate to the end of winter when the mustards start blooming. By noting these patterns every day, Allison creates a detailed record of the year. When the season is over, the calendar is filed away for future reference. She might not look at the calendar again until next year, or perhaps many years in the future. For example, the current year might have a hot and dry spring—so Allison will remember back to a previous year that matched that pattern, and refer to that year's calendar. She uses that earlier calendar to provide a point of comparison from year to year, informing how she might respond. She searches for patterns, finding clues from past vintages to compare to the current one. So, while most people use calendar planners to remind them of what's coming up in the future, Allison uses hers to remember what happened in the past. As she describes it,

When you look back at other calendars from other years, you see that it's different— different every year, but it is still the same progression. These cues can help you predict things a little bit better. I love looking at that kind of stuff, I think it's pretty crazy because there's a lot there that you couldn't really even research or scientifically study, it's just automatic, nature's programmed it to be that way.

Every moment of every season brings with it a multitude of decisions that affect the final product. So in addition to the use of a calendar, Allison relies on her senses. Leading up to the harvest, her goal is to help the vines produce the best possible fruit. She is out in the fields, in her broad hat and boots, checking the vines, deciding when to prune, tending to the soil, or picking blocks (sections of the vineyard) to be harvested. As the grapes mature, Allison tastes a lot of fruit, looking for variation between acres to map out flavors spatially. Each acre-based group becomes its own note in the resulting blend. She tastes to see if the grapes are developed and complex, looks at and feels the texture of the grape skins. She chews the skins and examines them between two fingers to see if their color is staining her skin, the hue of the stain a clue revealing the fruit's acidity. She also considers the intensity of the stain to assess how the winemaking process will extract all of those flavors, colors, and tannins. She notes the ripeness or brownness of the seeds, and tastes the seed to see if it's imparting some of its own flavors. Every bit of the fruit is examined, every sense is employed, and of course it's all written down in her calendar. As she points out, "All of these attributes will be magnified once we begin to make the wine, so we want them to all be harmonious. We want to know as much as possible about the fruit before we make the wine." All of the little bits of knowledge, from tasting the grapes to observing the direction of the wind, provide the material context for Allison's iteration. The details she learns from her close observations help her evaluate and plan the next step.

Of course, winemaking involves more than Allison, alone, strolling through the vineyards observing things. It's a team effort. Allison works closely with her vineyard foreman. So closely, in fact, that she describes their ability to communicate almost without any words—a kind of "viticultural telepathy." As she says, "He leads the vineyard crew to do amazing work, which I couldn't live without." There's a lot of hard labor involved in the process, as well as logistics and team management. A year in the life of the Colgin team moves from being consistently busy to being completely frenzied during harvest. It begins with pruning the vines at the beginning of the year to choosing when to mow the grasses, till the soil, and irrigate the vines, and deciding how and when to do each of these things to bring out the full potential of the season. Allison explains, "The when and the how are equally important. For example, not just when do we irrigate? But, how deeply shall we do it?"

Once it's harvest time, Allison transitions from sensory observation in the fields to the science of fermentation in the winery. There her notetaking continues, this time in a dossier for each wine. She explains,

I keep my own dossier for every wine—the nutrition of the fruit, tonnage, the berry and cluster weight, additions—it's somewhat technical. I keep that for every year. I have outrun the size of my cabinet with all of the notes. It's great to be able to look back. You can get really deep into a harvest and think it's all really normal, but when you look back at something from years before you may realize that those years you thought were normal were really unique.

Once harvested, the grapes are crushed, and Allison must choose how best to extract the juice—with higher or lower temperatures—and how much time to let the wine continue to macerate—a process by which the grape skins soak in the pressed juice—after the fermentation has completed. To decide, Allison returns to her sensory abilities:

All of these decisions are based on tasting the wine day by day. It's such a dynamic process, and you can't predict exactly how something is going to respond, so for me, it's important to taste again and again and again to see where the ship you're steering is headed.

Taste leads to choices about blending the wines, and when and how to move the resulting wines from vats to barrels to bottles. Each of these processes comes with many other steps, and the winemaker has to organize it all. In the fields they choose the blocks for picking during harvest by carefully watching and tasting the fruit, and in the winery they measure sugar levels and other chemical qualities. During each of these steps, there are a million things that can go wrong. This is where Allison's constant tasting comes in, to see where the slow "ship" of the winemaking process is heading, and making adjustments along the way. Allison's ship-steering metaphor is perhaps more accurate than the whitewater rafting one used earlier, given the slow cycle of the winemaking process, but with either metaphor Allison is responding to the natural context of winemaking, working with the flow of nature to produce great outcomes.

The science of fermentation in the winery and the farming practices in the field are ultimately in service of the art of making delicious and distinctive wines. Allison's sense of taste (meaning her taste buds, not style preference) is keenly attuned to how the flavors of grapes transform into wine, and how they work together in a blend (Colgin IX primarily produces blends, or wines made from multiple types of grapes), like pieces in a flavorful puzzle. Learning this takes seasons of tasting grapes as they turn into juice and into wine. Each year, the process is repeated, but the conditions of nature are constantly in flux, demanding flexibility in the process. One can't follow the same formula year after year because the raw materials—the grapes—are always responding to the changing conditions of nature. The senses, the science of fermentation and measuring levels in the winery, notes from previous years, and attention to every surrounding detail are all employed to coax the materials Allison works with into great wine. And to truly learn the qualities and behaviors of these materials involves iteration through years of winemaking, one vintage at a time.

Some vintages, however, leave a mark.

2011

Early in her career, Allison believed she should make very consistent wines that tasted the same from year to year, and that met certain expectations of Napa reds—like dark fruits or a full-bodied palate. But as the years went on, she realized that when nature veers outside the norm, it's better to go with it than against it. She told us, "Every vintage is supposed to be different. Every vintage is supposed to have an interesting story. Why do the same thing again and again?" She continues, "It's so fascinating to stay in the same place year after year, and to let the variations of each vintage take us to new places." There was one year in particular that took Allison to a very new place in winemaking, leading her to change her entire philosophy.

When you imagine California, what picture comes to mind? Whatever image it is, it's likely that the scene is bathed in sunshine. It's the warm, pervasive California sun that lends itself to the big, luscious, fruity reds of Napa. But, if you had decided to visit in the late summer and fall of 2011, you might have thought you were somewhere else. It was a cold and wet summer, with an unexpected damp fog that rolled in and refused to leave right before the harvest. These unusual weather conditions assured that the 2011 vintage would go down in infamy for the challenges it posed winemakers.

As *Wine Spectator* said, the 2011 growing season was "simply nasty."[6] "It was a horrible year for Napa Cabernet,"[7] said Chuck Wagner of Caymus Vineyards, another Napa winery. Or as Allison more calmly described it, "we had challenges." And the challenges were many. The spring was long and wet, delaying the vines' growth more than Allison remembers in her years of winemaking. The summer was colder and wetter than normal as well, conditions that can lead to the biggest enemy of grapes and winemaking: mold and fungi. The gray fungus *Botrytis cinerea*, or "noble rot," is welcomed in the practice of making sweet dessert wines, but for the wines Allison and many Napa winemakers cultivate, there's nothing noble about this mold and its cousins—it can ruin an entire harvest. To combat mold growth, grapes need to dry after rains. When unseasonable cold and frequent rains make this difficult, vineyards use leaf blowers to dry the vines in order to keep mold at bay. But the third threat of 2011's triple threat, the one that was impossible to solve with man-made means, was the unexpected warm fog that descended in early October and decided to stay. A million leaf blowers couldn't keep this wet fog blanket from wreaking havoc on the grapes.

Despite the impossible conditions, there was no second chance for Allison and the other Napa winemakers. Allison had to make some tough decisions, as grapes were swelling and bursting on the vines from the warm fog blanketing the region prior to harvest, even though the grapes were still not as ideally ripe as they could be. As Allison describes it: "I couldn't let the fruit ripen longer, so I had to judiciously decide how to proceed picking, acre by acre. Do you pick what's best right at the moment? Or do you go first to the things that are suffering? What do you do?"

What *do* you do? To make that wine, she needed to push the limits of her team and her timetable. As Allison described it, she was "picking a lot of fruit and making wine very fast." Exemplifying her tendencies to hedge a little bit, she picked the fruit that absolutely had to be picked or else they would burst or perish. At the same time, she looked for blocks where the grapes were better off and ready, and picked them too. She had also picked some grapes before the warm fog arrived, which were added to the blend. In the end, the wine was a mixture of the grapes picked before and after the fog, each set tempering the characteristics of the other. During those frantic days, Allison was engaging in Schön's "reflection-in-action"[8]—applying in the moment her previous knowledge and current sensory input, all working within the context set by her collaborator, Mother Nature. She describes her thought process:

There's just not any flexibility, so you ask yourself, okay—what do I have that is a strength? I have an amazing team that is just energetic and motivated and excited to be here, and I have incredible vineyards that are already going to make something special, and so drawing on all of that, what can we make out of it? And we made something that year that I am maybe more proud of than anything else.

Challenges are memorable, and they mark us. Psychologists have found that the greater the challenge, the prouder we are at overcoming it and the higher we value the results.[9] So it makes sense that Allison and her team are so proud of that 2011 vintage. It was a tough year; some vineyards brought in consultants from Bordeaux, where more adverse conditions are the norm. The Napa vineyards that did produce great wines that year did so through the skills of their winemakers.[10] As Allison put it, "When vintages are easy, it's kind of easy for everybody. But it's the years that are more challenging that you can really work harder and see the proof of your work."

The proof of Allison and her team's work was in the wines. Allison's efforts in 2011 turned out a very good wine, one that received great ratings despite it all. (While none had a perfect score, they were all very highly scored in the 90s.)[11] Allison reflects back on that vintage: "In some ways, it's cathartic to suspend your expectations and instead to seek, in that moment, where you can find beauty. Something you may have never predicted, but is still beautiful nonetheless."

The catharsis that Allison experienced during the near-disaster of the 2011 vintage ended up changing the way she makes wine. She and her team now have a stronger sense of the spectrum with which they work year to year. They know what the typically warmer growing seasons yield (big bold fruity grapes), and they now know what kind of wine a cooler season makes (bright, savory herbal grapes). Ever since then, Allison tries to make sure that every vintage has a small hint of those fresh, savory 2011 vintage flavors. She believes their complexity will help the wines stand the test of time.

Writing about that year, *New York Times* wine critic Eric Asimov asked, "When the weather switches up on you, do you embrace it and make wines that reflect the vintage? Or do you try to bend the wines to your will? From my point of view, harmonizing with nature wins out."[12] And that's what Allison did: instead of trying to bend the wine to her will, she found a harmonious way to work with nature while still achieving her goal: distinctive, great-tasting wines.

Winemaking requires working with what you're given—nature's patterns and the fruit and your senses and abilities to understand them—and finding the beauty in that year's vintage. Or in Allison's words, "What we do as winemakers is to explain exactly what happens with each season." The experience of the 2011 season pushed her to try new strategies, and in the process, to expand the way she makes wine. So while nature seemed to be working against her, it was actually revealing a whole new range of flavors she could play with. A new context.

Connecting the Dots

Over the years, Allison's perspective on winemaking has grown from her initial focus on the winery to include the vineyard and its surroundings.

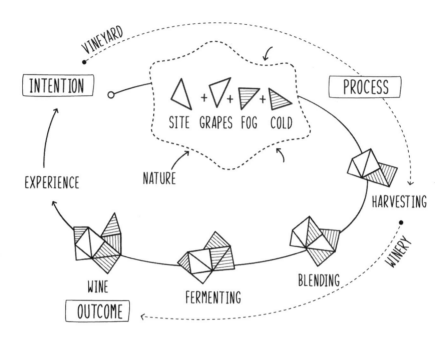

This expansion of **context** taught her how to be responsive to the dynamic situation of each new year, in large part by learning to identify nature's patterns and by trusting her senses. Nature is always changing, so within this flux, Allison finds balance between her **intentions** and her **outcomes** by developing a flexible and changing **process**. The cycle of the seasons is the engine driving Allison's work, and learning the range of conditions nature can provide involves iteration over the course of many years. Her process therefore emphasizes attention to detail guided by patterns that are only visible through the repetition of observation, note taking, and reliance on her senses to **evaluate** the characteristics of the grapes as they transform. Allison's detailed notes help her to see the patterns over the seasonal cycles from year to year, compare the range of conditions from the past to predict the future, and mitigate failure.

While Allison once strove for a uniformity in her wines from vintage to vintage, her philosophy has now evolved to respond to nature and the material qualities of grapes and winemaking in a more balanced way, seeking to enhance what nature provides. The process of finding balance has influenced her own outlook on life as well. Allison says, "When you are young, you are predisposed to one way, but as [I] get older, my life has sought to develop the rest of myself, to bring balance to [my]self." This process of finding balance between herself and the material conditions of the world involves paying attention to the details, looking back in order to mitigate an uncertain future, and working with—not against—nature. In other words, taking whatever nature provides, and making it delicious.

6 Reflective Contexts: Matthew Maloney, Animator

Though he may not have realized it at the time, Matthew Maloney's animation career began in a Blockbuster Video store. As a kid, Matthew was drawn to horror, sci-fi, and action films—none of which he was allowed to watch. And so he was left to imagine the stories found on the VHS boxes using the logos, airbrushed still images from the film, and a few sentences of hyperbole. Matthew tended to spend more time with the bombastic cover of George A. Romero's *Dawn of the Dead* than the muted imagery of Louis Malle's *My Dinner with Andre*. Both are important films, but the box art for dialogue-driven cinema didn't hold up in the presence of blood-drenched horror films. Horror films became Matthew's childhood obsession; there

Matthew Maloney. Photo by Shuangshuang Huo.

were amazing stories locked away in those VHS tapes, and in the absence of viewing the films, his imagination was left to construct fantastic tales from the box art.

Jump forward a decade, and Matthew enrolled in the Savannah College of Art and Design's (SCAD's) Computer Art program, where he began giving form to his stories in earnest. He studied with the stop-motion animator Hal Miles and the animation master Becky Wible Searles, and developed not only the craft skills for making films but the theoretical underpinnings for how moving images convey story, idea, and emotion. Matthew ended up sticking around SCAD for his BFA and MFA, and after a few years teaching and doing freelance animation jobs, he returned to SCAD's Atlanta campus where he now chairs the BFA and MFA animation programs.

During and around his teaching, Matthew has made several award-winning stop-motion films that travel the film and animation festival circuits: *King Rust*, a meditation on the human capacity for violence; *The Anchorite*, a surreal meditation on the struggles of creativity; *Loon*, a reflection on the ever-changing landscape of Hong Kong; and *Gryphon Animo*, his first foray into a fully 3D animated film, which interrogates the trope of the hero's journey.

As Matthew has said, "Good animation is style-driven, it isn't story-driven."[1] By this he means that yes, animations can tell stories (his so far always have), but that the sensory elements of sight and sound drive the medium, more so than the stories told. This is particularly the case of the short-form experimental animations Matthew creates. As he has noted, you can make a successful animation out of someone trying to find a book of matches, so long as the story is told with style. Matthew compares animation's relation to traditional filmmaking to poetry's relationship to literature; in the same way that poetry takes stylistic license with language in order to explore things beyond descriptive prose, animation can explore ideas and emotions that would be more challenging to articulate through traditional live-action filmmaking.

Matthew uses the term "experiential truth" to describe what he strives for in his films. He hopes to be able to share his emotional experiences, whether they are his experience of his own creative practice, his perceptions of a particular time and place, or the emotional experience of an object. Often, these experiential truths are difficult to put into words; and so, given Matthew's style-driven conception of animation, the logical entry point for creating these experiential truths is the image. His films then become poetic documents of a particular emotional state from a moment in his life.

One of the big challenges in Matthew's experimental filmmaking is that he doesn't focus on creating narratives with clear causal logic. Instead, he looks to create a particular mood or tone that allows him to explore broader ideas—creative practice, constancy confronted by relentless change, naive bravado in the face of adversity. Each scene in a sequence then works to establish an emotional tone that builds upon, shifts, or otherwise responds to the scene before it. This approach differs from the traditional reliance on associative linkage (the connections we make to understand the relationship of one thing to another) that help viewers construct a narrative logic by using information from one scene to help them understand the next. As playwright and filmmaker David Mamet has suggested, each scene answers the question posed by the preceding scene, and in turn asks a question that can only be answered by the next scene.[2] Most filmmakers have used this technique, dating back to Soviet montage theory and Sergei Eisenstein's sequencing of discrete shots. The implication of montage is that sequencing one shot after another builds the story, creating a cognitive understanding for the viewer. But when the sequencing of scenes and images is instead intended to create an emotional context, it is much more challenging for filmmakers to make their ideas visible. This is partly because the resulting sequences are less narrative-driven and more impressionistic and poetic.

From this perspective, it is not easy to locate where the filmmaker falls short of their expressive goals, or how the audience misses the intended emotional tone or impact. Matthew compares his approach to filmmaking to observational science—both are processes in which failure is not only possible but probable, and even at times desirable. This is why process is so important to both the scientific method and to animation—let's be methodical, as who knows, we may actually find something we need to reproduce. Stop-motion animation in particular is process-oriented. Each frame in a stop-motion film requires the animator to change character poses ever so slightly in order to create the intended sense of motion. For facial expressions, many stop-motion puppets have dozens of different heads that are interchanged to denote subtle shifts in emotional state. The setting and props in a stop-motion film require the same meticulous detail.

This attention to minutiae requires a precise methodology to make sure everything is just so.

Matthew approaches each film with an overarching question he hopes to answer. This larger question is then segmented into smaller questions posed by each scene, and within that scene, each shot, all the way down to each puppet and item on the set. Some of the questions are mundane— Does this sequence of frames have a continuity of movement that creates the illusion of the puppet coming to life? Formal questions arise as well around the medium—Can a story be told successfully along a single plane in the style of side-scrolling videogames? Can stop-motion puppetry be interleaved with live-action cinematography? Still other questions are more complex and compelling—Can this story of a two-dimensional character's journey capture the essence of a particular mood and emotional tone? Can a single character stand in for the rich history of a city?

Unlike David Mamet's notion of a linear question and answer from scene to scene, Matthew's questions stack and interweave, creating a depth that leaves Matthew knowing that he will not likely answer each question as well as he might hope. In this light, Matthew considers his films to be failures—not in the sense of being poorly made or unwatchable, but because he sets out to answer questions that aren't easily answered through experimental animations that eschew traditional narrative structures. These can be failures in reaching his intended outcomes, but also the failure of audiences to emotionally connect with the film. Even if a film connects with an audience, they will likely relate to different things, and have different emotional responses. But these types of failure are to be expected when pushing the boundaries of a medium and one's own creative practice.

Discovery through Repetition

This experimental approach to animated filmmaking is not without its challenges. Often, Matthew sets out to explore subjects in ways that lack obvious precedents and tried-and-true filmmaking techniques. To help him find the right embodiments and articulations of his ideas, he joins his iterative practices to a **reflective context**, using repeated close readings of the work of others in order to strengthen aspects of one's own creative practice. For Matthew, this takes the form of watching films, reading novels and short stories, playing videogames, and listening to music. Each work provides different lessons and inspirations, sometimes reminding him of important principles, other times revealing emotional potentials of film and animation, and still other times reconnecting him to a particular time, place, or feeling. While working on a project, he may watch a film repeatedly over the course of a couple of days, or even only once a year.

Matthew's creation of reflective contexts are his primary tool for mitigating the failures of affective communication inherent in experimental filmmaking. Once he finds examples in others' works that convey the emotions he hopes to share through his films, he will watch (or read, or play, or listen to) a work until he has internalized the power of the emotional note, but also the means by which the other artist has produced it.

Matthew is not alone in this sort of reflective ritual. Russian filmmaker Andrei Tarkovsky had a go-to film that he watched at the start of his own productions: Alexander Dovzhenko's 1930 film *Earth*. For Tarkovsky, *Earth* demonstrated how a filmmaker could capture a specific atmosphere in a film. Through rewatching it, he could revisit the strategies Dovzhenko used to create this poetic effect. As Tarkovsky said in his book *Sculpting in Time*, "Art is a meta-language, with the help of which people try to communicate with one another; to impart information about themselves and assimilate the experience of others."[3]

This gives us a window onto the use of reflective contexts: Through successive viewings, a creative practitioner can strive to understand and explore another's work as a means of strengthening their own. Tarkovsky sought poetic atmosphere in his reflective viewings of Dovzhenko's *Earth*. In other cases, filmmakers may look for particular cinematographic, sound design, or narrative techniques. For Matthew, it is more often than not an emotional tone or texture that he tries to experience. But in all cases, reflective iteration helps him to better understand his own filmmaking practice by bringing clarity to something he was struggling to understand or express.

Perhaps the most notable use of reflective iteration is Matthew's annual Halloween horror film tradition. Starting in the early fall, Matthew watches 100 or more horror films from the 1970s, 1980s, and early 1990s. He'll watch an entire franchise in order—*Friday the 13th*, then *Friday the 13th Part 2, Part III, The Final Chapter, A New Beginning, Jason Lives,* and so on up to *Part VIII*. In other cases, he will watch each horror film by a particular director in chronological order—the films of the Italian director Dario Argento, those of John Carpenter, Tobe Hooper, and so on. Horror films are not the first genre that one might associate with excellence in filmmaking. Still, there are a good number of well-crafted horror movies, many of them from the more than twenty-year period Matthew focuses on during his annual rotation. It is from these well-made films that another function of the annual viewings arises—recognizing the internal logic of a film's construction, and the individual flourishes and tricks that he might have missed in previous screenings.

These annual screenings allow Matthew to reconnect with the bravado of the passionate novice he once was. In the same way that the smell of a particular flower or the sound of a bell might trigger almost tangible memories of a time, place, or state of mind, Matthew's experiences looking at video covers have remained pivotal. While the films he produces now are decidedly better than the VHS-inspired films he'd imagined making as a child, there was a passion, wonder, and imaginative spark that had burned brightly. The annual screening ritual reminds him of those feelings and inspirations that began in the aisles of his local Blockbuster Video store. As a young child, his blissful unawareness of the challenges of filmmaking— the craft skill required, the financial and structural challenges, or even the mundane hurdles thrown in the way by daily life—allowed him to believe he could be as good a filmmaker as Romero, Carpenter, or Argento. Rewatching the dozens and dozens of horror films allows him to remember the origin of his passion for filmmaking.

The personal horror festival also affords Matthew an opportunity to reflect on how far he has come as a filmmaker. Each year, he has more practical experience making animated films, creating a wider and wider gap between where he is now and where he was when he first saw a particular film. Some years, a horror film will bring back the same emotions and feelings he had when he first saw it, while in other years, his childhood perspectives feel distant and even alien to him. This reflective iteration, spanning across the years, becomes a measuring stick of sorts for him to assess his own progress as a filmmaker.

Matthew has developed a series of reflective techniques that serves his work in different ways. One way he uses reflective contexts is what he calls "mental conditioning." This reflective mental conditioning is a form of training not unlike training for a sport, but with the focus on the mental rather than the physical. Matthew uses the analogy of Buddhist mantras to describe the role of this type of iterative reflection. By repeatedly reading, listening, watching, and playing works, he is able to get himself closer to his own understanding of them, which in turn prepares him for his own creative practice. Let's say he was preparing to make a film in the film noir genre. He would know exactly what he needed to watch and read: James Ellroy's *L.A. Confidential*, Dashiell Hammett's book *The Maltese Falcon*, and a couple of pulp novels. These would help him wrap his head around the genre and its use of language, tone, plot development, setting, and so on. His goal is to internalize the genre, making him conversant in its idioms and underlying aesthetic logic. If he were to catch himself speaking in a Sam Spade patois, then Matthew would know that his reflective consumption of film noir works had done its job.

At other times, he creates reflective contexts to help him break through creative blocks. His go-to film for this purpose is Akira Kurosawa's *Seven Samurai*. Matthew relies on a particular scene in *Seven Samurai*: the conflict that arises when the villagers realize their community is at risk, and a challenge is issued to keep them fighting. At a viewing of the film during graduate school, Matthew found himself completely wrapped up in the story, watching as viewer and not a filmmaker. A friend commented on the quality of the filmmaking, which pulled Matthew out of his attention to the plot, and redirected him to the underlying power of the film's construction. In the same way that rewatching horror films helps him get in touch with an earlier set of feelings, so *Seven Samurai* helps Matthew rediscover something in himself with which he sometimes loses touch—the need to think like a filmmaker, and the power that the medium can have.

Yet another model of reflective contexts is what Matthew calls "ambient viewing." Most times, while working on his own films, Matthew will have films on in the background while he works, in the same way that many people will listen to music while working. For Matthew, the film functions as a distraction of sorts, one he tunes into and out of while he works on his own film. Aware of his tendency to overthink or overwork an idea, he has sought out a means of keeping himself at just the right distance from his work. Having the films of others on in the background creates just the right amount of diversion to keep him from getting too caught up in his own ideas.

Getting to the Truth

Regardless of the particular application, Matthew's reflective techniques are all in service of his own creativity; they help him calibrate, focus, explore, and hone himself, his creative practice, and his films in the hopes of connecting with his viewers. Because the ideas he wants to explore aren't easily described or quantified, his only recourse is to watch and rewatch certain scenes in other films over and over until he understands them well enough to apply the idea or technique in his own work. For his stop-motion film *Loon*, there was a scene in Godfrey Reggio's *Koyaanisqatsi* that Matthew wanted to better internalize—the scene toward the end of the film when the rocket explodes over a soundscape of deep vocalizations. Matthew wanted to understand how auditory tone and text combined with color and motion to create an unexpectedly powerful moment. After innumerable viewings of this scene, he finally located its underlying structure and power, harnessing it to create a scene in *Loon* in which a view of Hong Kong is overlaid with a score of chanting monks.

Still from *Loon*.

Matthew begins all projects the same way: He watches films in which he has previously experienced the experiential truth he wants to explore in his new film. When he finds these emotional artifacts in other filmmakers' work, Matthew describes the feeling as being akin to seeing a face you recognize in a crowd; there is something unarticulated yet deeply resonant in that moment of the film. Once he finds the precise moment, he repeatedly watches the film to calibrate his thoughts and the visual and emotional tone of his own film. For *Loon*, Matthew watched *Koyaanisqatsi*, a number of Argento films, Panos Cosmatos's *Beyond the Black Rainbow*, and a few John Carpenter films. This viewing was less for the visual style than for the sound design and scoring of the films—they all shared synthesizer-driven scores that related to the style, texture, and tone he wanted to capture in *Loon*. The scene in *Koyaanisqatsi* that Matthew reflected on is the moment when the intense, chaotic imagery and score of a bustling city give way to the silence of a hot air balloon floating through the sky. From this, Matthew wanted to understand the buildup of tension and its release through stillness and silence rather than explosion.

This process is very much in the spirit of Matthew's mental conditioning process—he seeks out examples that help him better understand and then express the ideas and feelings he hopes to capture in his films. Once he has absorbed what he was seeking from the slate of films, he creates a style frame for the new animation. In this image he strives to capture a particular emotion, one connected in some way to a memory. Once this image embodies the experiential truth Matthew is going for, he then develops a plan to get himself to that particular moment in the film. And, as necessary, he returns to the inspirational films to keep him in touch with that experiential truth.

Making a Side-Scrolling Fairy Tale

Matthew's *Gryphon Animo* provides a useful example of reflective iteration within his creative practice. He began the film because he wanted to create a fairy tale in the tradition of the Brothers Grimm: a character-driven story in which the character grows as a result of a journey. But unlike a typical Campbellian "hero's journey,"[4] Matthew wanted to subvert the trope by allowing his character to move through the world unscathed, slicing through all conflict without strife or hesitation. For Matthew, this was a way to explore the complexities of life and the unforeseen, often unfair challenges that come our way. At the same time, he wanted to push back on the absurd notion that "character-building" challenges necessarily lead to strength and fortitude.

To start the process, Matthew read a lot of fairy tales. One in particular, "The Griffin" by the Brothers Grimm, jumped out at him. The tale is rife with non sequitur challenges and journeys forced upon its hero, Hans—carrying apples, building a boat that travels on land, herding 100 rabbits, plucking a feather from a sleeping griffin. Matthew thought the story provided the perfect narrative with which he could subvert the hero's journey. So he streamlined the tale to give his hero character, Roland, a single task—retrieving a feather from a griffin. To really stack the deck, he equipped Roland with a tommy gun, which allows the character to move unscathed through the obstacles standing between him and the griffin.

This review of the Grimms' fairy tales serves as an important example of reflective contexts in Matthew's practice. With an idea in mind—creating a fairy tale that subverts the Campbellian hero's journey—Matthew read a good number of fairy tales in order to find inspiration. Through reading the stories, he was able to more fully capture the idioms and structure of the fairy tale narrative form. And with "The Griffin," he found a perfect foil for his critique of the hero's journey.

Gryphon Animo takes place in a two-dimensional world not unlike the classic 2D platformer videogame series *Mega Man*—another important work Matthew reflected on. Matthew liked the idea of using the always-moving-forward progress of side-scrolling platformers as a way to express the inevitability of his hero's unscathed journey. He played *Mega Man* over and over to get himself familiar with the tropes of the side-scrolling platform genre. As he played, he began thinking about how the game unfolds like a piece of music—flowing in a single direction with a progressional inevitability.

Matthew also wanted to better understand the way narrative thresholds were established in *Mega Man*: The player character always moved forward, with the only pauses happening around major "sub-boss" encounters. The "threshold guardian" moments leading up to these encounters were an established trope in 1980s and 90s side-scrolling hack-and-slash games; sub-boss fights were almost always preceded by chaotic, intense combat accompanied by up-tempo music. Matthew noticed that to create narrative tension, everything would grow calm just before the sub-boss entered the

The Lake Giant in *Gryphon Animo.*

screen. The music would then rise as the player and sub-boss engaged in battle. This calm-before-the-storm trope can be seen in the Lake Giant, one of the sub-bosses Gryphon encounters on his journey. Everything quiets as the scene changes to a vast lake from which emerges the Lake Giant—a monster so large he can stand on the bottom of the deep lake and still have his massive head completely above the water.

Matthew as well wanted to draw upon the flat art style typical to games of that era. Particularly in the early 8-bit games, *Mega Man* inhabits a largely flat world composed of parallel planes. The worlds are sparsely populated, with the setting limited to only the essential environmental and character elements necessary to thwart the progress of the player's characters. Matthew creates a similarly sparse world for *Gryphon*, even if the graphic style differs radically. To prepare for this, he played the game over and over to help him internalize the basic logic of side-scrolling video games and their use of discrete planes to at once create depth and define the movement of characters and objects.

Matthew equally drew inspiration for *Gryphon Animo* from the shallow sets of live puppetry. When translated into film, these wide but shallow spaces complement the forward motion of the platformer game. Quintron and Miss Pussycat's stop-motion film *Trixie and the Tree Trunks* was an important reference for Matthew in this regard. The sets in the film have the feel of a puppet world, with the action happening on parallel planes, and within spaces with never more than a handful of different planes of action receding from the camera.

Trixie and the Tree Trunks also served as inspiration in one other important way—its sound design. The low-fidelity electronic soundscape had a rough-hewn, raw feel throughout the film. The characters' voices were similarly distorted and blown out, as if they had been recorded too loudly for the equipment being used. Matthew studied the film to think through how this recording technique helped build the tone and spirit of the film, as he hoped to achieve a similar effect in his own. He felt the low-fidelity sound quality created a layer of absurdity that fit his critique of the hero's journey.

Matthew describes *Gryphon Animo* as "Imagine if Yuriy Norshteyn created a pinball game."[5] This allusion points to one last pivotal influence for *Gryphon Animo*—Yuriy Norshteyn's *Hedgehog in the Fog*, a stop-motion film from the 1970s. The simplicity of form in Norshteyn's character designs had long fascinated Matthew. Unlike in contemporary animation, Norshteyn's characters had simple bodies and faces, which maintained a limited set of facial expressions and poses. But instead of constraining the emotional range of the characters, Norshteyn's simplified faces opened up the potential for more complex emotional responses. The less emoting his characters performed, the more space there was for audience interpretation, and the more likely the audience would be drawn into the characters' emotional state. *Hedgehog in the Fog* became an important touchstone for Matthew for all of his animated works, and so it is a film he watches again with each project to remind him of this and other lessons he learned from the Russian master.

Matthew began the *Gryphon Animo* project in 2010 and completed it in 2018. He worked on the film over the eight-year period as opportunity presented itself during breaks from his teaching and leadership responsibilities at SCAD-Atlanta. Each time he restarted the process, he revisited *Mega Man*, *Trixie and the Tree Trunks*, and *Hedgehog in the Fog*. They became part of his ritual for making the film, getting himself recalibrated back to the experiential truth he hopes to explore in it. He watched or played them before he undertook each task related to an aspect of his filmmaking process—*Mega Man* when considering space and movement, *Trixie and the Tree Trunks* when working on sound design and score, and *Hedgehog in the Fog* when designing characters and working on animation. Together, these helped Matthew more quickly return to the headspace necessary for creating *Gryphon Animo.*

Connecting the Dots

Matthew's creation of reflective contexts is a practice borne from seeking inspiration and guidance from the work of others to inform his own work. Matthew uses wine as an analogy: "It's like tasting wine, and after you've been to a part of the country and you've never smelled a certain flora and then you go back and taste the wine again, and now it tastes a lot like this flower from the region, and now your vocabulary is expanded."

But unlike in oenology, Matthew's **intention** isn't necessarily to seek out terms to assign to the intangibles of his filmmaking; instead, he looks for the experiential truths he wants to explore in a film. Sometimes he looks for genre conventions, and at other times he seeks out tone and emotional states and the techniques used to produce them. The **process** to do this is, as Matthew points out, not unlike meditation mantras—the practice of repeated viewing of films, reading, and/or playing games opens him up to better understand what connects him to the work, with the hope that this will guide him to the desired **outcomes** in his own filmmaking practice.

The heart of reflective iteration is a set of anchoring works that contain important lessons, techniques, or expressive acts. This mental "catalog"

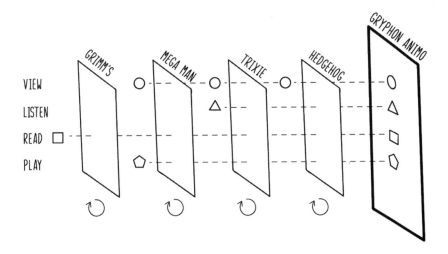

becomes an important part of Matthew's iterative practice. This catalog includes horror films and videogames from his childhood, but also selected works that have influenced him in his education and career—films like Kurosawa's *Seven Samurai* and Reggio and Glass's *Koyaanisqatsi*. Given the experiential intentions behind Matthew's filmmaking, reflective iteration allows him to discover ways to combine image and sound to articulate emotional and intellectual themes. His approach is akin to recognizing a face in a crowd, or feeling a tug of connection to something you'd felt or observed in the past. His reflective consumption of others' works assists Matthew in **evaluating** his own ideas, and helps him know when he has found the right way to embody his ideas in scenes, scores, characters, and so on. The best tool for reflective iteration, then, is to maintain a steady diet of films, books, games, music, art exhibitions, food, and so on. One never knows where those truths and epiphanies await.

7 Targeted Intentions: *Radiolab*

As Jad Abumrad sees it, journalists are obliged "to not know anything."[1] But in the absence of knowledge, what remains? A methodology for learning, a structure for presenting what has been learned, and a style for presenting that information. This is where *Radiolab*, the radio program and podcast hosted by Jad and Robert Krulwich, has made its mark: It is a striking combination of a methodology driven by deceptively simple questions, a conversational structure that models the learning process, and a style driven by illustrative and evocative sound design.

As the name hints, *Radiolab* is a radio program about science. But it has also been a lab for radio as a storytelling medium, even if that wasn't Jad's intention when he named the program. Instead of treating public radio as

a traditional sound-based journalistic outlet, the creators of programs like *This American Life* and *Radiolab* have turned expectations on their ears; these programs looked for ways to replace the traditional "inverted triangle" of journalistic reporting with storytelling practices to give new perspectives on what radio could do and be. This layered technique—intertwining the hosts' conversations, interview segments conducted by the hosts or other *Radiolab* staff, sound design, music, and extensive audio manipulation— has become a frequently imitated style.

Traditionally structured journalism begins with the "lede," the important idea at the center of the piece, which is followed by a broadening base of background information and facts. *Radiolab* instead begins with a question that is explored but never fully answered. This unfolding question is developed through conversation between the show's hosts, interviews with expert guests, and perhaps most important for the *Radiolab* style, sound design and scoring that bring a rich, illustrative sensibility to the show. And rather than presenting a story based on evidence that leads to understanding, *Radiolab* episodes use these methods to make visible the nuances of the original question. The kinds of questions the show explores cannot necessarily lead to evidential understanding, but more often lead to a greater appreciation of the complexities at the intersections of science and metaphysics.

Jad and Robert stitch together the people, the stories, and the unfolding question by talking their way through ideas. This approach isn't so unusual, as it mirrors the investigative journalism process and bears similarity to the popular talk radio format. What's different with *Radiolab* is the implicit "beginner's mind" that remains present throughout the story. Robert explains the challenge:

We want our listeners to hear what it's like to not know something, what it's like to be curious and how you stumble about feeling awkward or stupid on your way to knowledge. That's what we're modeling for our audience, what it feels like to learn. … We don't know. We learn. We wanted our audience to hear us earning our authority by learning right in front of them.[2]

This is the structure of each episode: Jad and Robert work their way through a question as a means of performing their attempts to answer it, but also sharing with their listeners the stories that give form to the process. They want the journey through the question to feel real and organic, and so they strive to embody the beginner's mind as they work through the conversation and reflection on the interviews.

Questions about the Unknowable

After a decade of tinkering and experiment, *Radiolab* has a polished, well-received approach to long-form radio journalism. It is the product of what we call **targeted intentions** applied to an iterative process incrementally moving toward a specific outcome. *Radiolab* poses questions to which the answers are *more* questions. That's because the kind of ideas they consider don't have pat or simple answers, nor should they. The world is a complex place, and to think we can distill natural and human phenomena into simple explanations is foolish. Jad, Robert, and the rest of the *Radiolab* staff try to impart this complexity and uncertainty even as they help us get a better handle on the world around us.

A *Radiolab* episode is an auditory investigation of a given topic—a "performance" in the sense of the retelling of the story of asking questions, finding answers that lead to other questions, eventually leading to a balance of understanding, wonder, and uncertainty. In Jad's words,

That becomes the process: You iteratively move through a set of questions looking for the better question. ... In that way, *Radiolab* stories start small, maybe with a stupid question, but it's the question you got, and then they expand slowly as the question becomes more and more interesting, until finally, you're at a question that encapsulates something big and profound and universal. But it takes a long time to get there, and I like constructing stories where the listener gets to walk with you, because I feel that is useful, that's life, it's about being dumb, and then being less dumb, and then being a little smarter, and the smart question is the one that make you feel the most dumb.[3]

One of the driving motivations behind *Radiolab* is to produce wonder, and by extension, an inquisitive interest in the world around us. As Robert sees it, they "use that power to tell stories that are sophisticated, or complex or mathematical, or dense."[4] Where science usually intends to build understanding and add to foundational knowledge, *Radiolab* seeks to stir up more questions than answers, and thus to produce a sense of wonder in its listeners. *Radiolab* is, after all, a science journalism radio program, and so the first part of that makes sense: explaining how things work. But the second part—creating wonder—doesn't necessarily follow the logic of the scientific method. As Jad puts it, "there's just more mystery. There's just more randomness. There's just more fluctuations. ... In some way, this represents infinite possibility, that we can't ever know."[5]

A big part of this process is "calculating on the unforeseen," Rebecca Solnit's rephrasing of an idea first expressed by Edgar Allan Poe. Solnit expands on the idea:

> How do you calculate upon the unforeseen? It seems to be an art of recognizing the role of the unforeseen, of keeping your balance amid surprises, of collaborating with chance, of recognizing there are some essential mysteries in the world and thereby a limit to calculation, to plan, to control.[6]

Radiolab looks to strike the right balance between humble knowledge and awe in the face of unending complexity. To do this, the *Radiolab* team approach radio journalism, an auditory medium, as music. As Robert Krulwich put it, "for us, telling a story, finding a theme, changing moods as we go, hitting highs, pausing, breaking, pulsing, the silences, the peaks, holding the moment—we treat our stories in good part as musical exercises. We think, in a modest way, we are making music."[7]

Finding "Something Different" in the German Forest

The story of how *Radiolab* came to be is oft-told.[8] It began in 2002 when Jad, a musician by training with early career aspirations of film scoring, was given two hours a week to fill with documentaries when no one (literally)[9] was listening; Jad and Robert, a veteran radio and TV journalist with a penchant for innovative storytelling, met through work-related happenstance, and over breakfast one morning[10] the two developed a segment for Jad's show[11] and otherwise schemed about doing radio stories together; soon thereafter, in 2004, Robert joined as cohost; and some years later, after a series of fits and starts, *Radiolab* became a George Foster Peabody Award-winning radio program[12] followed soon thereafter by Jad's winning a MacArthur Genius Grant.[13]

Of course, this rise to fame didn't happen overnight. Though the process was slow, and the exact goal vague (to create "something different"—but different from what?), there is an underlying logic to how Jad, Robert, producer Ellen Horne, and all the rest of the *Radiolab* team developed the program's process and approach. We consider this to be an example of targeted intentions to address a specific goal—the creation of a new approach to radio journalism.

Radiolab started when Jad was given four days to pull together a new radio program. His charge? Create something unexpected and different from standard science documentaries aired on public radio. Given the resources available, Jad started by stitching together existing audio documentaries curated around shared themes. He had lots of questions to start this process: What kind of host would he be? What were the interesting stories? How could he integrate music?[14] These questions all touched on things Jad had done before, but if he was indeed going to create something different, he knew he was going to have to find new ways to combine his radio persona, his journalistic storytelling skills, and his background in music composition.

In a 2015 interview for the *Radiowaves* podcast, Jad brought up Parker Palmer's concept of the tragic gap.[15] The tragic gap is the space between your abilities and resources, and your intended goal. When the goal is something more easily articulated and measured—say, "Increase the stickiness of this glue by 25% while decreasing its costs by 12%"—there are concrete markers to go after. But even then, there is no guarantee of the means by which to achieve these goals. When the goal is more open-ended—do "something different" with science reporting—the method and the outcome are both in need of definition. And the only way he was going to sort this out was by making radio—which is a good thing, because that's what he had to do, week after week.

In the case of *Radiolab*, the goal was simultaneously defined and explored through the creation of radio pieces. At first, Jad did this alone, working "without a template"[16] to meet his boss's challenge. There weren't clear precedents for doing something new with radio science documentaries, so Jad had to find his way while still creating weekly episodes. He developed themes to which he connected existing documentary pieces, stitched together with interstitial dialogue. A breakthrough in his pursuit came with the assignment to create a one-hour primer on Wagner's four-part, fifteen-plus-hour dramatic opera cycle *The Ring of the Nibelung*.[17] Needless to say, explaining a notoriously complex work of art in an hour is a challenging assignment, but for Jad it tested the limits of his abilities as a radio journalist. Every time he thought he had figured it out, a request would come in to make sure to include another aspect of the opera and its intricate story involving more than thirty characters and its nuanced, tightly constructed music developed from a series of no less than 175 leitmotifs.

This task isn't an unusual one for a journalist—rapidly developing an understanding of a complex subject, and then communicating a concise explanation that maintains the integrity of the topic. But for Jad, this was also a struggle with the medium of radio. How can radio be used as a stylized platform for long-form culture reporting? How does one present such dense material in audio format? What are the ways music and sound can illustrate and supplement meaning-making and comprehension?

Working on the piece was infamously challenging for Jad,[18] leading to the phrase still used at *Radiolab*: being lost in "the German forest." They use the term to describe feeling lost in a project, uncertain of how to make it all come together, how to make it good, how to even bring it to a conclusion. For Jad, listening to the Wagner piece, "The Ring and I," after it was complete, he heard something he hadn't expected: his voice, his point of view, and an approach to making *Radiolab* "something different."

In his 2012 Third Coast Conference talk, Jad plays a portion of the Wagner episode in which a music expert helps him understand Wagner's use of motifs. Using the leitmotif for Wotan's spear as an example, Jad and the expert talk through Wagner's use of recurring musical themes to signal a particular character, object, or idea. The technique emerges from the interleaving of Jad's interview with the expert, passages from the *Ring* cycle, and then follow-up from Jad. Though the episode lacks some of the polish and precision of *Radiolab* in its prime, the seeds of a path forward are present and visible. Most importantly, a vision for *Radiolab* became clear to Jad, providing a mile marker in the journey to develop *Radiolab*'s voice. As Jad put it, the German forest "is a tool. It is a place you have to go to hear the next version of yourself."[19] As he also notes, the experience is never easy, and is always terrifying, but after several trips through it, you learn its value.

One important lesson coming out of "The Ring and I" had to do with time. Up to that point, *Radiolab* was a weekly program with thirty-one episodes produced in 2002 and thirty episodes in 2003. But in 2004, the year of the Wagner incident, Jad produced only two episodes in total. This was an important part of developing the "something different" that became *Radiolab*: taking the time to really dig into a topic or question, and to allow the fits and starts of creative exploration to exist alongside the successes. This slower, more patient pace would feel familiar to investigative journalists, but for Jad, whose background was in music composition and film scoring, this was a process developed through trial and error in his attempt to bring a new point of view to radio-based science journalism. Time was important to the development of leads that go down sometimes fruitful and sometimes frustrating paths. Closer to Jad's previous work as a film composer, time was also necessary to edit together the episode, and to add the layers of illustrative and affective sound design and scoring.

Not all visits to the "German forest" led to breakthroughs, however. Early in their friendship, Jad and Robert were asked by Ira Glass to contribute a two-minute piece on the theme of Flag Day for an episode of *This American Life*.[20] Jad and Robert agreed, and began work on a piece anchored by an early 1960s recording about the rules governing interactions with the American flag. They decided to play portions of the recording intercut with humorous skits reacting to the instructions. In the piece, augmented by Jad's sound design, Robert plays a host of characters that bumble their way through the handling of the flag. The feedback from Ira Glass and *This American Life* producer Julie Snyder was that the piece was awful—it had no throughline; it didn't make a point; it was silly, complicated, and confusing. Julie made an important observation about *Radiolab's* slow development: She could see how the piece was connected to the eventual *Radiolab* voice, even though it was an example of a path that got them further from the eventual solution.

What "something different" meant became clear as time passed, allowing the show's focus to eventually shift from figuring out what Jad's producer wanted him to change about radio journalism, to how to reproduce the discovery of understanding when trying to answer complex scientific and metaphysical questions. As the target shifted, the intentions became the development of a process that would result in a *Radiolab* episode—a mix of conversation, interviews, and sound design to explore one big question per episode.

By 2005, Robert and Jad had found the basic structure of a quintessential *Radiolab* episode: One or the other of them have a question about a broad topic—How does the mind work? What is the impact of stress on our bodies? Why do we laugh? The two hosts set about discussing the question, and trying to answer it through their own conversation and through sidebar interviews with experts, which lead back to more conversation and questions by the two hosts.[21] Weaving it all together is a level of sound design, foley, and scoring not usually associated with public radio. The quintessential *Radiolab* episode uses music and sound to create atmosphere and mood, and to illustrate actions and ideas.

How to Make an Episode of *Radiolab*

The *Radiolab* format is in itself an exercise in targeted intentions. Each episode tends to pose a single question—How is a personal identity formed? Can losing sometimes be winning? What happens when people are forced to "play god"? The hosts explore the question through conversation,[22] it is expanded upon through a series of stories that dig into aspects of or angles on the core question. In this way, each episode is itself guided by a targeted intention—pose a question about a scientific concept or phenomenon that is explored through a conversational form of storytelling supported by an incredible amount of research and illustrated through sound design and musical scoring.

In many ways, all the elements of the *Radiolab* approach are present in the very first episode following Robert's joining the program, "Who Am I?"[23] The episode begins with a "cold" opening (launching straight into a story without explanation) told through a conversation between Jad and a guest, illustrated by light sound effects that bring the story to life. The story leads to Jad posing the question that the remainder of the episode will attempt to answer. At that point, Robert enters the picture, and he and Jad talk through the question, with periodic branches into stories that explore particular nuances within the larger question.

"Who Am I?" poses the question, "Where is 'me' located?"—an exploration of how our brains construct an understanding of self. This is a classic *Radiolab* topic, as it combines science with the lived experience in a way that few other outlets ever attempted. It is a subject full of intangible concepts, complicated scientific concepts, and deep metaphysical musings. The topic lends itself to the unique mix of discussion, interview, and illustration.

The targeted intentions underlying *Radiolab* are twofold: first, the long arc of developing the show based on the prompt to create "something different"; and then the repeated cycle of developing each episode around a particular question or idea. In many ways, the intentions are one and the same, with the initial prompt leading to the development of a process for creating "something different" that has played out over dozens and dozens of episodes over a course of several years. And once that "something different" took form, the process that was developed played out with each new episode.

Because of the complexity of the ideas and questions investigated, and the wide-ranging nature of the stories, Jad and Robert's conversations become the connective tissue. They use a human-scale means of explaining and working through often-complicated scientific material from a quasi-metaphysical perspective. Their back and forth takes on a conversational tone, not unlike two friends talking through an idea. Robert refers to their ability to have conversations that sound natural, but that actually take place after a good deal of discussion, debate, and preparation of the episode. This natural quality gives the audience the sense they are along for the ride as the two hosts work through the question or issue.[24]

But to get to those stories, Jad and Robert have to find the people who can tell them. And how are these people with the stories found? Often by happenstance, or maybe because their story was already out there in some other media form. Once a critical mass of people with stories are identified in relation to a given question, an episode can start to take shape. These stories tend to happen on an individual basis; someone on the *Radiolab* staff finds a person with an intriguing story, and the staff member interviews them. The raw files of these interviews are shared with the full staff for group discussion. Everyone discusses what they do (and don't) hear being discussed, how and where moments of emotional connection are (and aren't) found in the material, and whether or not the natural rhythms of a good story are present. Jad refers to this process as "individual search punctuated by group reflection." After group conversation, the staff member goes back to refine things and further explore the underlying questions. Sometimes this means returning for additional interviews, other times it means finding other related stories and people, and sometimes it leads to a dead end.

Most episodes involve four separate stories that together tease out the nuances of that episode's underlying question or theme. To get to those four stories, the *Radiolab* staff seek out as many relevant story ideas as they can. If they are seeking out four, they increase their odds of getting to four by pursuing more stories than they need—akin to placing multiple bets as a hedge against losing. Sometimes there are only four to chase. Other times there are eight or twelve. As Jad put it,

If you do enough of those bets, you begin to change, because enough of them pay off, and they'll explode your idea of who you are. But you can only do that if your odds are fifteen to four—you chase fifteen, you get four—which means you are killing eleven in the process. I would love to get to a place where we are chasing twenty to get four, and maybe four of them fall out and sit on the shelf, and the other twelve just die because they aren't good enough. And maybe one of those four is the one you thought would never work, but just blew your mind, and you emerged out the other side a totally different person.

This process of starting with a lot of "bets" on stories and angles to help explore a question requires an openness to the unexpected and unconsidered. It also requires a receptiveness to failures, false starts, and dead ends. Confidence is necessary to not just see the value in assumed failures, but to believe that enough of the "bets" will work out.

Once all the conversations and interviews are recorded, the episode is "illustrated" by using sound design and musical scoring. The *Radiolab* team describes the audio-only quality of radio as allowing "co-imagining": Instead of the imposition of image over ideas that TV and film produce, radio allows the listener to participate in giving form to the material.[25] Jad has described the function of radio as "to paint pictures in people's heads. It's not pictures you show them, its pictures they make."[26] The extravocal sound design functions as the connective tissue, but also as a form of intonation, elucidation, mode, and style. Jad thinks of the sound design in terms of "musical interpretation" and "augmented audio."[27] Regardless of what we call it, the sound effects, music, and audio editing are vital components of *Radiolab*. This aspect of the show points to one of the powers of radio, going back to earlier days in the medium when dramatic stories were told using sound effects we now associate with film.

Perhaps the most recognizable example of this illustration-meets-musical interpretation is the opening sequence that begins every *Radiolab* episode: "Wait … you're listening to … *Radiolab*, from WNYC." If spoken at a normal pace, without interruption, it takes maybe two or three seconds to utter. But in the show opening, it takes seventeen seconds, extended by a series of repeated lines, word snippets, and sound effects. The end result is a multilayered communication: the basic information of the show's title and where it is produced; a hint at the conversational flow of the show; an example of how augmented human speech and sound effects can establish mood, style, intention, and content; and a hint at the number of people and ideas it takes to unravel a *Radiolab* story.

If you listen to a sampling of *Radiolab* episodes over the nearly fifteen years of its existence, you will hear at least three different versions of this opening sequence. Earlier versions are less refined and polished, but with each new version, it gets closer to the signature opening used today. The targeted intention to develop "something different" extends from *Radiolab* as a whole to each of the component parts. With the show opening, the *Radiolab* team worked to develop a short introduction that both conveyed information—the name of the program, and where it was produced—and a sense of what it is like to experience the program. It shouldn't be a surprise that the opening changed over the years, as Jad and Robert's understanding of their program, how they made it, and what they hoped to provide their audience also changed and refined as they worked through the creation of each episode.

Connecting the Dots

Iterative practice driven by targeted **intentions** begins with a known, identifiable goal—in the case of *Radiolab*, this was do "something different" with science journalism on the radio. While the intention was understood, as was the medium, the **process** to get to "something different" wasn't clear. And so Jad at first, and later with Robert, Ellen, and the rest of the staff, did what they knew how to do: make radio. Each episode was an attempt both to figure out what "something different" meant for long-form radio journalism, but also to get close to that goal. Sometimes they found clues about the "something different," sometimes they lost sight of their goal. But with each episode, they learned something about their goal and how to obtain it—even if that learning was "nope, that's not it." **Evaluation** of each episode, and the work that went into it, became an important process of reflection and reorientation. Repetition was the pivot point for their targeted iterative practice: They made science documentary radio in pursuit of an open-ended **outcome**—create "something different."

Context also played an important role. The *Radiolab* staff had to operate within the resource constraints of public radio—financial, of course, but

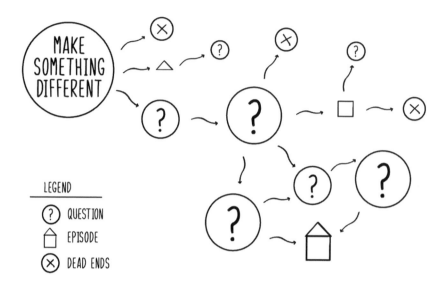

also the equipment available and, perhaps most important, the time available before the next episode needed to be broadcast. Jad, Robert, and the staff—the **actors**, in our parlance—were another form of context. Early on, Jad was working alone on the program, which made for slower progress. As the program grew to include Robert, and a growing staff of producers, the "something different" became clearer and more easily pursued.

8 Exploratory Intentions: Chef Wylie Dufresne

Wylie Dufresne started working in his father's restaurant at the age of eleven, and has been in kitchens ever since. His family restaurant and food service jobs throughout high school and college gave him ample opportunity to learn the techniques and methods of how food is conceived of, turned into menu items, and then prepared and served over and over. After getting an undergraduate degree in philosophy from Colby, Wylie enrolled at the French Culinary Institute in New York and formalized his already deep practical experience. By the end of culinary school, Wylie had the methods and on-the-job expertise from the family business, laced with a philosopher's itch to question assumptions, and backed up with formal grounding in refined culinary technique and aesthetics.

Wylie Dufresne. Photo by Shuangshuang Huo.

His immersion in technique and culinary aesthetics continued through the mid to late 1990s when Wylie worked for the French chef Jean-Georges Vongerichten at Jean-Georges in New York City and at Prime in Las Vegas. Where traditional French cooking is typically heavy, with rich sauces and near alchemical transformations of ingredients, Vongerichten's focused on lighter, simpler preparations of quality ingredients. And where classic French cooking used simple presentation, Jean-Georges's approach foregrounded the plating and presentation of dishes.

It is from this tradition that Dufresne's own style of cooking emerged—classical training in service of contemporary dining. Wylie began finding his own voice in 1999 as the chef de cuisine at his father Dewey Dufresne's restaurant, 71 Clinton Fresh Food. Located in the Lower East Side—a neighborhood known at the time more for punk clubs, bodegas, and laundries than restaurants—71 Clinton quickly became a sought-out dining destination. In 2003, Wylie opened WD~50 in the same neighborhood. There, his voice as a chef became clear and distinct—what Wylie calls "modernist cuisine" that emphasizes unexpected use and preparation of ingredients plated with great attention to visual surprise. In 2013, Wylie opened Alder in the East Village of New York City. Instead of WD~50's multicourse meal approach, Alder emphasized "a la carte" small dishes that played with expectations around bar and tavern food. But as at WD~50, the dishes all carried Wylie's signature culinary modernist twist. WD~50 closed in the fall of 2014 when the building was sold and torn down. Alder, too, came to an end a year later, another restaurant lost to the fast-paced, high-rent world of the New York City restaurant scene. More recently, Wylie has opened Du's Donuts and Coffee, a Brooklyn shop where he and his team reimagine the humble donut through the lens of modernist cuisine.

The innovative dining that Wylie became known for emerged from an **exploratory intention**: to reimagine the possibilities of cooking. Wylie's approach to cooking is a melding of science and culinary art. Not unlike scientists, who we imagine in lab coats puttering around with test tubes and atom smashers looking for "eureka!" moments, Wylie and his staff probe the foundational structures of cooking and food science. In so doing, they push the field of cuisine toward exploratory questions that seek and expand the edges of their discipline's knowledge.

While Wylie's dishes provide sustenance, they also go well into the subsistence-plus territory of aesthetic experience. When interacting with more utilitarian things, aesthetics don't usually factor into someone's expectations—no matter how awful the interface on an ATM is, people will still deal with it to get their money. But with modernist cuisine, the aesthetic considerations are just as important as—if not more important than—the utilitarian concerns of sustenance. And when you go into such subjective territory, you are bound to make mistakes in your attempts to create for others' tastes. Iterative techniques are a large part of this kind of exploration, as the answer to whether or not your creation will connect with its audience is only knowable after it is placed in front of them.

Wylie's craft presents an intriguing intersection of exploratory intentions guided by aesthetic (rather than scientific) reasons within the practical constraints of running a business. This kind of exploration is akin to a painter asking questions about the basic properties of oil, pigment, brush, and canvas in order to find new potentials for painting. Wylie's approach is very much a foundational inquiry into the how and the why of cooking.

The deep explorations of a field or medium is not without its risks. Early reviews of WD~50 suggested the menu was too intellectual, and too focused on showiness rather than tastiness. As William Grimes's *New York Times* review put it, "I'd like to see a little more pleasure and a little less intellect."[1] While there was no question Wylie and his team were breaking new ground with their research, there was a tension between the expectations of his diners and the boundary-breaking dishes put on their tables. Thus, an essential challenge in the early years of WD~50 became balancing "tasty"—Wylie's shorthand for foods people enjoy eating—with the intellectual experimentation driving his work. Not all discoveries in their research led to tasty food, but all discoveries added to the team's knowledge, which sometimes contributed to tasty dishes further down the road.

Failure, then, is inherent in this process. Not every experiment will yield tasty results, let alone the necessary criteria for a dish included on the menu. In fact, most experiments will not. That is to be expected when engaging in exploratory work like Wylie and his staff's. This is the heart of Wylie's exploratory intentions for cooking: learning from and contributing to the shared knowledge about the potential of ingredients and techniques that may not all immediately result in tasty food, but that can eventually contribute to a well-received dish.

Asking How, and Why, to Make Pudding

At some point early in his career, Wylie realized that he knew how to cook, but was fairly unclear on why food was prepared in the ways it was. As he put it, "Knowing mechanically how to poach an egg but not what's happening to it while poaching it is almost an empty knowledge."[2] The science of cooking—a mix of physics, chemistry, and biology—was far less understood by Wylie than were the set of cooking practices learned through training, mastered through repetition, and applied within the constraints of a restaurant. The philosopher in Wylie met the chef, and a career of asking "how" *and* "why" began.

Wylie asks not only "how," but "why" when approaching a dish, an ingredient, or a technique. Typical "how" questions relate to the preparation of foods, the techniques used to cook them, and that sort of thing—how to steam broccoli, how to poach an egg, how to set a pudding. Asking "how" gets a cook to a certain level of knowledge and skill, allowing for a range of possibilities. "How" gets a chef to a reproducible dish created under time and resource pressures demanded by restaurants.

"Why" questions look beyond "how" to explore the possibilities for food preparation. Instead of just accepting broccoli is steamed by putting a steamer in a shallow pot of boiling water, someone asking why might see what happens when broccoli is cooked in a rice cooker. "Why" questions upend what we think we know about a dish, including its ingredients, preparation and presentation. This requires exploration—what scientists might call basic research—into what is and is not possible, and an expansion of what we know about the chemical, physical and biological properties of ingredients and what happens when they are subjected to traditional and unexpected cooking techniques. The end result? Dishes like fried mayonnaise or shrimp and grits in which the shrimp *are* the grits.

Wylie wasn't alone in knowing how but not understanding why. Much of this has to do with the ways restaurants are organized, and how chefs are trained. In many ways, restaurants are a vestige of a centuries-old workshop-style training process that emphasizes technique over inquiry and understanding. There is the chef-de-cuisine, the executive chef, sous chefs, line cooks, prep cooks, all organized in a clear hierarchy. Pretty much everyone starts at the bottom, and works their way up the ranks. Once you get past the bottom rung, you are at once a student and a teacher—you are trained by whomever is above you, and you train those below you. This mostly happens "on the job"—you learn by doing as you serve the restaurant's customers. The system places emphasis on the steps in the process rather than knowing the reasons why those steps are done. As people move from restaurant to restaurant, practices spread and are absorbed into the already-established workflow of the new kitchen.

This workshop methodology—one that hasn't substantially changed in nearly a century—is built to clearly answer the "how" of cooking, but isn't conducive to exploring the "why." To do so would expand and reshape the bread and butter of the restaurant business: striking a balance between providing sustenance and an aesthetic experience in a way that is both economically sustainable and reproducible from plate to plate and night to night. Yet that is exactly what Wylie and many of his contemporaries strive to do.

Wylie's intentional explorations of food and dining operate within the larger field known as molecular gastronomy: a discipline of the food sciences focused on developing knowledge about the biology, chemistry, and physics of food preparation. The term molecular gastronomy was first used in the late 1980s by French chef and chemist Hervé This and Hungarian physicist Nicholas Kurti. Together, they started the Molecular and Physical Gastronomy meetings where chefs and scientists gathered to share their research around the science of cooking. Instead of accepting the standard processes for cooking eggs, making mashed potatoes, or cooking meat, these food scientists wanted to know how eggs react to different temperatures, what happens when a potato is subjected to the physical acts of boiling and mashing, and what goes on at a cellular level when a cut of meat is heated.

For Wylie, this was the first step in a process of learning the full range of materials and techniques with which he could pursue his aesthetic goals. Wylie tends to think of his explorations as "playing with food."[3] This isn't in the sense of pushing it around your plate, or making smiley faces out of pancake batter; instead, he plays with the potential of food. Once you understand the chemistry, physics, and biology of your ingredients and your preparation techniques, you can find new ways to prepare and serve food. This knowledge informs and changes the "best practices" learned in kitchens over the years—bringing meat up to too high of a temperature dries it out, overheating coffee makes it bitter, freezing certain fruits and vegetables hurt their structural integrity. Wylie and his team combine the frameworks of the traditional "workshop" structure of a kitchen with the experimentation of a food scientist's laboratory. With the knowledge of what causes green beans to first brighten and then brown, or eggs to firm up after a certain temperature is sustained for a period of time, Dufresne and his staff conduct a second wave of exploration that builds upon the foundations established by the molecular gastronomists.

Wylie never tires of finding new ways to play with eggs, for example, always pushing on the "how" and "why" to see what can be done—a fried egg sandwich that looks like grilled cheese,[4] poached eggs with the texture of fudge,[5] raviolis in which the filling is scrambled eggs and the shell is made of egg yolk.[6] Extending the playing with food analogy, Dufresne's team establishes the boundaries of their play space—the newfound learning derived from food science coupled with traditional preparation techniques; there, they play with the tools, techniques, and ingredients in order to see what unexpected spaces of possibility they might discover.

Exploration without guiding principles or goals is more tinkering than anything else (which of course is perfectly acceptable in its own right, but isn't really research in the strictest sense). Guiding principles are necessary to structure and guide the research. Wylie's exploration of the potential of food and dining are anchored by a couple of aesthetic goals. The first is recognizing the importance of people's expectations about food, what he calls the "givens"—most people enjoy sweets, certain combinations go well together, people have "comfort foods" that are go-to choices. Beyond the foundation of taste preferences, there is a more specific set of goals guiding their basic iterative exploration: as Wylie describes it, taking the familiar and serving it in an unfamiliar way, or taking the unfamiliar and serving it in a familiar way. This play on diner expectations is challenging, as Wylie and his team get into territory guided by childhood and family memories and the very deep-seated nostalgia for food.

With these guiding principles as a baseline, Wylie sets out to "question what can and cannot taste good together and in combination with each other."[7] Informing this interrogation is a wry sense of humor about our expectations of food—like blood orange creamsicle donuts, or hollandaise sauce served as little fried cubes with English muffin breadcrumbs.

Together, the traditions of food preparation and cultural tastes provide a surprising range of potentials when you consider the dishes, ingredients, and techniques available to a chef with an expanded understanding of what cooking is and can be.

"An idea is not more important than delicious" is a guiding principle for Wylie's teams. By this, he means their experimentation is ultimately driven by the restaurant, its menu, and most importantly, their diners' enjoyment. And so if a dish doesn't actually taste good, regardless of the cleverness or seemingly obvious truth of the idea, they will not put it on the menu. For example, Wylie and the team had an idea to combine yogurt and bacon. While in theory it sounded like a good idea, it proved to not be delicious, and so they moved on. Still, the exercise was invaluable, as it proved their process works to pose questions, test, and evaluate ideas in addition to providing new knowledge about food combinations to inform future ideas.

A good example of how Wylie's aesthetic intentions drive his exploration is the "everything bagel with smoked salmon and cream cheese" that was on the menu at WD~50. When the plate arrived, it looked like a tiny everything bagel with smoked salmon and cream cheese. But when you touched it with a fork or spoon, you realized it was ice cream. Yet, when you put it in your mouth, it actually tasted like an everything bagel. The team captured the essential flavors of the bagel, salmon, and cream cheese in an ice cream, put the ice cream in a mold, and used a little food coloring and seeds to create the look of the bagel. As Wylie said of his hopes for WD~50, it was "a place where you could get delicious food that made you think, that made you smile, that it was fun [sic] place to eat."[8]

In many ways, Wylie's approach to his restaurants is part and parcel of his basic research of food and dining. What kind of context is most conducive to this dining experience? What is the "ask" Dufresne can make of his customers? There are, of course, self-proclaimed "foodies" seeking culinary adventure, but they are a small subset of the population, and not necessarily a large enough constituency to sustain a restaurant. As a result, springing the unexpected on a diner is not always going to work out well. Dufresne then simultaneously experiments with dishes while creating in his diners a literacy around his modernist cuisine approach to cooking. This is where the aesthetic drive of making the familiar unfamiliar and the

Everything bagel with lox and cream cheese. Photo by Eric Medsker.

unfamiliar familiar surfaces. It creates a framework within which diners can make sense of what is going to arrive on their plate, and end up in their mouths.

The experience began with the menu, itself an exercise in reductiveness at WD~50: Dishes were not described, but instead were represented by a list of ingredients or component parts: "squid, banana-Ritz, parsley," or "American cheesecake, green tomato, white bread."[9] This set the stage for customer anticipation: How would Wylie and his staff reimagine and combine these ingredients into a dish?

Next comes the plating, which creates visual cues for diners. Diners were treated as if being presented an art exhibition, one dish at a time. Each plate was carefully planned and executed, seemingly to be admired as much as to be eaten. Plating, combined with the menus' focus on ingredients, creates a sense of wonder around each dish. With only the ingredient lists on the menu and the visual presentation to guide diners' understanding, each bite becomes an act of discovery, consideration, and interpretation of the flavors and textures. The mantra "Make the familiar unfamiliar, and the unfamiliar familiar" leads to surprises and discoveries, and stirs up taste memories from one's previous dining experiences. Wrapped around this is a sense of playfulness and humor that begins with the visual and moves into the realms of flavor, texture, and sensory interpretation. All of this was only possible due to Dufresne's intentional explorations in the aesthetic potential of modernist cuisine within the larger field of the culinary arts.

Creating Dishes as a Team Sport

A big part of what enables this exploratory approach within a business setting is Wylie's attitude about restaurant kitchens and how they work. He points to sports teams as an example; in the same way that sports teams first have practice and then the game, there is prep and then service in a restaurant. Most important, the exploratory iteration Wylie and his staff conduct is a cyclical process. Every day, they start again. And so if mistakes were made (and they almost always are), the new day provides the opportunity to do it again, but to do better than the day before. As Wylie put it, life in a restaurant can feel quite repetitive and can only be enjoyable "if, like Sisyphus, you can find joy in pushing that rock up the hill and knowing it's going to be at the bottom every morning."

And so this knowledge that every day is a new opportunity is important to allowing the sometimes risky experimentation (at least from a business perspective) that governs Wylie's approach to running a restaurant.

Wylie looks to the staff to help generate ideas and to participate in the research process. Indeed, the origins of WD~50 was "the funk tank"[10]—what Wylie and his original team (Sam Mason, Miguel Rosell, and Glen Goodwin) called Wylie's home kitchen during their period of experimentation and design for the restaurant's original menu. The team worked together to review and experiment with ideas tucked away in Wylie's numerous notebooks. Packed with ideas, questions, recipes, new techniques, and notes about ingredients and dishes, the notebooks served as a starting point, with the team adding their own ideas and tastes along the way. This exploratory approach developed techniques, dishes, and a process for how WD~50 would operate as both a basic research lab and a restaurant serving diners. Once WD~50 opened, the practice continued, and even expanded.

Wylie speaks of his mother's advice: "creativity is not linear."[11] By this, she meant you can't necessarily plan for or schedule creativity; it is important to be prepared for moments of inspiration. As part of the process to create a dish that makes it onto the menu, the team methodically records each attempt at that dish and the results that came from that attempt. Once they get to a recipe they like, that is recorded as well. The team also records mistakes in execution or outright failed experiments. These mistakes are just as important as the successes, as they can keep the team from making similar mistakes in the future, or serve as inspiration for new ideas.

All chefs and cooks in Wylie's kitchens carry waterproof notebooks to capture inspirations, ideas, adjustments to recipes, and whatever else makes sense.[12] If an employee leaves for another job, their notebook is copied and then given back to them so that the restaurant can keep the institutional wisdom developed during their time on the staff. These seemingly small details are an important part of establishing a culture of experimentation and open collaboration.

While Wylie and his executive chefs are in the position of leading the experimentation and dish development, the whole team is encouraged to participate in the process. This might mean suggesting an idea for a dish, giving feedback on an in-progress idea, or tasting a dish as it moves through the experimentation process. Sometimes the process starts with a staff member learning about a new tool or technique that can provide new avenues for exploration. To some degree, this openness to teamwork is borne from Wylie's belief that ideas are less important than process. As he puts it, "The inception point is almost irrelevant, because it is the process that's the important part."

Wylie and his staff have a number of processes for how they conduct their basic research, but it usually begins with a question about a particular ingredient, dish, or technique. A good example is their questioning of the traditional combination of steak and potatoes. Wylie and one of his sous

Bundle of chef's notebooks from WD~50. Photo by Eric Medsker.

chefs, Ryan Henderson, had been talking about a dish in which potatoes were put on a tartare. As they began to explore the idea, they liked the contrast of hot potatoes and cold beef, and the interplay that would happen at their point of contact. At some point in the process, the classic dish shepherd's pie entered the conversation. This led to additional conversations about what vegetables the cooks associated with shepherd's pie. Jon Bignelli, the executive chef at Alder, joined the conversation, and started turning the basic idea into experiments. Over a period of several weeks, the team iterated their way through a reimagination of shepherd's pie as a tartare. They tried different combinations of vegetables, different ways to prepare the potatoes, and different meats for the tartare.

Central to this process is balancing an idea with taste—both in the sense of tasting the experiments, but also with people's tastes in food. Certainly, the five basic taste centers (sweet, salty, sour, bitter, and umami) play a role in this, but there are subjective interpretations to be made about what is a "good" idea and what is a "bad" idea for a dish. The team has intuitions about what will be tasty and interesting, but they then have to consider what their audience will enjoy or be willing to try. So a dish like the shepherd's pie tartare goes over well because of the ease with which people can imagine the dish. At Alder, the staff began "Test Kitchen Tuesdays," which featured a weekly R&D lab for recipes the team was developing.[13] This was a logical step in Dufresne's approach to experimentation, as it allowed the staff to test their opinions and assumptions against those of customers.

In the end, some experiments lead to dishes on the menu, while others simply add to the knowledge acquired by the team about techniques, preparations, ingredient properties, and so on. They also learn things to avoid, like the yogurt and bacon experiment. It is all part of Wylie's explorations into new directions for modernist cuisine.

The Journey to Warm Ice Cream

One of the more emblematic of Wylie's research projects was the quest for warm ice cream. The team wanted to keep all the properties of ice cream—its mouthfeel, texture, the flavor—but with the dish served warm instead of cold. Once they had this basic concept—one that plays with the familiarity, nostalgia, and humor—they set about understanding the chemistry and physics of ice cream. What is it: a gel, a foam, an emulsion? (The short answer: It's a foam.) Central to their investigation was understanding the changes that occur when a liquid, a sugar, binding agents, and flavors are subjected to churning at cold temperatures.

Some basic principles came to the forefront: The cold forms an emulsion, thanks to the binding qualities of the fats, creating a colloidal structure; churning introduces air into the mixture, which adds the volume and texture of ice cream (and gives it its status as a foam); keeping the ice cream at a cold temperature maintains the binding, which in turn keeps the texture; stabilizers like carrageenan or xanthan gum produce an even, consistent distribution of the fat, which creates the creamy mouthfeel; and the colder the temperature at which ice cream is stored, the harder it will be.

The challenge for Wylie and his team was to maintain the binding of the fat elements, the churning that introduced air, and the constant storage temperature—and to achieve all this through the use of heat instead of cold. Fats react differently to heat, which causes them to loosen rather than bind. As a result, the team had to conduct experiments to investigate other materials to take the place of fats in the binding process. And if that didn't work, to find other methods that would result in the same combination of texture, taste, and mouthfeel.

Wylie and his team have been pursuing warm ice cream for quite some time, but the closest they have gotten was a warm soft-serve custard. In the process of experimenting, though, they have invented numerous techniques that produced gels, foams, and emulsions that they have used in a variety of other dishes. The most popular were the tofu noodles that

Miso soup with instant tofu noodles, from WD~50. Photo by Eric Medsker.

customers squirted from a small bottle into a warm miso broth. The pursuit of warm ice cream exemplifies Wylie's exploratory intentions. The team posed a question, then researched and experimented to find answers, always keeping in mind the overarching values of the restaurant as well as the specific questions of the dish. Instead of being one-off experiments, these explorations are used by the team to learn new techniques and approaches, even when menu items aren't generated.

That this research into warm ice cream hasn't yielded a perfect outcome does not mean the process has resulted in failure. Instead, it is what is to be expected from exploratory iteration. Each step along the way—even when the original intention didn't pan out—created knowledge for the team. The only real failure would happen if the experiment weren't carried out until it produced knowledge. Otherwise, Wylie's exploratory intentions are always productive, even if they don't result in a new dish on the menu.

Connecting the Dots

The underlying concept in Wylie's iteration is an adaptation of scientific basic research combined with the workshop organization and operation of restaurant kitchens. Both begin with exploratory **intentions**, but where scientific study is generally about broadening our understanding, Wylie's focuses on his aesthetic goals for his restaurants. This involves drawing on scientifically derived knowledge about the biology, chemistry, and physics of food, but also on knowledge derived from centuries of cooking. This all happens within the **context** of Wylie's restaurants, involving the participation of almost everyone on the staff. The **actors** in this case are the chefs and cooks in the restaurants, who must fit the exploratory work in and around the regular duties of preparing food for and serving the restaurant's customers.

Wylie and his staff developed a **process** that uses the science of food in conjunction with the techniques and materials of the culinary arts. This is an iterative process, anchored by exploratory intentions, in which scientific methods are harnessed toward aesthetic ends. The process cycles through four "gates" of **evaluation**: Is it feasible? Does it meet their aesthetic goals? Is it reproducible in a resource-efficient way, allowing it to appear on the menu? And once on the menu, is it popular enough with diners to remain there?

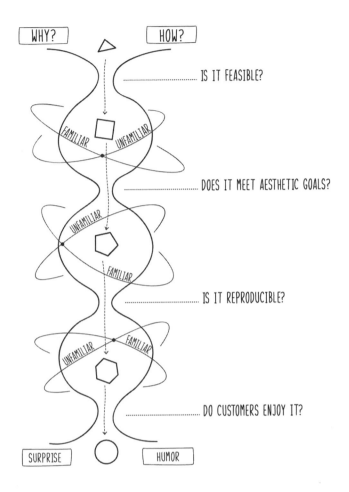

WHY?   HOW?

.... IS IT FEASIBLE?

FAMILIAR   UNFAMILIAR

.... DOES IT MEET AESTHETIC GOALS?

UNFAMILIAR

FAMILIAR

.... IS IT REPRODUCIBLE?

UNFAMILIAR   FAMILIAR

.... DO CUSTOMERS ENJOY IT?

SURPRISE   HUMOR

Along the way through these four evaluative gates, there are numerous potential **outcomes** beyond the development of a new menu item. Perhaps Wylie and his staff learn a new technique, or confirm certain chemical or physical properties of an ingredient. Maybe, as with the warm ice cream project, they fall short of their initial intention, but along the way find unexpected paths for further exploration, or even dishes they hadn't imagined possible.

9 Methodological Processes: Nathalie Pozzi, Architect, and Eric Zimmerman, Game Designer

The players frantically tossed large cardboard boxes in an attempt to block their opponents, who in turn were trying to get two balls linked with rope across the field. They were playing *BlockBall*, a fast-paced strategic sport created by game designer Eric Zimmerman. He invited architect Nathalie Pozzi to this early playtest of the game so he could ask her advice on the play space and the design of objects in the game. As Nathalie would relay later, "it was looking pretty bad."[1] The rules of the game were fine, but the way the play interacted with those cardboard boxes and the linked balls was disastrous. Yes, it was a prototype, so the materials weren't the focus. But even so, Nathalie was responding to the scale, the shapes, the length of the rope connecting the balls, and most importantly, how the physical

Nathalie Pozzi and Eric Zimmerman. Photo by Shuangshuang Huo.

elements related to the human bodies that interacted with them. They were all *off*—they just didn't communicate the drama of the game to the players. Nathalie's input turned a somewhat clumsy prototype into a much more spatially aware *BlockBall* in its debut at the 2009 Come Out and Play Festival, a street game festival in New York City. And so a collaboration between the architect and the game designer began.

Since Nathalie's invaluable consultation on *BlockBall*, Nathalie and Eric have created six installations—the term they use to encapsulate the shared disciplinary concerns of games and architecture about space, material, and social interactions. Their projects have been installed at venues like New York City's Museum of Modern Art, the Smithsonian American Art Museum in Washington D.C., La Gaîté Lyrique in Paris, and the Museum of Science in Boston. The installations include *Cross My Heart and Hope to Die*, a labyrinth with no right angles where individual team members form walls to protect or hunt creatures from Greek mythology; *Flatlands*, where participants debate the aesthetics of 200 vintage board games contained within a sleek, modular archive; and *Starry Heavens*, a competitive fable involving large steel plates and giant floating weather balloons. The installations often have a subversive element to their play, enabled through the architectural design of the playspace. In *Interference*, players meddle with other players' adjacent games, stealing pieces from each other as they mischievously look at each other through a perforated screen. The installation *Sixteen Tons* is a circular gambling pit where contestants bribe one another with the cash they have in their pockets in order to move large steel play pieces. *Waiting Rooms* is a theatrical meditation on bureaucracy and all its trappings, starting with, of course, a waiting room. The architectural elements of Nathalie and Eric's installations often eschew straight lines and right angles for a sculptural impact that is as playful as the activities that take place within and among them.

Game design and architectural design merge to create a complete experience, often shown in an art context. These dynamic installations bring play and interaction, laughter and exclamation into museum and gallery spaces typically reserved for quiet contemplation. However, while Nathalie and Eric's installations might encourage unhindered playfulness, there is a consistent, methodological process that went into the development of each of them—a methodology that merges the best practices of architecture and game design.

Nathalie's architectural practice was influenced through her studies in Venice and her upbringing in a small mountain town in the Italian Alps. In the Alps, traditional architecture followed the needs of the family and the dictates of harsh winters, integrating the barn into the living space to take advantage of the warmth of the animals. As she describes it, "the house was a machine for a specific type of living." Nathalie's grandmother's home was designed in this way—and it helped Nathalie form an appreciation for functional designs with a monastic simplicity of form. She brought these influences into her architectural studies at the Università Iuav di Venezia, where functional design based on tradition and history was coupled with a contemporary use of material and form. In her time at the university, she was introduced to a wide array of practices, including those of artists and sculptors using architectural language to explore abstract concepts.

Nathalie was particularly influenced by the work of Ilya and Emilia Kabakov and their installation *The Man Who Flew into Space from His Apartment*. In it, one walks into a messy studio, where there is a chairlike catapult in the center of the room, above which a hole bursts through the ceiling. Nathalie's collaborative work with Eric would be influenced by the implied story of this installation, expressed solely through the space: a cot, a workbench, a hole in the ceiling, and debris on the floor from the catapulting. Her interests—the utilitarian and vernacular design of her grandmother's home and the conceptual explorations of installation art—found their way into her practice, fusing both architecture and the arts, coupled with a precise eye for material and craft. She moved to the United States where her practice has spanned residential architecture for clients and sculptural projects with artists, consulting on installations for the Yokohama Triennale of Art, the Florence Biennale, and the Royal Academy of London, to name a few.

Eric Zimmerman always made games. As a child, he would create elaborate games with army men for his friends to play. He went on to study painting in college, but by the time he was graduating, he says, "I was doing things that really looked like games."[2] After graduating with an MFA in art and technology from Ohio State University, Eric found work at R/GA Interactive in New York City where he collaborated with game designer Frank Lantz on the videogame *Gearheads*—a sort of chess played with windup toys—reminiscent of those games with army figures Eric had invented in his childhood basement. This was the first in a set of game titles that innovated either through new styles of play or unusual content. *Sissyfight 2000*, for example, was one of the first online social games to be played on the web, and perhaps the only game of its era (or any era, for that matter) to explore the politics of young girls in a playground. He went on to cofound his own company, GameLab, best known for the time management game *Diner Dash*. Eric forged the path for independent game design—exploring games more deeply as culture—and also came up with new kinds of gameplay. He coauthored the influential *Rules of Play: Game Design Fundamentals* which established a philosophy of games as systems with rich meaning emerging from their play.[3] The book cemented a design methodology focused on the player, and a prototype-playtest iterative design cycle. After GameLab closed, Eric helped found the NYU Game Center at New York University, where he is currently a professor. Eric continues to pursue a variety of independent game projects (including an ongoing collaboration with the authors of this book through the company Local No. 12).

All of which catches us up to Nathalie and Eric's collaboration.

Possibility Spaces

Nathalie: No more grids.

Eric: As a game designer that's where I start from, the grid.

Something you quickly realize when talking to Nathalie and Eric is that these are two people who truly respect what each brings to the table, but they are also not afraid to disagree with one another to advocate for something that they strongly believe in. In fact, when asked how they resolve creative conflicts, Nathalie's answer was, "We fight a lot." (As Nathalie said this, Eric laughed and agreed.) The fighting, however, is of the productive kind. They push each other to question their field-specific assumptions. Often this takes the form of a challenge, like the ultimatum "no more grids"—Nathalie's challenge to Eric came from her sensibility as an architect, pushing against traditional forms. But for Eric, the grid is a go-to in game design, the ur-form upon which most games are built (think of chessboards, football fields, even pixels on a screen).

When Nathalie challenged Eric to stop using the grid, she provided what is known in game design—and design in general—as a constraint[4]—a rule

Interference screen. Photo by Maxime Dufour Photographies.

that would force a playful solution. Interestingly enough, the emphasis on rules in their methodology mirrors the rules one finds in their installations. The paradoxical relationship between rules and play[5]—that strict rules lead to playful creativity—is found throughout their collaborative practice. In other words, they have derived an ordered methodology to generate playful installations—rules to generate play. For Nathalie and Eric, constraints take the form of rules presented as a challenge or a goal. Not using a grid proved to be a fruitful constraint (as design constraints tend to be), radically influencing the look and feel of the microthin screens for their installation *Interference*, in which participants interfere with the games of other players by stealing their play pieces. Suspended, microthin steel screens act as vertical game boards with organically arranged holes resembling biological cells. Competing players paired on either side of the screen face each other and insert cylindrical wooden pieces into the cells on the screen. By eschewing the grid, Nathalie and Eric created a striking set of cellular-like spaces—as they call them, "cell colonies"—to play within.

One of the primary constraints Nathalie and Eric work with is the context of each installation—where it is located, when it will take place, and who will play it. Because their work is installed in various locations, the space each installation will exist in is a key consideration in its design. In architecture, context (or "site") provides a defining constraint to work with. Returning to the example of *Interference*, the location was a transitional space between a staircase and a bar in Paris's digital arts center, La Gaîté Lyrique. Observing how individuals flowed through the room gave them the idea of creating a passageway—a space you would move through. The context of the space provided the form for their installation—one that would work with and direct the flow of human traffic. Nathalie came up with the idea of gossamer-light steel screens bisecting the space, and dividing players from their opponents, as they interacted through the cells in the screen. The passageway context, then, informed how players would interact with the piece.

A performer calls numbers in *Waiting Rooms*. Photo by Ida C. Benedetto for Nathalie Pozzi and Eric Zimmerman.

Their most recent project, *Waiting Rooms*, on the other hand, didn't start with a location, but instead was designed to be played in a variety of contexts. However, there was still a constraint: no reading of rules. In fact, this constraint was the origin of the piece—Nathalie and Eric wanted to create an installation that would allow participants to simply begin playing. The constraint materialized from something they had learned from their previous projects: Deciphering rules is a barrier to participation. (If you've ever played a new board game, you would likely agree that reading game rules is not the most scintillating activity.) Without anything more to guide them than the fact that they wanted to avoid rules reading in their next project, they began conceptualizing. As they explored solutions to the challenge, they landed on the idea of a generic waiting room, inspired by Nathalie's experience with the U.S. visa and immigration process. Visitors (the term they use to describe participants) would be assigned a number and begin the game in the waiting room, awaiting the calling of their number. Once called, they explore different rooms, performing according to instructions provided by actors positioned throughout the building. Nathalie and Eric have shown *Waiting Rooms* at a variety of museums and in a variety of other buildings, each time customizing the activity to use spaces for various moments in the experience. The experience itself is disorienting in the way that bureaucracies can be—a maze of arbitrary rules and unclear outcomes. While participating, many ultimately seek to subvert its systems, seeking a way to "win," even though the goal is left ambiguous. And that's exactly the point.

Nathalie and Eric's work puts into relief the systems that underlie our everyday experiences. These systems might be bureaucracy (*Waiting Rooms*), labor (*Sixteen Tons*), or even games themselves (*Interference*). Their installations become a metaphor for the challenges of the contemporary human condition. On their surface, the installations look like minimalist, abstract structures, but once they are engaged with, the metaphor becomes clear. However, in these metaphoric experiences Nathalie and Eric insert a twist: the opportunity to playfully subvert the rules of the system. In *Waiting Rooms*, for example, this subversion is exemplified by how visitors either resist or follow the rules they are subjected to, or how they attempt to set their own goals in the absence of a clear goal defined by the experience. Often the experience of the installation calls into question the structure of games and rules themselves. As Nathalie describes:

Our games are austere, classical, they often feel like classical strategy board games, on a large scale. But we also like to break the rules of how games usually work, we like to play with what's proper, so in *Sixteen Tons*, you are taking real money out of your pocket, and bribing people, and at the end of the game the rules don't tell you what you're supposed to do with the money. With *Interference* you are actually stealing the pieces from other people's games (interfering with their games), so you are actually reaching and taking pieces from other people's boards on another part of the wall.

When we interact with Eric and Nathalie's installations, we activate them through our participation, in the process transforming them into something else—a performance, a happening, a dance party, a role-played meditation on life. Their installations "break the rules" in games, architecture, and the human experience to create something new.

Nathalie and Eric combine material built environments and immaterial rules to create a "possibility space."[6] While they use metaphors to guide our interpretations of their designs, it's up to each participant to create their own playful strategies within the space provided by the rules and the built environment. In games, a possibility space is an abstract decision space containing all the possible moves at any given time during play—all the moves a player could make in a game of chess, for instance. The possibility space of architecture is generated through the interplay of form and function, context, and the needs of the community or client occupying that space. In essence, humans play within the built environment,[7] and they play within the rules of games. To design buildings and games is to recognize the possibility spaces they create. And to be able to recognize and manage all of these possibilities involves … playtesting.

The Proof Is in the Playtest

Nathalie and Eric share a consistent methodology that stitches together their fields and helps them manage the complexity of the possibility spaces each project opens up. They use constraint (no grids) and context (a passageway) to establish their intentions and focus on a specific outcome. They begin with a concept from real life, or see one emerge metaphorically in play. But in order to "see" their design and the possibility spaces it opens up, they incorporate playtesting.

Playtesting is an all-important and well-known step in the iterative process of game design. We've looked closely at this in our book *Games, Design and Play: A Detailed Approach to Iterative Game Design*, where we identify the four main steps in the iterative cycle: conceptualizing, prototyping, playtesting, and evaluating the results.[8] While it is at times painful to see players struggle, playtesting is a necessary, important, and often revelatory step in Nathalie and Eric's methodology. As Eric puts it, "Ideas are cheap, but playtesting is truth."

First, a bit of background on playtesting within the field of game design. Playtesting, as it sounds, is testing the way a game plays. In essence, a game is a dynamic system that only takes form when it is activated through play. When it's not being played, a game is little more than a set of written or coded rules, or perhaps some objects like dice, cards, balls, and markings on a field. To see the dynamics of the rules and objects come together, someone needs to pick them up and play with them—otherwise it's almost impossible to imagine how the gameplay will look and feel. This is because the rules in games often generate emergent outcomes that are difficult to anticipate—possibility spaces! Different people have different play styles and use different strategies—often ones that the game designer would have never anticipated.

Playtesting is something that should happen early on and quickly in order to, as designers call it, "find the fun." In game design, to get to a playtest, one first needs a prototype—a playable version of the game. It's ideal to prototype as quickly as possible to get to the playtest—and it's relatively simple to prototype a game to see if it's working. One can simply describe a rule—rock beats scissors, scissors beats paper, paper beats rock—and then immediately test it. Even technologically advanced 3D videogames are often prototyped simply and effectively on paper.

Within the field of architecture, "playtesting" is not an operable term, even though designing spaces also involves an understanding of systems dynamics and the complexities of human and social behavior. Architecture is materially difficult to prototype and playtest at human scale. To build at scale simply to test a design would be a Borgesian task—like creating a map that is the same size as the territory.[9] To prototype their ideas, architects create representations in the form of sketches, models, and renderings. In many cases, games and buildings share simple origins on paper. Architecture is also tested in that representations, in the form of renderings, are presented to clients and, in some cases, to other stakeholders impacted by the impending structure.

Other strategies architects use to mitigate failure and "playtest" are based on history and experience. Nathalie describes the closest thing to playtesting in architecture as the lessons that can be learned from already-completed buildings—picking up hints from materials, motifs, and scale from architectural history, the work of others, and their own previous projects. So while playtesting is a well-defined practice in the domain of game design, in architecture, testing designs encompasses a variety of activities, from studying built environments and their use to presenting plans and renderings to clients and stakeholders.

Despite these differences, playtesting is an integral part of Nathalie and Eric's collaborative methodology. As Nathalie puts it, "we have to make a project say something we want to say." But how does one use the abstract language of architecture and games to say something? The answer is to have a strong methodological process that hinges on iterating through successive prototypes and playtests to get closer to what Nathalie and Eric want to say. And it's through playtesting that failures in the design—large and small—become painfully evident. As a case in point, we'll look at the process in designing the "no grids"–inspired *Interference*.

The spatial and sensory effect of *Interference* is stunning, with thin vertical steel screens resembling a futuristic interface upon which the secret language of the game moves in an irregular, biological pattern. The early iterations, however, were completely different.

Through conversations with staff at La Gaîté Lyrique, where *Interference* was commissioned, Nathalie and Eric knew that they would be creating a piece for a particular context—a long passageway. They began thinking about an activity that took advantage of the length, and a form to sculpt the space. As soon as they had a vague idea—a wall or line to divide the space and the players—they developed a rough prototype to see if that could form the basis for a game. An early prototype of the activity started in a park with bamboo sticks laid on the ground to represent a wall, and a ball used in a fashion similar to a bocce ball. Participants were asked to pretend that the sticks were a wall that was separating them, so they all looked down to the ground and played along the walls. Nathalie describes the moment they started playtesting as a total disappointment. Witnessing how antisocial the gameplay was, with everyone looking down and not at each other, brought her to tears. Indeed, this kind of heartbreaking

Interference. Photo by Maxime Dufour Photographies.

moment occurs often in a playtest, when you actually "see" the game for the first time.

Pain is an integral part of Eric and Nathalie's process. It's difficult to observe players struggle to make sense of rules that to you, the designer, seem perfectly clear. As Nathalie describes it, playtesting is "cruelly revealing," largely because it puts into plain view the things that aren't working. Eric explains,

While playtesting is cruel, it's healthy that it's cruel; it forces you to confront the truth of your design. Ideas are cheap, but playtesting is truth. So you might have what you think are brilliant ideas, but when you get someone actually interacting with it, it's just shit that breaks on the rocks of reality.

Playtesting can surface a variety of ugly realities in a design: The goal is unclear, the rules are easily exploited, it simply is not a fun or engaging experience. It's painful for the designer, and it's not always a pleasant experience for the player, either. It takes time and experience to cultivate a taste for playtesting. Eric likens it to developing a taste for spicy foods; you begin to look forward to the pain. Remaining open to players' comments and, beyond that, listening and observing intently for clues to improvements in the design are part of the art of playtesting. Learning to evaluate playtests is similar to a doctor observing symptoms and homing in on their underlying cause. Playtesting is like a pathology for prototypes; when something in the design fails, it provides the designer with the data they need to evaluate the cause and find a solution, a path toward their next prototype.

So, rather than give up, Nathalie and Eric responded to the devastating playtest for *Interference*, when players looked at their feet and not each other. They established a new constraint: to make a game where people *are looking at each other*, in a social event context. To try to model this, Eric went to the hardware store and bought some pegboard walls, the kind used to hang tools. They began prototyping games involving pushing wires through the holes. The perforations in the pegboard enabled players to be on either side and see what the other player was doing as they pushed their wire through the hole. But, as Eric puts it, "Nathalie hated the grid the pegboard came with." This was the impetus behind the "no grids" constraint. And it was then that *Interference* really began to take form.

They started prototyping games that had more organic layouts. To start, instead of trying to create an organic pegboard (this would take too long—game prototypes need to be quick and dirty to get to the all-important playtesting), the installation was rotated to lie flat on a table with an organic layout drawn on paper. They used tiles from a preexisting board game as the play pieces. They were also busy researching cellular structure and behavior, and Nathalie was thinking about using thin perforated screens as a way to create the board, so that players could be on opposite sides but still see each other, encouraging more social interaction to answer their first design constraint. She found a fabricator in Italy that creates one-millimeter-thick steel screens, and began the process of prototyping with small samples of

Early prototype of *Interference*. Photo by Eric Zimmerman.

the screen material. The design question at this point was, "What can we do with cells?"

The idea of a territory-based game about collecting spaces inside a cell led them to board games like *El Grande*, where players fight for control of regions in Spain. Much of the prototyping process involves looking at precedents—at times, other games that explore a similar question—similar to the way that architects use history to guide their designs. Precedents for architecture might also come from material research, such as new technologies in steel screen fabrication. And finally, precedents might be found in a completely different context from architecture or games—like cellular structures, or the nature of bureaucracy.

One could stop here, to make a perfectly playable game that answers these questions. But the primary underlying motive behind everything Nathalie and Eric do is to enable playful subversion of the experience. A breakthrough came in a playtest, as players ran out of pieces and began stealing pieces from other games going on around them. This created a subversive hook for the piece, a metaphor, and the installation's title, *Interference*. The idea of messing with other games in progress, and of some outside event messing with your game is commonly referred to as "interference"—especially in sports, when something unexpected or not allowed gets in the way. The lesson learned, and one learned in playtests over and over again, is that some of the best ideas can come from players. The trick is to remain open to the possibility spaces each playtest explores.

Finally, after multiple prototypes and playtests, the installation was saying what Nathalie and Eric wanted it to say. It had a subversive and playful element that asked players to reflect on their own expectations. The combination of the game's rules, the sculpting of the space, and the materials led players to look at each other, socialize, and otherwise interact on the organic playing field. The design came together as a result of trying to respond to constraints and context through prototyping, playtesting, and evaluating. All this was guided by their individual training, the practices of their creative disciplines, and their personal and shared interests. Many of the constraints and the overarching metaphor weren't articulated before the project, but instead came up as part of a dynamic iterative methodology that continues to guide their process.

Nathalie and Eric's strong methodology embraces the cruel truth of playtesting in order to find the truth in their design. Their methodological embrace of iterative prototyping and playtesting also helps them connect their diverse practices, finding a new language to merge the material and immaterial aspects of their crafts. Nathalie and Eric fuel their process by challenging each other with constraints ("no grids"), designing for context (a passageway, for instance), and finding life metaphors (bureaucracy) to guide their subversive play goals and the participants' experiences. And finally, they use research—both in terms of materials and other game-based precedents—to inform their process.

Connecting the Dots

To guide their collaboration, Nathalie and Eric employ a methodological process that stitches together their respective fields of architecture and game design. Their methodology includes a series of repeated steps that get them from intention to outcome. Nathalie and Eric's intentions are often formed by challenging each other with constraints, designing for **context** and exploring metaphor to guide their subversive play goals and the participants' experiences. The context, constraint, and metaphor can start a project, emerge at some point midway, or even come about at the end as they cycle through prototyping and playtesting.

They give form to their ideas through prototyping, creating scale models, materials tests, or rules tests with stand-in materials (the pegboard used for *Interference*, for instance). They then playtest the prototype with a variety of people so that they can **evaluate** whether their intentions are coming across, and identify emergent **outcomes** they might not have foreseen. **Actors** participate in the installation to bring it to life—whether in playtests or in the final version.

Successive cycles through prototypes and playtests help them hone the experience for participants. Within and around these cycles, they conduct research into materials, architectural and game precedents, and ideas and

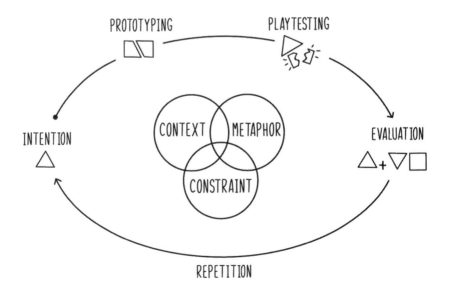

concepts that can form the metaphors underlying the installation. Each time a project is installed leads to improvements or new ideas and constraints leading into other projects. For instance, *Waiting Rooms* was born from the challenges participants had learning the rules before participating. As Nathalie observes, "Architecture, once it is done, it's done, but with the reinstall, it gets better." Iterating within projects and from install to install, their methodology helps them fully explore the possibility spaces in their designs. You might say that because their methodology remains consistent, they can embrace the inconsistent and at times chaotic results of their play-tests, finding their way through faith in the process to creating unique and meaningful experiences. Without the use of grids.

Andy Milne plays piano. This statement has been true for as long as he can remember. As a small child, he would sit and improvise tunes on the family piano, and when he turned six he began taking piano lessons, as all the Milne children did. But Andy's lessons went very differently than his siblings' lessons: His parents never had to force him to practice. He just loved to play.

As a teen, Andy didn't really know what a career as a musician would be like—no one in his family was a professional musician. But he knew that he wanted to pursue music, and so he went to York University in Toronto and got an honors degree in music under the tutelage of renowned jazz

Andy Milne. Image: Kabeer.

musicians such as Pat LaBarbera, Don Thompson, and Oscar "O.P." Peterson. After graduating, Andy received a scholarship to Banff Centre where he met saxophonist Steve Coleman, who encouraged him to move to New York to join his ensemble. So Andy did, and that unknowable career as a musician began to take shape.

Steve Coleman is known for a distinctive way of thinking about music called the M-Base concept (short for "macro-basic array of structured extemporization"). The ideas Coleman and his contemporaries were exploring through the M-Base collective incorporated both improvisation and structure to express life experiences using non-western musical ideas and philosophies as inspiration.[1] Playing with Coleman night after night led Andy toward developing a personal harmonic and rhythmic vocabulary—the content of their verbal and musical conversations generated new insights and philosophies that drove his improvisational approach. They worked together, touring internationally, recording, and collaborating for the better part of ten years.

During the early 1990s, Andy began leading his own groups, putting into practice the concepts he had absorbed from his time with Coleman. In 1999 Andy created Dapp Theory—a group formed to "tell passionate stories, promote peace and inspire collective responsibility towards uplifting the human spiritual condition."[2] Dapp Theory was named after the "dap," an expression of solidarity and equality through handshake variations that originated among black GIs in the Vietnam war after the Black Power salute was forbidden by the military.[3] Andy describes the connection between dap and Dapp Theory:

The concept behind the name of Dapp Theory comes from the 60s, from Black Power—you give someone dap, some props, some recognition. I think that within that idea there was some connectivity to how you conduct yourself. I used to think of it how my mother would sternly suggest to "do unto others as they would do unto you." The Golden Rule.[4]

Whether musician to musician, or group to audience, the Golden Rule prevails. The theory behind Dapp Theory provided the foundations for an improvisational golden rule that Andy refers to as "recognize and respond." Dapp Theory uses this golden rule of improvisation to guide their music, which blends the boundaries between jazz, hip hop, heavy metal, folk, and classical.

Andy's work embraces collaboration and the ways in which improvisation brings together different cultures and influences. In addition to his work with Dapp Theory, Andy has established an award-winning career composing and performing with collaborators such as Grammy-winning jazz singer Dianne Reeves, renowned poet Sekou Sundiata, and folk-rock icon Bruce Cockburn. The latter collaborated with Dapp Theory in 2003's *Y'all Just Don't Know*, an album that melds the heartfelt sociopolitical folk of Cockburn together with the rich melodies of Andy's compositional style. Another collaboration, *Strings and Serpents*, brings together jazz pianist Benoît Delbecq, animator Saki Murotani, and Japanese koto players Ai Kajigano and Tsugumi Yamamoto. In the performed piece, jazz improvisation coexists with traditional Japanese music, and animated visuals based on musical patterns and the mythology of the rainbow serpent.

Andy cites influences from jazz greats like Thelonious Monk to lyricists like Joni Mitchell, and his compositions and performances have traversed an equally wide array of styles and forms. He has recorded several critically lauded solo albums, including *Dreams and False Alarms* (2007), which includes renditions of two Joni Mitchell songs, as well as reggae, folk, and pop classics. He's composed the music for *Star Trek* star William Shatner's documentary film *The Captains* and several subsequent documentaries by Shatner, and has even performed at *Star Trek* and sci-fi conventions (yes, Andy is a sci-fi fan). He has experimented with new technologies via a collaboration with pianist Benoît Delbecq in *Where Is Pannonica?* (2008) using 5.1 surround sound as part of the recording process to position musical elements in different sonic spaces.

Andy finds inspiration all over the place—in politics, philosophy, comedy, science fiction, and even homeopathy. *The Seasons of Being*, a ten-piece ensemble and work commissioned in 2015 by Chamber Music America's New Jazz Works, explores the healing principles of homeopathy through improvisational structures designed to respond to each member's emotional musical state.

In addition to his influences, collaborators, and musical philosophy, Andy's music ultimately extends a tradition at the heart of jazz: improvisation.

We're Always Improvising

What is jazz? Musician and educator Wynton Marsalis gives us a breakdown:

The main three components are the blues, improvisation—which is some kind of element that people are trying to make it up—and swing, which means even though they're making up music, they're trying to make it up together. It feels great, like you're having a great conversation with somebody.[5]

Of the three components Marsalis describes, improvisation is at the center of jazz's origin story. Jazz is an improvised combination of African American and Afro-Caribbean musical traditions with European instrumentation, reflecting the diverse cultural mix of its birthplace: New Orleans in the late 1800s.[6] Improvisation is also what jazz musicians do—they make up music.

Everyone has a small claim to improvisation—even if it's not music that they're making. Andy says, "We're always improvising, even if we're not making sound." Choosing what to wear in the morning, making coffee on a campfire, coming up with a pun while chatting with a friend—these are all ways in which we improvise in response to a situation (dressing, camping, and chatting). Improvisation is a skill we all use in life.

Andy uses improvisation to attain his goal of expressing the human experience through music. But to be able to express human experiences first involves being human. And to be human is to experience failure. To Andy, failure is simply part of the process. In fact, he believes it might be a necessary ingredient. As he points out, "It's good to have some adversity to help you grow. If everything was going along smoothly all the time, maybe you wouldn't recognize that you could be doing even better." Perhaps because failure for a musician is simply part of getting better, Andy was happy to dive into the topic. As he puts it, "No one's going to get hurt if you go for it. You might have an embarrassing performance, you might spend a week questioning if this is the right thing for you to be doing, but it's okay. No one will have permanent damage from a bad performance."

In jazz, failure is not going to hurt anyone (except, perhaps, the musician's ego). Yet, while we're not talking brain surgery, a career in music is still a risk. You do need to "go for it" if you're going to make it, and making it often means a constant enterprise, from gigging to collaborating, to commissions and commercial work. In the midst of all this activity, failure is inevitable. But perhaps jazz musicians are particularly suited to dealing with failure—because when one fails, one often has to improvise a solution.

In jazz as in life, improvisation finds a way to transform failure through an appropriate response. When a guitar string breaks, the music must go on. However, to choose the right response, particularly in the moment, takes skill. To know how to respond to failure involves recognizing what is going on around you. This is where the golden rule comes in: Do unto others as you would have them do unto you. Andy breaks this down further into two steps: "recognize" and "respond." Improvisation is about recognizing what is happening in the moment, and responding in kind.

This philosophy is also carried through in Andy's work as an educator. A big part of Andy's life is about playing music, and an equally big part of his life is teaching how to play music. He teaches at three different schools in New York City: Columbia, New York University, and the New School. Andy identifies learning from failure (or failing to learn from it) as part of the attentiveness involved in improvisation. He says that "a big part of being a great musician is being a great listener."

Although failure is part of the process and is essential to learning, sometimes the student doesn't see—or hear—when failure happens. This is another form of recognize and respond—seeing the situation for what it is, and responding to it appropriately. Failure in music is not always as obvious as a broken guitar string or an off note. Because music allows for such a range of expression, being able to see and hear where your performance is subtly failing and needs to be improved is challenging: "The number-one challenge that my students have is that what they play is fine—it's how they mix it up, it's how they integrate everything that's the pass/fail barometer in terms of whether the music is actually successful from the point of view of being cohesive."

Cohesiveness is, in part, connected to context: recognizing what's going on around you and responding in a way that fits into the flow preceding it. Andy provided this example: Imagine you are a lifeguard. You witness someone in the shallow end of the pool flailing their hands. They're surrounded by friends who are laughing. The flailing person eventually stands up, giggling, too. It becomes clear in a matter of seconds—they were a group of teenagers horsing around, pretending to drown. Contrast this situation with someone caught up in high waves in an ocean, and the same gesture—flailing hands—demands a completely different response by the lifeguard. You'll need to jump into the ocean and help them out, whereas the teenager in shallow water would benefit from a verbal admonition that pretending to drown is not to be taken lightly. The lifeguard had to intently observe the situation in order to recognize what was happening, and within a matter of seconds, respond by either jumping in and saving a life, or scolding the teens. The lifeguard's observation had to also include the context—what's happening around the flailing person—to respond in an appropriate manner.

Of course, music making isn't a matter of life or death, but improvisational music *is* all about the same process of recognizing and responding in the moment, appropriate to the context. This involves plenty of practice with one's instrument, and it also involves practice playing improvisationally, over and over again, to become better at it. The saying "Practice makes perfect" implies that imperfection—failure—is the prerequisite to perfection. Being able to recognize failure and respond to it appropriately is the first step in learning how to improvise well.

Learning to Listen

Andy uses travel as an analogy for the skills needed to improvise. Have you ever tried to get somewhere and your mode of transportation breaks down? You need to figure out how far is left to go, how long it will take to walk, and other ways to get there. Chances are, you've been in a situation like this, and you still figured out how to get to where you were going. This is because, as Andy points out, we're always improvising. And we usually improvise in response to something that didn't go according to plan—we improvise to respond to failure. Imagine this scenario: You need to rescue scientists in a crumbling subterranean lab where an explosion has broken open a giant vat of sulfuric acid. There's no time to spare, but there's a candy machine. What would you do? Well, if you were the fictional character MacGyver, you would plug that deadly sulfuric acid leak with some chocolate, which due to the chemical properties of chocolate, works like a charm.[7] It was an improvised solution in response to a failure.

Not all of us understand chemistry well enough to be able to improvise as effortlessly as MacGyver. Similarly, not all of us can use our voices with as much acumen and groove as Ella Fitzgerald, or play a sax solo as fluidly as Charlie Parker. As Andy tells his students, the first step toward effortless, intuitive improvisation is to learn your instrument. As he puts it, "You develop it [intuition] by having fewer impediments between you and your sound production." Whatever way you make sound is a technology, whether it's voice, clarinet, or computer. Learning how to use that technology to make the sounds you want is the first step. This involves practice— it's learning a language. Becoming fluent takes a while; Andy calls it making your instrument "invisible"—in other words, being able to use your instrument to make the sound you want without having to stop and think. As Andy says, "that invisibility is your ability to play that instrument, and utilize it and have that vocabulary to just make a sound and not have to be saying, 'wait, hold on, I have to …' Because every time you do that, you're interrupting your ability to just be present."

In addition to practicing and ultimately developing fluency with an instrument, being present, in improvisation, means having the bandwidth to listen. British comedian Paul Merton once said, "The thing about improvisation is that it's not about what you say. It's listening to what other people say."[8] Whether it's used in comedy or jazz, improvisation involves a keen sense of what is going on in the moment—listening, observing, and, the first half in Andy's two-step process, *recognizing*. And once you recognize, the next step is to respond as fully as you can. That includes the context (where, when, why are we playing?) and the probable meaning of what you are responding to. In fact, becoming "fluent" in improvisation is a lot like being a good conversationalist. As Wynton Marsalis says, "It feels great, like you're having a great conversation with somebody."[9]

This all might sound relatively simple, recognize and respond, as easy as having a conversation. But in practice, there's more to it. There are so many potential responses, and in the flow of a performance, only a split second to pick and enact one. Of course, there's also the importance of listening well, getting the context and tone right, so that one can respond cohesively. Any delay can take you out of the moment. Andy calls the time between recognizing and responding the "sample buffer." In computers, a sample buffer or data buffer is the time it takes for the computer memory to move data between an input and an output—for example, how long it takes to process sound coming into a microphone on the computer and send it out through the computer's speakers. The length of time this process takes is called "latency." Using this metaphor, Andy strives to limit the latency between recognizing and responding as much as possible. Musicians are always pushing the limits of that buffer, trying to improve their ability to respond in ways that express their own sensibility, as well as their contribution to the group. Andy likes to describe this idea of pushing the limits of your own sample buffer as riding the thin line between perfection and failure, using piano tuning as a reference:

One slight turn too much and you've lost it. Like a tuned racecar, right to the edge of its performance ability. So knowing, what is your sample buffer, and pushing right to the edge of that. Trying to find that sweet spot. You're growing and pushing but also realizing that I only have this much sample buffer. As we're all playing together, we're trying to suss that out—we're not putting numbers down in a spreadsheet, but intuitively gauging how that works. I think each of us should be trying to understand ourselves a little bit that way, because it helps maximize our effectiveness.

Recognizing and responding well involves plenty of practice to remove as much latency as one can in one's ability to perform. It also requires recognizing the context and tone of what's being played in order to respond cohesively. Failure is part of the process—which is mitigated by practice. As mentioned earlier, failure isn't always as clear as a wrong note or a broken string—it can be subtle. Learning to listen and know whether one's response is cohesive or not—being able to hear one's own failures—is important too.

Slow Motion Improvisation

If live improvisation is like tuning a racecar—testing the limits of one's buffer between recognizing and responding—the process of composing music is the slow-motion instant replay. As Andy describes it:

Improv performance is real time, whereas [composition] is happening in a sort of time lapse over the span of a day, or years. But the reflexes, the work that goes into it to create a sound composition, you're still dealing with the same evaluation, it just is happening in slower time. There's more of an opportunity to pause, so there's this thoughtfulness that can take place that one wouldn't have the luxury of in a live performance, but at the same time, you eventually do have to make a decision, or the composition is never complete. And so that recognize-and-response reflex is informed by your studies of music, your studies of the material, the instrumentation, and if there's a predetermined context in which the music needs to be performed—i.e., for this ensemble, this film score, this commercial, whatever the purpose of the music is. Whatever those parameters are, they influence how I make these decisions in slow-motion time.

If composition is improvisation slowed down, then improvisation is composition sped up. Composer and jazz musician Roscoe Mitchell draws the connection: "To be a good improviser, you have to study composition as a parallel. Because what improvisation is, on a high level, is spontaneous composition."[10]

Andy's work moves between the real-time, spontaneous speed of live performance and the slow-motion speed of composition. Both involve the improvisational skills of recognize and respond—both are about inventing responses to the sounds that came before, but in different scenarios and contexts. In live performance, composition happens in real time, with other musicians adding to the mix—this collaborative real-time composition *is* improvisation. During the act of composition, improvisation happens as well, by iterating and trying different combinations of notes, and building musical structures. Another distinguishing characteristic of composition— it is often a solo activity. Ultimately, improvisation in live performance is like having a conversation (to use Marsalis's analogy),[11] while improvisation in composition is a lot like writing, taking one's time to find the right words.

Sometimes, composition is about taking an existing song and making it one's own. One aspect of jazz is taking "standards" or songs from *The Great American Songbook*—a variable grouping of classic tunes that we've heard jazz musicians take and transform since the beginnings of the form. These songs by composers such as George Gershwin, Cole Porter, and Irving Berlin from the 1920s to 1950s, with their strong melodies, lend themselves to reinterpretation while still being recognizable. One could say that jazz musicians recognize something in these songs and respond to them in their own style.

In *Dreams and False Alarms*, Andy supplements *The Great American Songbook* to include pop, folk, rock, and reggae. There's "I Shot the Sheriff" by Bob Marley, "The Times They Are a-Changin'" by Bob Dylan, and "Amelia" by Joni Mitchell—all songs that were important to Andy growing up. When asked about the inspiration behind the album, he said, "Artists like Bruce Cockburn, Bob Marley, and Joni Mitchell use their songs to speak about important things that need to be heard in this world, yesterday, and today. I guess I'm drawn to them for their courage and ideology."[12]

In addition to the political and social messages these sounds contain, these songs, in the tradition of *The Great American Songbook*, also have a strong and recognizable melodic structure ripe for improvisation—which connects directly to Andy's sensibilities. As he told us, "I like music that grooves, I like music that has strong melody, and I like music that incorporates improvisation and has the capacity to move people." The songs included in the album are moving in melodic structure as well as message—and Andy's renditions recognize these melodic hooks and underlying meanings, and respond with his own movement—or groove—that makes them something else entirely.

To look more deeply at the improvisational process that went into the songs in the album, we focus on Andy's rendition of The Police's 1980s hit "Message in a Bottle."[13] His take on the song is slower in tempo, with more space between the notes, echoing the sentiment of a "lonely castaway" through simple instrumentation—a solo piano. However, trying to capture the feeling of the song with words proves the maxim, "Writing about music is like dancing about architecture."[14] So instead of reaching for further explanation of how the music feels, we'll do our best to capture the process: how Andy used the improviser's tools of recognize and respond to create his own rendition of the song.

In order to truly appreciate Andy's approach to the song, we need to look under the hood to learn more about his process. To start, one might imagine that when someone makes an arrangement of a popular tune, they would write the entire thing down in sheet music. But this isn't how Andy approached his reworking of "Message in a Bottle." Instead of making changes to the song in a linear fashion from its beginning to its end, he created a modular structure that would enable improvisation, allowing him to play it differently each time. In other words, he composed for improvisation. His approach to the composition was twofold: reimagine the rhythmic structure that underpins the melody, and make harmonic changes to the inner movements of the song.

Andy found patterns within the rhythm and melody that he could take and manipulate without compromising our recognition of the song. The harmonic patterns in the melody allow for plenty of variations, since the original song uses short melodic phrases that repeat. These repetitions can be riffed on, played with, and resequenced. These "harmonic shifts," as Andy calls them, are developed and woven into the piece so that they happen in the inner movements, where the chorus repeats. As we listen to Andy's version, we hear extrapolations on the familiar chorus ("sending out an S.O.S."). Sections of the chorus diverge from the original tune altogether, creating a new melody, but one that ends up slipping back again to the familiar tune after a few bars. Andy calls these departures and returns to the original melody "pop-ins." In Andy's words, "It's more like an allusion— rather than bold, firm new directions that take you for a long weekend, they're like a pop-in."

Andy's approach to the rhythmic structure of "Message in a Bottle" was to take the 4/4 structure of the melody, and add a 13/8 rhythm to the bass line underneath. If you know a little bit about music, this dual-rhythmic structure is pretty mind-bendingly skillful—like being able to pat your head and rub your belly, but harder. To explain, Andy describes it as being like a puzzle, along the lines of "two trains leave the station bound for Toronto at the same time, one from Chicago, the other from Vancouver, but one has a stopover in ..."—remember those questions? The beats, like the trains, will converge at times and diverge at times, or as he describes it, "There's points where things meet, and points where things have fake cadences and semi-cadences and then there's a conclusion." For Andy, creating and playing with these rhythmic patterns is a reflex—it's like being able to answer the train puzzle intuitively and not having to work the math out on paper.

"The trick to doing all of this well," Andy says, "is to be able to do them where it doesn't overshadow the melody. One of my teachers said, 'You can't dis the structural integrity of the melody.'" He describes the process of composition as being like building. When one departs from the structural integrity of the song, it can fall apart. As Andy puts it, "That's the artfulness—being able to play and have a little fun and explore something but not to bring the second story down." The key in composition, as in live improvisation, is recognizing the structure and context of the song and responding to it in a way that's cohesive.

While it's interesting to learn how Andy constructed his own improvised "pop-ins" and the diverging and converging rhythmic cadences, the really exciting part is why he made these changes. He took the original harmonic and rhythmic composition of "Message in a Bottle" and made them modular and reconfigurable. In other words, he turned the song's structure into an improvisational playground.

When Andy's "Message in a Bottle" is performed, it's never the same composition twice. For this reason, he doesn't simply create sheet music to be followed. The key to his entire compositional process is that instead of taking the piece and writing a new version from start to finish, he constructed

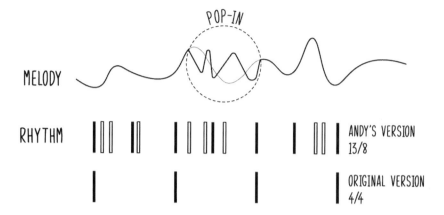

a modular framework—creating elements that could be inserted into the larger overall narrative of the song. He already understood the relationships between how the thirteen- and four-beat phrases would work, so he wrote those down and practiced the song with that shift. Then, after coming to an understanding of some of the harmonic shifts he would make, he made each allusion, or "pop-in," which becomes an insert in the whole arrangement. He then practiced those. Each change to the song was practiced so that Andy could develop an intuitive understanding of how his modular changes could be played and improvised in performance. This approach is similar to a tennis player practicing specific kinds of shots, like a two-handed backhand or an overhead volley, so that when it's time to play a game, each move can be used as appropriate during the game's flow. Again, we see the connection between practice and improvisation—in order to improvise, one must first be fluent in the expressive capabilities of one's instrument. In the case of Andy's version of "Message in a Bottle," Andy had to practice the modular elements of the song to fluently weave them together in performance.

Because the composition's modular framework allows the song to be different every time, "Message in a Bottle" was recorded for the album based on how Andy wanted to configure the rhythmic and harmonic elements at that moment in time. The process Andy went through to recognize the patterns in the original Police song and find his own compositional response to it also laid the groundwork for live performance. Now, when he plays this piece in live performance, he'll improvise on the fly, moving parts around—as if he's quoting himself. He says, "I could play verbatim, or I could choose to reference it, or I could choose to just let my memory of it influence what I would do today." In a way, each time Andy plays the song, he is improvising with himself.

Connecting the Dots

In improvising, playing your part isn't about creating a monologue; it's about engaging in a conversation (from musician to musician, or in our parlance, **actor** to actor). Improvisational processes begin with the **intention** to recognize the structure of the situation (which could be a musical note, a concept, or a feeling) and to respond with an appropriate expression as the **outcome**. Andy defines this **process** as "recognize and respond." To respond fluidly in the musical **context** is the goal. Failure, in the case of jazz improvisation, is a failure to listen—to recognize—and in turn, a failure to respond accordingly. Improvisation happens in the moment, so it demands honing responsiveness through advance preparation—for example, learning one's instrument and learning how to improvise by practicing, over and over again. Practice is how one shortens the "buffer" between recognize and respond, enabling more fluent improvisation.

Composition is improvisation slowed down. Composition is about recognizing the musical structure and responding to it: The composer **evaluates** each response as it builds on the musical foundation. At first, Andy practiced his modified rhythmic structures underlying "Message in a Bottle" and the harmonic "pop-ins" within the chorus as separate elements. By doing this, he could call upon each section to create an improvised sequence

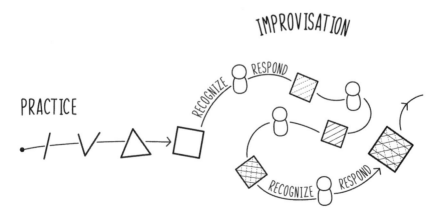

that responds to the **context**—whether in the recording studio or performance. He practiced these structures in order to enable improvisation.

Finally, improvisation, as Andy points out, is something we all do, whether it's choosing what to wear in the morning or finding a new route to work. Applying some of the "in-the-moment" practices of jazz improvisation can help develop an intuitive ability to manage unpredictable situations and respond to them appropriately. In other words, when things around us fail, we all learn to improvise.

11   Internal Evaluation: Amelia Brodka, Professional Skateboarder

Like many young people, Amelia Brodka became hooked on skateboarding at an early age. Seeing a group of young women skating at the X Games (ESPN's showcase and competition for action sports) really caught Amelia's imagination—she realized that skateboarding was for her, too, and not just for her brother. From that point forward, skating[1] became a central part of her life. Growing up in Poland and then in the United States, in Maine and New Jersey, Amelia couldn't fully commit to the sport due to the limitations of the weather and the lack of skating facilities. Given these limits, Amelia focused on street skating—skateboarding both literally in the street and on other constructed obstacles (curbs, benches, sloped walls, staircases, and so on) and in small skate parks that bring these same elements into a designed

Amelia Brodka. Photo by Shuangshuang Huo.

environment. She moved to Los Angeles for college at the University of Southern California, where she could simultaneously continue her education and pursue a skating career. She transformed from a street skater to a vert skater (skating in environments where the upper edges of the environment are perpendicular to the flat bottom) and a park skater (e.g., skating on skate ramps, pools, and bowls designed for skating).

As she improved and moved into the skateboarding elite, Amelia hit an unexpected glass ceiling: Women's skating receives far less support and resources than men's skating. The main income streams for pro skaters come from sponsorships, competition purses, sales of endorsed products, and—for the lucky few—their own product lines and companies. These income sources are predicated upon publicity and exposure—in skateboarding magazines, in YouTube videos, at events, and in competitions, particularly those with large audiences like the X Games. Compared to men's skating, media exposure opportunities for women's skating are very limited. The big contests tend to emphasize the men—to the point that most casual fans probably wouldn't realize there were women's competitions at all. The same goes for the magazines and websites, creating a vicious cycle that stunts women skaters' careers.

The 2011 X Games was the straw that broke the camel's back. Soon after Amelia received an invitation to compete, the women's skateboarding events were canceled. Once again, women were denied an opportunity afforded the men. This cancellation catalyzed Amelia to do something about this inequality. Her documentary film *Underexposed* brought attention to the challenges facing women in skateboarding in the early 2010s.[2] And her organization, Exposure Skate, filled the void in professional skateboarding contests for women starting in 2012. Today, in addition to its annual tournament, Exposure Skate uses skateboarding to educate and empower young women while raising funds for victims of domestic violence. Amelia's efforts, and those of other women in the sport, have led to an increase in opportunities for women, and a growth in the number of girls and women participating in the sport.

Despite the challenges in getting a foothold in the professional skateboarding economy, Amelia has continued to skate and work to increase opportunities for women and girls to skate. Her drive to skate is at once personal and communal; she loves the experience of skating in all its forms, and wants to share her love of the sport with others. Amelia is an innovator within the community, and an ever-present figure in women's skating, whether it be at competitions, events, or in the constant flow of skate videos. Her enthusiasm for skating is coupled with a determination to open doors for women and girls to experience the joys and benefits of the sport.

Skating with Confidence

If you watch most skaters during a run, they probably have a look of determination on their face. But Amelia? She smiles. "Your best skating comes through when you feel like you are being yourself. And for me, that's smiling and being happy and not putting too much pressure on what I'm doing."[3]

Often you can tell if she is smiling without seeing her face—most of the time, the smile reflects her relaxed, seemingly effortless style. She seldom makes abrupt movements, her pose is always relaxed, and she has a sense of peacefulness about her. Someone who doesn't know the sport could mistake her appearance and smile as an indication that she isn't taking her skating seriously, but that is far from the truth. That is Amelia's approach to skateboarding and, really, the positivity with which she lives her life. Her smile reflects an inner focus, a centeredness that places her attention completely in the moment. Amelia's positivity isn't a carefree optimism, but a determination to be the best skater she can, and to make skating more inclusive. She brings a positive determination to all of these pursuits, an attitude and disposition encapsulated in her smile, the purest expression of her commitment to positive change.

Though the untrained eye may only see the similarities among skaters' practice, skaters can see individuality and self-expression in one another's skateboarding. Lizzie Armanto, a contemporary of Amelia's and frequent participant in the Exposure Skate tournament, has a calm demeanor that is manifested as an elegant fluidity in her movements and lines. Then there is Julz Lynn Kindstrand, who brings a confident flair to each skate session. Julz's quiet confidence makes her at once fearless and adaptable to new skating environments.

The bottom line for elite-level skateboarding is confidence—confidence in one's abilities, in one's strategies for mitigating the unexpected, in one's ability to see a situation in a split second and to assess the best response to safely land or bail on a trick. This confidence is sometimes braggadocio, but more often, it is earned the hard way through practice and experience. Like many sports, skateboarding requires a fine-tuned self-awareness, and an ability to assess and refine one's performance on a macro and micro level. In other words, Amelia's practice is one anchored by **internal evaluation**.

Trying, Falling, Doing

Where does internal evaluation begin for skaters? Paradoxically, it starts with the skating community. Skating is, for most, a communal activity—people skate together, developing camaraderie, encouragement, and community. One of the more prized values of the skating community is progression—being able to push oneself, and therefore everyone else, forward. Amelia explains:

Skateboarders feed on progression, and the concept of progressing, and innovating, and pushing the sport. That is the driving factor for every skateboarder. No matter how good you get and how many tricks you learn, nearly every skateboarder will be thinking about the next trick moments after finally accomplishing the trick they were working on. Every new trick is a building block for the next trick. The motivation doesn't come from being the best or doing the biggest trick anyone has ever done, but from a personal gratification of progressing in a sport that you love.

This is an important aspect of Amelia's internal evaluation—she is driven to become a better skater, a goal that can most fully be achieved in the context of the larger skating community. Yet only she can make it happen. There is only one person on the board, after all.

A great example in Amelia's skating is her approach to the Crail Slide—a trick in which the skater rides up the ramp wall, pops their board into the air at the top, and instead of immediately pivoting around for reentry, grabs their board to slide along the coping (the lip of the ramp) on the board's tail before dropping back onto the ramp. Most skaters do this trick by using their back arm to grab the board's outer front edge, which helps rotate the board as well as keeping their balance with the body's weight over the front of the board. When Amelia does this trick, she reaches around both legs to grab the outer edge of the board as opposed to between her legs, as the trick is traditionally done. This movement increases the complexity of the trick, as it lessens the arm's role in creating both balance and force. It also increases the style factor, making Amelia's Crail Slide one her most photographed tricks.

Amelia doing a Crail Slide. Photo by Michael Burnette.

Amelia did this trick for years without realizing she was doing it differently from everyone else. This illustrates the internal evaluation of
skating—no one can do a trick for you, so you have to figure it out for
yourself, and whatever works for you is the right way to do a trick. The most
granular level of skating is the "trick," skaters' word for a repeatable maneu-
ver done while skating. A trick can be really simple—like doing a wheelie—
or incredibly complex—launching off a ramp, then doing two full rotations
in the air before landing back on the ramp. The process of learning a trick

begins by watching other skaters performing it, whether in person or in the millions of skate videos or in photo sequences. The process of translating something you observe into something you do is both mental and physical.

For Amelia, the internal evaluation process begins with thinking through the trick. How should she approach the trick? What movements will she need to make? Where do her feet need to be on the board? How does she move the board and her body? Are there other tricks she already knows from which she can build the new trick?

Just as important is the environment in which Amelia will learn the trick. Is it best learned on a ramp with a slow transition from flat to vertical? Or is it better learned in a concrete pool, where tighter transitions require faster trick execution? Or maybe on a small quarter pipe, where there is less risk of injury? Would the trick benefit from having a metal lip on the ramp or bowl, which provides slicker, faster surfaces? Or is it better learned on concrete pool coping, which has a textured surface that slows down some tricks? With a trick like the Crail Slide—which involves the skateboard sliding along the lip of the ramp, bowl, or pool—two features stand out as helpful during the learning phase. First, a slower lip reduces the likelihood that the board will slide out from under the skater, therefore allowing more control. Second, it also helps to learn a Crail Slide in a bigger environment where you can approach the trick with more speed and use the larger, gentler transition to ease reentry. Knowing these seemingly subtle factors of a trick's performance and the characteristics of different skating environments is a big part of what separates elite skaters from more casual hobbyists.

Attempting a new trick begins with trial and error—trying it, and seeing how the skater's mental impression of the trick translates into execution. A trick like the Crail Slide requires full commitment; in order to pull it off, the skater has to put their weight out over the front of the board, which commits them beyond return. (To not put their weight forward can cause the skater to fall backward.) Once the weight is pushed forward, there are only two options—make the trick, or fall head-first back into the ramp. As Amelia puts it,

You learn from each attempt. So maybe the way you come out of the attempt, you see where your body is, and "well, okay, my body isn't square with the board, so this time, when I try, I need to shift my shoulders this way." So each attempt gives you something new, teaches you the next step you can take towards making the trick.

Early in learning a trick, there is a lot of thinking. But at some point, for the trick to really be mastered, the skater has to transition into executing without a lot of thought about body position, entry point, and so on. In part, this is due to the speed with which skating tricks happen. Many of them only last a few seconds, even when they involve multiple components, each with one or more body and board movements. As Amelia puts it: "You have to shut your mind off, and let go of fear." The only way to stop thinking about performing a trick is to attempt it over and over until it can be performed fluidly. This process is akin to a dancer being able to perform a piece from "muscle memory," or a musician being able to play a song without actively thinking about what the next note is.

On to the second part of Amelia's statement: "let go of fear." The biggest enemy of skaters is fear—not the healthy, instinctual fear that keeps us safe from imminent danger, but the kind of fear that overrides the well-honed instincts that keep skaters safe. As Amelia puts it,

> There is certainly a lot of trial and error in skateboarding. It can be frustrating sometimes, but in the back of your head, you know that once you get that trick, once you are able to move past that frustration, or that fear, or whatever it is that's stopping you from landing that trick, everything is going to be better, it's totally going to be worth it.

Another big aspect for learning a new trick? Knowing how to safely fall. Particularly when first learning tricks, skaters are more likely to fall than to land the trick. Thinking through the environment in which they are skating, how the body is moving, what its relation to the skateboard is, and where the center of gravity should be—all are necessary to know how the body is likely to fall, and where the skateboard is likely to be during the fall. Skaters call this "bailing"—the act of getting out of a trick as painlessly as possible. It is the most universal skateboarding skill. Knowing how to fall minimizes injury, allows skaters to improve, and in a more fundamental way, simply allows the opportunity to continue skating. Learning to bail from the top of pools, bowls, and ramps is often learned before the most basic of tricks, like dropping in from the top onto the transition or onto the curved surface that leads to the flat bottom of the environment. The importance of bailing to skateboarding is all the proof needed to understand the deep connection between failure and the sport. Once bailing becomes intuition without requiring thought, then the skater is ready to start learning tricks.

Different skating environments lend themselves to different approaches to bailing. Street skating? Bail by tucking and rolling, or simply trying to push the board away and run off the momentum. Skating on ramps, pools, and skate parks with big transitions? Knee slides are the best bet, followed by sliding on your butt or sliding like a baseball player. All skaters learn to turn their bodies to get into a position that allows them to hit the ground knees first, as if in a kneeling position. This allows the body to slide into the fall, avoiding direct impact by relying on the knee pads and the tops of their shoes to create friction to slow their momentum. This isn't an intuitive way to fall. First, the skater has to make catlike moves to turn their body to face forward, with their legs beneath their torso heading in the direction of the surface. At the same time, the more relaxed the body is, the less tense the body is, the more easily the impact will be absorbed.

Sometimes there is no avoiding a bad fall. Instincts alone aren't able to protect skaters, and so injuries are not uncommon, even—and perhaps especially—for the best skaters. Some injuries don't stop a skater—a bruised shin, a tweaked ankle, a skinned elbow—but many others will force a skater to stop skating for a longer period of time—a concussion, a pulled back muscle, a broken forearm. For Amelia and many others, being grounded with an injury is the hardest part of the sport. Skating is an important part of her life, and so not being able to skate interferes with her life. Being off the board also leaves time for the skater to dwell on their injury, to develop fears about the trick that led to the injury, and to generally over-think things. Once the physical injury is healed, the skater has to mentally prepare themselves for getting back into the flow of skating, and to relocate the right balance between instinct, intuition, and the forethought of internal evaluation. These instincts are all that separates a skater from rolling away from a well-done trick and a slam that could lead to injury. In Amelia's words,

Figuring out the trick, trying it, even trying it hundreds of times, you realize there are adjustments you need to make with each attempt. Sometimes the only thing holding you back is being too scared to commit to the trick because you know if you decide you want to put that trick down [pull a trick off], you will either roll away or slam. Committing to a trick often means making the decision not to bail under any circumstance. You have to come to the decision that you do not care whether you slam. Oftentimes, just committing to a trick even if you slam is a victory within itself. If you do slam, you brush yourself off and realize that you are okay; this allows you to brush off the fear and continue to commit to each attempt until you roll away successfully.

Skating clearly requires a high degree of bravery coupled with a tolerance for pain. Both are deeply embedded in the culture of the sport. The importance placed on safety equipment is one of the more obvious indicators. The changes in the design, engineering, and production of skate parks and ramps over the last thirty years have primarily been driven by the need to make skate parks as safe as they can within the bravado spirit of skateboarding's extreme sports culture. One source that provides outsiders with insight into how skating communities approach the clear dangers of their sport is the "Hall of Meat," a feature started in *Thrasher* magazine that celebrates outrageous falls. There is a reverence for bombastic and spectacular failure inherent in skating. Things like the "Hall of Meat," and the lavish attention paid to big failures on Viceland and *Thrasher's* streaming series, *King of the Road*, serve as reminders of the ever-present risks in the sport, and promote a devil-may-care attitude.

Skateboarding's culture of bravado is not without its problems. Skating started as a "boy's club," with few women present—the first woman to turn professional was Elissa Steamer in 1995, some twenty years after the first male pro. The old boy's-club attitude, the overemphasis on the macho absorption of pain, and the sexist and misogynistic elements live on, perpetuated by small skating communities but also by some of the more popular skating publications. One of the ways this sexism plays out for female skaters is having "to prove you can 'hang,'" as Amelia puts it.

Organizations like Exposure Skate are changing these attitudes, but it takes time, growing with each new young girl picking up a skateboard, with each new competition and event, and with every woman-owned company. One of Amelia's personal and communal goals with Exposure Skate is to create more infrastructure to support girls new to competitive skating. By creating more low-level opportunities for them to participate in events, Exposure Skate enables women and girls to gain experience, to meet other skaters, and to garner some of the all-important exposure that propels careers.

Flowing through a Crail Slide

Skateboarding is at once a sport of precision and infinite variation. Each trick requires specific movements that leave little room for error—yet error is inherent in the sport. Performing and landing a trick in precisely the same way every time is simply not possible. The variables are too great for this—the environment (which park, which ramp, which bowl, which pool, which bench), the climate (inside, outside; the temperature, the weather), the state of equipment (new shoes, old board, middle-aged wheels), the skater themselves (recovering from hip bruise, sleepy, stressed about a family trip), and the conditions of the run (coming in to the trick too fast, slightly off balance, imperfect foot position). As a result, every attempt at a trick is different, impacted by what happened before it, and in turn impacting what comes next. All this requires a keen internal evaluative sensibility not only to identify the contextual differences, but to also know how to handle them.

The "big picture" evaluation comes in preparing for a run, particularly those in competitions. Some skaters choose to plan out the sequence of tricks in great detail based on the particular environment in which they will perform. Others prefer to "wing it," and make their trick choices during the run. Amelia takes a middle approach. Rather than plan out her runs in great detail, she instead puts together sequences of tricks that she knows work together due to the speed they require, the angles they are best approached from, and so on. She also works out contingency plans for when tricks don't turn out as intended. For example, if she comes out of one trick too fast, or at the wrong angle, she'll have a series of options for what trick she will attempt next.

These evaluations have to be made in a scant second or two in the amount of time it takes to come out of one trick; roll down the transition; cross the flat bottom of the pool, bowl, or ramp; and then launch up the opposite transition wall. There is very little time for deep consideration, and so the evaluation and decision have to be made almost unconsciously. Skaters like Amelia develop instincts for adaptability, being able to evaluate their options while launched three feet in the air above a twelve-foot-tall ramp, while rolling at twenty miles an hour across the flat of a ramp, or while hurtling toward a staircase railing. All of this requires skill, training, and above all, trust in oneself and one's skills. There is no room for indecision. As Amelia puts it,

Oftentimes you can interrupt the process of a trick by thinking too much instead of understanding that your body knows the trick, you've practiced it a million times, you practiced your run a million times, and you know intuitively that you can do it. But sometimes, one little stray thought or one slight hesitation will mess you up and make you miss the trick or slam.

This need for adaptability and decisiveness points to the importance of "flow" in sports like skateboarding. Psychologist Mihaly Csikszentmihalyi introduced the concept of flow to describe the mental state a person enters when fully engaged with an activity.[4] More than just engagement, the flow state merges action and thought, bringing the person's full faculties to the task at hand, and providing a sense of empowerment. The concept is well known among skaters: "Flow is definitely a term skateboarders use on a day-to-day basis," Amelia confirms. "It refers to moving from wall to wall or from obstacle to obstacle in a way that seems fluid while completing tricks flawlessly."

It is the flow state that enables skaters to disappear into their runs, to become connected to and in control of their boards and their bodies, and to work with the environment in which they skate. In his article "The Physical Genius," Malcolm Gladwell explores the idea of physical mastery by looking at the expertise of a brain surgeon, a hockey player, and a musician.[5] Gladwell discovers in his investigation the way practice converts into mastery. This mastery allows the practitioner to "see" a situation, to quickly assess their options, and to respond flawlessly in the moment. One of the factors that Gladwell targets is the way physical geniuses (a term he coined) are able to intuitively see or consider things others might not, often because these considerations aren't visible at all to everyone else. In skateboarding, this physical genius is captured in the way a skater moves through their environment, the understanding they bring to that environment, to their own abilities, and how to execute.

Csikszentmihalyi's concept of flow and Gladwell's physical genius suggest that elite levels of the sport require an iterative mindset driven by rigorous evaluation. To that end, Amelia's skateboarding embraces an iterative mindset anchored by internal evaluation. The challenge, of course, is developing the physical abilities to perform at a high level alongside the development of the cognitive understanding of the sport and the ability to not just see, but quickly assess the particulars of the situation. This is where internal evaluation comes into play. As much as skateboarding is communal, it is from the individual's physical, cognitive, and instinctual skills that excellence emerges.

The best way to make a name for oneself is by taking an existing trick and doing it on an obstacle that no one has ever pulled off—on a longer set of stairs, a wider gap, a bigger ramp or pipe, and so on. In this light, the fact that skateboarders prize innovation within their tradition shouldn't be a surprise, even with the sport's countercultural reputation. Skateboarders make names for themselves by doing tricks a little differently, by adding their own style or flair to a trick, and through the style they bring to their skating in general.

This process requires a good deal of internal evaluation. To be able to innovate, a skater first needs to master the basic trick. As described with Amelia's approach to the Crail Slide, mastery requires a lot of trial and error; without an iterative mindset, a skater is likely to get frustrated and give up. The best antidote to this frustration is developing a keen internal evaluation process that puts the skater more in tune with both their mind and their body. Developing these skills takes time and patience.

So how can a skater get to the point where they can not only master a trick, but also add something new to it? In the spirit of innovation within tradition, skateboarding tricks are often built from other tricks. Take the 5-0 Grind—a trick in which the skater "grinds" the rear metal truck on the edge of an obstacle while keeping their front wheels aloft.[6] This trick

Amelia doing a 5-0 Grind. Photo by Dan Sparagna.

is built out of three other tricks: an Ollie (when street skating), a 50-50 Grind, and a Manual. Ollies are tricks in which the skater gets their board into the air without using their hands by tapping the tail of the skateboard off the ground and then simultaneously pushing the nose of the board forward with their front foot while jumping upward. The end effect is that the skateboard appears to stick to the skater's feet as they jump. A Manual is the skateboarding equivalent of doing a wheelie on a bicycle. And finally, a 50-50 Grind is a type of grind trick in which both trucks grind across the edge of the obstacle. To perform a 5-0 Grind on the street, the skater has to know all three of these tricks, and then work to put them together. First, the skater must Ollie up onto the surface of the obstacle. Once in the air, the skater has to adjust their body and board to be parallel to the edge of the obstacle so that they can land in a Manual, or wheelie. Once the back trucks make contact, the skater then Grinds with their momentum moving forward across the obstacle's edge, and with their weight balanced over their board.

Traditionally, 5-0 Grinds are done in street and park skating. The 5-0 Grind lends itself to environments where the skater can approach an obstacle parallel to the edge on which the trick will be performed. In bowl and ramp skating, skaters are approaching perpendicular to the edge, making the trick more challenging. Amelia adapted the trick from street to bowl and ramp, and in the process, brought an innovation from one form of skating to another. In many ways, this makes a lot of sense, as Amelia had far more opportunity to street skate early on—her family lived in New Jersey, where skate parks were not common. And so when Amelia had more opportunity to skate pools, bowls, and vertical ramps, it stood to reason that she would adapt tricks from street skating to these new environments.

As Amelia puts it, "Everything is skateable, everything. Even a wall. It's just a matter of what you're going to do in that situation, and how you are going to skate on that everyday object." This statement is really the key to understanding Amelia's skating. She is, at heart, an East Coast street skater turned West Coast vert skater. Amelia's strongest set of tricks are lip tricks like the 5-0 Grind, which shares attributes of street, park, and vert skating environments. She combines the spontaneity and adaptability of street skating with the fluidity, speed, and sequencing of vert—all done with a smile and a fierce determination to be a better skater, and to open doors for other women and girls.

Connecting the Dots

Amelia's skateboarding demonstrates internal evaluation within an iterative mindset. Writ large, Amelia's **intention** is to be a top-tier, internationally recognized professional skater. But zooming in closer, we see she has a more general intention to grow and progress as a skater, and within that, to refine and expand her existing repertoire of tricks. These intentions directly inform her desired **outcomes**—participation in international invitational and open competitions, in order to gain national and international ranking, make incremental improvements to her skating, and learn new tricks. As Amelia puts it, "a lot of skateboarding is definitely intention, but it's intention combined with allowing the tricks to happen and skateboarding with flow."

Achieving these outcomes requires a **process** anchored by internal evaluation, an analytic and reflective mode with one **actor**—the skater. Amelia draws upon a wide range of **evaluation** techniques to help her make sense of the **context** within which she skates (meaning the environment, but also the purpose of that particular skating session), the tricks she attempts, and how she reflects on the entire experience to better herself as a skater. In her skating, Amelia has to determine which trick to try, and how to approach and execute that trick. Among the many factors she must evaluate are the environment in which she skates, the qualities of the run thus far, and which trick she hopes to land. Within each trick are innumerable moments of internal evaluation, assessing her body position, speed, her

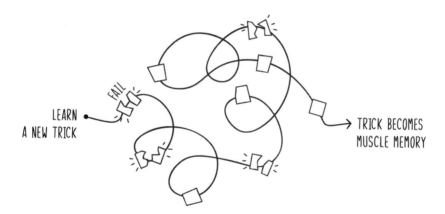

relationship to the environment, and so on. This evaluation all happens in a split second—Should Amelia adjust her trajectory slightly to better approach a crail slide? Or does her speed indicate she should instead go for an air (tricks in which the skater flies up above the environment)? Or should she bail on the trick?

Iteration is a central component, as each skating session is a new loop through the process, as is each attempt at a new trick or improving an older one. The repetition of internal evaluation continues after the run is over, too. Amelia will inevitably reflect upon aspects of her day's skating to see what she can learn. As Amelia puts it,

You never get it perfect every time. Even if you make whatever it is you are seeking to accomplish with the trick, you are always going to want to do it better, or do a harder trick, or apply that trick to a different obstacle. There's always a way to do it better, and to do more, and to be more innovative and creative.

12 External Evaluation: Baratunde Thurston, Comedian

Baratunde Thurston has made a career of seeing the humorous irony underlying power relations—in writing, on stage, on the screen, and all over the Internet. When he was growing up in Washington, D.C., power was as everpresent as the White House, a few miles down the street from where he lived. And so was keeping power in check. While some might see this as a contradiction, for the Thurston family, working for the government and questioning its power was a way of life. As he points out,

I have ancestors who belonged to the government, who rebelled against it in the form of literacy. My grandmother went on to work for the government—she was actually the first black employee at the Supreme Court building. My mother protested outside of its walls, but also entered it as an employee. And then she gave birth to

Baratunde Thurston. Image credit: Shuangshuang Huo.

my older sister who would chronicle government as a journalist, and then me, who takes all that and comments on it, through satire and technology.[1]

Baratunde's mother raised him and his sister largely on her own, and while Baratunde forged his own circuitous path to comedy, her influence is striking. "Question Authority," said the bumper sticker on Baratunde's high school locker, a gift from his mother. The irony of a parent giving their child a bumper sticker that calls for the questioning of authority is obvious, but it was par for the course in the Thurston household. Racial politics and politics in general were always present and discussed in his family. He describes his mother as a "pro-black, pan-African, tofu-eating hippie" who, in addition to the bumper sticker, gave him the book *Apartheid and How It Works* at the tender age of eight. In addition to raising a young activist, Baratunde's mother was a computer programmer for the U.S. government, back in the 1980s—before computer programming was a typical career. Baratunde says, "It always struck me that my mother being a programmer was a big deal—I mean, in a way she was the original Black Girls Code."[2] His house, in a mostly black and Latino neighborhood, was the only one with a computer (an Apple IIe).

Baratunde credits his mother for his own atypical life, saying that "because of her, I grew up in a house full of fun contradictions rather than stereotypes."[3] In his bestselling book, part memoir, part tongue-in-cheek instruction manual *How to Be Black*, Baratunde points out how his version of "being black" both reinforced and departed from the stereotype:

Yes, I grew up in the "inner city," at 1522 Newton Street, and I survived DC's Drug Wars. Yes, my father was absent—he was shot to death in those same Drug Wars. But it's also true that I graduated from Sidwell Friends School, educational home of Chelsea Clinton and the Obama girls, and Harvard University. I love classical music, computers, and camping. I've gone clubbing with the president of Georgia, the country, twice.[4]

Baratunde's mother also introduced him to comedy at a young age, spending family road trips listening to an eclectic blend of comedy tapes on the car stereo, ranging from Garrison Keillor to Richard Pryor. The influences in Baratunde's youth thus included an upbringing where politics and activism were a way of life, computers a household fixture, and comedy a common soundtrack on road trips and family vacations. In retrospect, the building blocks were all there: activism, technology, and comedy—a triad of interests that have come together in Baratunde's career as a political comedian. But first and foremost, Baratunde is a writer.

Writing is where Baratunde's comedic voice got its start, beginning with the high school paper at Sidwell Friends School, then for the student-run daily the *Crimson* at Harvard. It was at Harvard that he started to get funny. One of his articles for the *Crimson*, called "Why Life Is a Scam," analyzes the ice-to-drink ratio at restaurants, daylight savings time, the aerobic phenomenon Tai Bo, Serbian war criminal Slobodan Milošević, ethnic cleansing, and, of course, Harvard (the subject of most *Crimson* articles).[5] Baratunde was a philosophy major at Harvard, but writing and editing for the *Crimson* was where he found his calling. He was about to begin a summer internship at the *Washington Post*—and a career in journalism—when it all came to a halt. As his career was about to take off, he developed a bad case of carpal tunnel syndrome—a repetitive stress injury writers often get. The cure? Stop writing.

He had to give up the summer internship at the *Post*. To occupy himself that summer, he enrolled in a theater program. It was there that he realized he liked being on stage, and his comedic voice blossomed. That same summer, he took a job at a strategy consulting firm, riding on the tech boom wave of the late nineties. His position as a technology analyst/strategist would turn into an eight-year job that built the foundation for his current entrepreneurial and online work in comedy.

So, while it might have seemed preordained from his upbringing that Baratunde would forge a career as an activist-technologist-comedian, he arrived at these endeavors due both to his upbringing and to that chance affliction with carpal tunnel syndrome. Baratunde learned from his time working in tech that he could mix his love of writing, his onstage comedic voice, and his technology interests into a unique form of disruptive civic engagement. Or as he says it, to use comedy as "an educational, media, and cultural hack."[6]

This mission to use comedy and technology in the service of activism has driven his work as a comedian, a bestselling author, and an overall purveyor of "pro-justice comic expression."[7] Baratunde has worked in media, as director of digital for *The Onion*; as supervising producer for the *Daily Show* with Trevor Noah, overseeing original digital content; and as a correspondent for the documentary series *National Geographic Explorer*; and he was nominated for an Emmy award as host of the Spotify/Mic series *Clarify*.

He cofounded the company Cultivated Wit and the *About Race* podcast. He wrote a *New York Times* bestseller (the aforementioned *How to Be Black*), and was a director's fellow at the MIT Media Lab, exploring the intersections of comedy and emerging technology. This is just a small selection of the many things he has done. Baratunde keeps busy.

For the sake of this case study, rather than try to pin down one of his activities, we'll focus on the single thing that unites his work—his comedic voice. Baratunde's practice employs a form of **external evaluation** in which he uses audience reactions to help him "edit" his work—whether it is written, performed, or otherwise presented. Or to put it differently, he engages in conversation with others to see if what he says is funny, clear, and politically provocative. This helps the editor in him know what to keep, what to cut, and what to continue honing. Baratunde works like an author: absorbing the world around him and sharing back what he sees in his own words. But, while he ultimately creates the material, everything he does is in conversation with an audience.

The Comedic Voice

The content of Baratunde's conversation with his audience is often political—drawing on a long-standing comedic tradition. From Aristophanes' satirical plays to *Saturday Night Live*, political comedy has used humor to keep power in check. Comedy has a way of slicing through the most serious, ingrained, and taboo subjects. When applied to politics, humor has the power to cut to the truth by surprising us about our own assumptions. Actor and social commentator Will Rogers said of the political climate in the 1930s, "Everything is changing. People are taking their comedians seriously and the politicians as a joke."[8] Baratunde echoes Rogers's words when he says, "There's a lot of straight lectures and philosophizing and proselytizing and politicking out there that are less trustworthy than the comedic voice. That's what I stumbled into early and I've stuck with for the last twenty-something years."[9]

Philosophers, psychologists, neuroscientists, and comedians have tried to figure out how humor and the comedic voice work. Some have used theories to describe why we find things funny—we laugh to release tension, or to feel superior to others, or to transform shock and surprise to laughter as we try to resolve incongruities between concepts.[10] Neuroscientists study humor by telling jokes to people in MRI scanners, comedians by telling jokes to people (usually not in MRI scanners) and hoping for laughter. But no matter the context, one thing is true: Funny needs an audience. Baratunde finds his audience through a variety of channels—from his extremely active Twitter account to appearances on television news. As he admits, he's still exploring a variety of platforms, trying to find the right one:

Is it blogging, is it jokes on Twitter, is it the comedy hackathon type of events that my company helps produce, which is putting humor in code and making interactive comedic creation, is it standing on the stage in front of drunk people? Is it standing on a stage in front of sober business people? (Drunk people are better.)

No matter the endeavor, though, the measure of the resonance of his comedic voice is found through a process of communication and what comes back, whether it's laughter, more discussion, or even, silence. From writing to corresponding to stand-up, social justice through the comedic voice is Baratunde's forte, and the ideas that drive it come from a process of communication, editing, and refinement that is inherently social, in conversation with a variety of audiences. Through their response—hopefully involving laughter—the audience contributes to Baratunde's evaluation and refinement of his voice.

Baratunde's humor might be critical, but underlying it is always an optimism that there's a solution to our problems and that through humor one can find clarity. He says, "A big part of my motivation is clarity. It's also sharing good things." The good things he shares, in addition to laughs, are insights on the world informed by his voracious appetite to learn about and understand it, and presenting those insights with comedic clarity. To describe his process for finding clarity, he says, "I ingest the world. At least I try to, and I want to spit back out something that makes more sense." For him, the key is to share his discoveries with others:

There are a lot of answers out there about our problems, like the future. Someone once said about the future that it's already here; it's just not evenly distributed. I think that's true about solutions about some of our problems—the answers are out there. We know how to fix the planet, we know what to do about prison situations, and we know how to raise children to not be demonic assholes at this point. But it's very unevenly distributed, given the population of demonic assholes that runs free.

To Baratunde, the promise of technology is one of the reasons to be optimistic. His mission is to spread social justice through comedy *and* technology. For him, technology embodies the idea that equal access to information is at the heart of our democracy. He discovered this as a middle school student writing for the Sidwell Friends School paper, where he had the opportunity to report on the school's connection to the Internet: "The system itself is rather loosely organized with no one really 'in charge.' As computer coordinator Ross Lenet put it, 'It's amazing it even works at all.'"[11] Baratunde believes that to make something work, whether it's the Internet or democracy, involves knowledge. The only thing keeping us from making the world a better place is lack of knowledge—not a lack of tools or will. He points out, "My interest in tech is not gadget-based; it's freedom-based."[12] And since that first introduction to the Internet in 1993, it has been a place where his comedic voice found an audience.

In 2006, Baratunde cofounded *Jack and Jill Politics*, a black political blog whose coverage of the 2008 Democratic National Convention is archived at the Library of Congress.[13] He also writes a special series called "Active Citizenship" on Medium, the online publishing platform that serves as a virtual town square. He "live-hate-tweeted" every film (except the first) in the *Twilight* series.[14] The Internet is where Baratunde lives. It's a space where ideas can be shared and evaluated in real time, with an audience that can be anywhere. In fact, the ideas explored in his book, *How to Be Black*, began as a Twitter conversation. The Internet is the perfect platform for a comedian like Baratunde; sending a tweet results in a response—and becomes a step toward honing his comedic voice. This is one way that Baratunde can receive feedback every day, or in other words, seek external evaluation from an ever-present audience in real time.

The feedback Baratunde seeks online can sometimes be a distraction. He's widely known for living without the Internet for almost a month, despite its being his most prolific platform (he averages thirty-two tweets a day). In an article for *Fast Company* documenting his twenty-five days offline, he describes his love of connecting to the "global hive-mind," and at the same time, his need to take a break:

In choosing to digitally enhance, hyperconnect, and constantly share our lives, we risk not living them. We have collectively colluded to take this journey, but we've done so inches at a time, not realizing that we have traveled leagues in the process. For 25 days, I pulled back far enough to see that distance.[15]

Pulling back to see things from a distance is a recurring theme for Baratunde. He needs the Internet, but he also needs time away. It also describes his process; in addition to a need to bounce ideas off an audience, Baratunde finds the need to return to ideas after some time away, distancing himself from himself, so to speak, so that he can see his ideas with a fresh perspective. This distancing is similar to shifting from writing to editing, two modes he knows well.

It Starts on Paper

Baratunde began developing his comedic voice by writing in middle school, and he continues to start everything as a writer does—on paper:

Humor for me was honed in writing first, and around current events, news, and the idea of sharing that news with people who didn't know it but I thought should know it. It evolved from there and became much more personal, more performative on stage from stand-up to speaking and things, but it starts on paper.

His process begins with writing down what he calls a "fleeting thought." Fleeting thoughts happen out in the world—not alone on a mountaintop—and often through conversation with someone: during lunch with a friend, or watching something online, hearing a speech, reading an article. He describes these fleeting thoughts as "reactive inspiration." Reactive inspiration is always in dialogue with something or someone else. If he is inspired by an idea, he writes it down so that it will not forever evaporate. Sometime later, when the right moment appears, a fleeting thought may get developed, connected, and expanded into a tweet, an article, a part of a stand-up routine, maybe as part of a book, or a company project.

Once fleeting thoughts are captured, the hard work of editing begins. Baratunde was known at the *Harvard Crimson* as a speedy but precise editor. After four years of working on a daily student paper, it's no surprise these are sharpened skills. He revels in the editing process, and says that he'll often write too fast just to get to the fun of cutting out the bad stuff that he knows is there. He edits on the computer, but when he's feeling super rigorous, he'll print out his work, get a pen, and mark it up, old-school style. Seeing his words on paper helps him see what he calls "the gaps" in his thinking. As he describes it, "when they're in the same medium that I first created them (on the computer), I'm more precious about it, and I can't see the gaps." Baratunde needs to transpose his words from one format to another to edit fleeting thoughts into a coherent written piece or set to be performed.

Once a work starts taking form, Baratunde shares it with an audience so he can evaluate the work in progress. The good thing about comedy is how quickly a joke can be assessed, as audience reactions happen in real time. The performance is not the end of the process, though—it's the middle. Baratunde always listens to the tapes afterward. He does this because he has a difficult time hearing himself talking on the stage—not that he literally can't hear himself, but he isn't able to simultaneously deliver the material *and* evaluate it. So he plays back the tapes later to hear himself and the audience's reactions more clearly.

When he's at his best, he says, he is rigorously reanalyzing the raw material of his words and the reactions of the audience. The editing process becomes a collaboration with the audience—he speaks the words, and they react. Together, the two components give him a clear picture of the whole of his performance. He describes the recording as "the data"—harkening back to his career as a tech analyst—necessary to improve his sets. As he listens to his recorded performances, he pays equal attention to what he said, how he said it, and how the audience in turn responded. This helps him make sure he is hitting his goals of funny, relevant, and informative. He is bouncing his comedic voice off others and listening to what comes back. Baratunde describes this call and response with others and himself as a kind of "echolocation." Ultimately, he evaluates and edits his comedic performances through this process of echolocation with an external audience to hone his comedic voice.

In some ways, one could say that as he evaluates his work, Baratunde talks to himself—not in the way you might think (although he might, when no one's watching). He talks to himself through a process of relistening, review, and speaking back through new projects and performances. Even if he's editing alone, he's transposing his writing to another format so that he can, in some sense, externalize it.[16] It is an "internal-external" evaluation—a method used to "see the gaps" in his writing with fresh eyes. This process used for writing is similar to his review of his taped performances—but in that case, he listens for the gaps between his words and the audience's reaction. Whether it's a written piece or a performed piece, the evaluation and editing process begins by transposing the medium—words on a computer to words on paper, words on paper to words performed, words spoken to words recorded and listened to. To evaluate his work, he needs to be at a slight remove, similar to the way a painter moves back from their painting and looks at it from a few steps away.

There's one more strategy Baratunde employs to externalize his work: *time*. Baratunde often needs the remove of time between his performance and relistening. As he puts it, "I need immersion, and I need time. And I need a gap between the first spillage of creativity and coming back for the edit and the synthesis." By "immersion," he means immersion in the material—reviewing and editing his work—and then the opposite: time away from the ideas. By creating a gap in time between moments of immersion, Baratunde is evaluating an earlier version of himself.

Speaking of time, it took Baratunde years to finish his book, *How to Be Black*. The deadline came and passed. He was stuck. To help himself get unstuck, he spent time listening to his interviews, talks, and political commentary. He needed time away from the book, and he needed to hear himself, in order to evaluate his ideas and reimmerse himself in writing the book. Delivering clear, funny ideas about complex politics is challenging, especially because politics, the news cycle, and social media discourse happen in an instant. Despite the temptation to work quickly and respond right away to the political fires, some work, like *How to Be Black*, takes time. Baratunde describes the lesson he took away from this process: "I have learned what I do well, I have learned a bit about how I do it. It requires time—and that's frustrating. When I don't give myself enough time to walk away and come back, it's going to be worse."

Walking away and coming back—like quitting the Internet, or taking time to edit and develop ideas—is a key theme in Baratunde's process. It's a way of evaluating himself and his ideas from a different perspective. Rebooting, so to speak, to gain clarity.

Each step in the process—fleeting thought, writing, performance, review, immersion, and time—isn't always part of a linear project or a single piece of work, and not all of the raw material that goes into a given project is completely worked out in the way described earlier. A performance is more planned and procedural, whereas conversations and interviews are more improvisational. Stand-up requires collaboration with the audience, while writing is a solo process. Ultimately, however, his work is about making connections—between fleeting thoughts and more developed ideas, between himself and the audience. As Baratunde describes,

Knowing where I'm starting, having the direction but not knowing where it's going to take me. And finding jokes, analogies, metaphors or connections between things, when I think about what I actually really do better than most of the things I do, it's the synthesis.

And that synthesis—to refine, clarify, and make complex political topics funny—takes time to externalize and evaluate.

Baratunde's process might sound relatively methodical. Fleeting thoughts from a variety of sources are noted, expanded, edited, and written or performed. The "data" from the writing or performance is externalized and reviewed by transposing the format (recording, paper) or taking time to gain perspective. Immersion in the material is contrasted with time away from it, to gain an "internal-external" perspective on the work. It's a method that seems failproof. But as you might have guessed by now, nothing truly is.

Crickets

One night, it happened: the stand-up comedian's nightmare. Baratunde walked onstage and there were three people in the audience. Only three people. He recounts the fateful night:

I remember a very early show, and it was an audience of three, which is not a good scenario. You're almost going to fail anyway, because they feel bad. An audience that feels sympathy for the performer—that's not a good thing. You don't want them feeling sorry for you. They're not in the right space to laugh emotionally, and they're just like cringing, judging, wondering why they're the only ones—are you really so bad that they're the only ones?

But, as they say, the show must go on. But a few minutes into his political stand-up routine, one of the three audience members interrupted to say: "Stop, stop, stop, we don't know what you're talking about. Talk about something else." As Baratunde put it, "It violated all the rules! I'm up here, you're down there, but there's just the three of you. We're basically peers at this point, so I guess your heckle—it was like one-third of the audience told me to stop."

Being a civically minded person attuned to the mechanisms of democracy, Baratunde heeded the will of the people. He departed from his well-honed set and improvised. He asked them questions, and he let them ask him questions. During the process, as painful and scary as it was, he found a whole new set of jokes.

The evaluation from the audience that night was a shock. But without it, he might have carried on, losing the audience in the process. He needed their reaction to know whether his ideas were getting across—whether there was clarity. The audience feedback left him with no choice but to react in real time. Thanks to a little tough-love external evaluation, what began as a failure to communicate became something else—a fun, improvised conversation with the audience.

Whether it's on Twitter or onstage, Baratunde hones his comedic voice through conversation. As the game designer Chris Crawford describes it, "a conversation is an iterative process in which each participant in turn listens, thinks, and expresses."[17] Crawford was interested in conversation as a model for realistic and robust interactive experiences—in effect, teaching computers to converse with people. Conversation is an integral part of Baratunde's evaluation process; in the beginning of his process, conversation can help generate ideas and fleeting thoughts that catalyze his work—this is what he calls "immersion." In the middle of a project, conversation helps him find the gaps where he hasn't yet found the synthesis between humor, clarity, and provocation. Here, Baratunde adds a step to Crawford's three-part conversational model: time. He is immersed in listening, thinking, and expressing, and in between these loops, he benefits from time away to gain perspective. However, when a situation looks dire and there's no time to step away, like that night in front of an audience of three, Baratunde's skills in conversation can resolve differences and even become inspiration.

Baratunde's process involves both the real-time feedback from others and the extended time and/or transposed format of his own external evaluation. Conversation between Baratunde and his audience is iterative: moving from listening, to thinking/writing (fleeting thoughts), to expressing, and whenever possible, time away for evaluation (is it funny and clear?).

Sometimes his process fails. But once he receives the external signal back, he is quick to respond. That fateful night, he edited his routine in real time and turned it into a collaborative bit—a conversation. By the end of the night, everyone learned something, and everyone had fun.

Connecting the Dots

Many people imagine comedians are inherently funny, able to produce laughs off the cuff and on the fly. And there is probably some truth to that. But, as one can see when considering Baratunde's **process**, behind the scenes it also can take plenty of work, lots of edits, and many repetitions through his iterative loop. Being funny involves editing and time to externally **evaluate** whether his ideas are getting across. For Baratunde, honing his comedic voice with the **intention** to create social change is an iterative process, punctuated with moments of performance and some really great jokes. But the humorous quip is the tip of an iceberg of edits, evaluation, sometimes failure, reworking, and time. As Baratunde points out, needing to take time to gain perspective can be frustrating, but ultimately, time is an important part of his process, and it is what allows ideas to finally clarify.

His process begins by capturing fleeting thoughts. Multiple sources and **actors** are involved: whether the news, discussions with friends, or a heckler from an audience of three. Fleeting thoughts come from the world outside, but they are honed and sculpted through the internal conversation of his own editing process. Baratunde keeps a notebook to write down fleeting

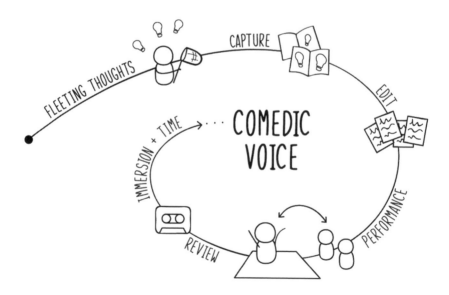

thoughts. Fleeting thoughts are often the starting points for a joke, a project, even a book.

The response from his audience comes back to him as a kind of "echo-location," in the process guiding him to home in on the right voicing and delivery. For Baratunde, reviewing "the data" is essential to reveal where ideas are clear and where they need work. Whether it's listening to a tape of public speaking or his own stand-up routine, playing it again—just like printing out a piece of writing to edit it—places his words in a new **context** to help him see them in a new light. Editing is a particular skill, one that Baratunde developed over years on a daily student paper. This is a process of both internal and external evaluation—he needs immersion to edit himself, but ultimately he also needs transposition (printing, or time away) to pull back and see his own work with greater clarity.

13 Convergent Outcomes: Cas Holman, Toy Designer

She'd made it. The Museum of Modern Art (MoMA) Design Store wanted to sell Geemo, a flexible magnetic sculpting toy that Cas Holman designed in grad school. For industrial designers, getting a product into the MoMA Design Store is a definite bucket list item. For Cas, it could be the break her new company, Heroes Will Rise, needed. Using money saved from freelance work, Cas put the toy into mass production. She was sure that Geemo's arrival in the MoMA Store would spark interest from other stores. And with Geemo's likely success, other products would certainly follow.

But when the toy launched at MoMA, it was, as Cas describes it, "tumbleweeds." There was no big splash, and she couldn't get the price low enough to gain traction with other stores. Over time, it eventually sold in

Cas Holman. Image: Shuangshuang Huo.

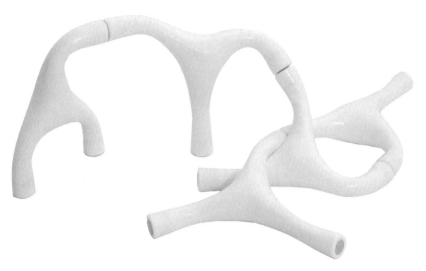

Geemo. Image: Heroes Will Rise.

respectable quantities at MoMA, but nowhere near the numbers Cas had projected. While she had reached a high point for product designer aspirations, she saw Geemo as a commercial failure.

Soon after, her wounds still fresh, Cas was struck like a bolt of lightning by an *Onion* headline: "Failure Now an Option."[1] A new world opened inside that headline. "I think I cried with relief," Cas said. "I took all of them [the newspapers] and cut it out [the headline: 'Failure Now an Option'] and posted it all over my house."[2] Despite *The Onion*'s ironic intentions, "Failure Now an Option" became a mantra for Cas. From her experience with Geemo, she learned to see the bigger picture. Just as important, she began to reckon with the different kinds of failure that happen at different scales and times within a project, from the initial prototype to product launch to sustaining a business. In a business centered on products, success is measured in units—the more you produce, the cheaper each unit's cost, the bigger the profit, but also the larger the risk that you will end up with a warehouse full of products no one wants to buy. Geemo was successful as a concept—kids loved it, it got picked up by MoMA—but at the business scale, the level of success didn't meet up to Cas's expectations. She explains:

I like to set [a toy] up for "ideal"—so I say, okay, I don't know how many of these are going to sell, so I price it based on 10,000 and based on 1,000. You scale—you do

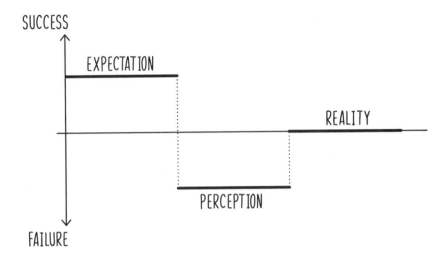

SUCCESS

EXPECTATION

REALITY

PERCEPTION

FAILURE

both. But ultimately, if you set something up for an ideal, and ideal is up here [points above her head] and as you go you end up slightly lower [holds hand low], it feels like failure, because you set up for this [the higher point]. But what's important, and what I try to remind myself is that this [a point between the high point and the low point] is still better than this [points even further down]—so in fact it's still a huge success, comparatively.

Of course, failure in business is expected—to the point that it's cele-brated in much of the business literature. But what is unique about Cas's formulation of failure, as both a business owner and a designer, is her view of failure as a continuum. Failure and success are not opposites. For Cas, failure exists in degrees. Ultimately, there are many levels of success and failure. For example, Geemo is still on the market today;[3] its failure, mea-sured in degrees, was a failure in its creator's perception, but not in reality. Geemo showed that critical success and commercial success are not always correlated. If Cas hadn't come to this realization so early in her career, her future projects and the ultimate success of her company might not have come to pass. The lessons learned from Geemo found their way into the design of her subsequent toy projects. But to understand how Cas ended up designing toys at all, we must start on the Galapagos Islands.

After an unsuccessful first attempt at an undergraduate education, Cas spent a year and a half on the remote islands of Galapagos. She liked the natural sciences but had no idea what she was going to do with her life, so she went to help her scientist aunt and uncle count the land iguana for a biodiversity study. The land iguana population was decreasing due to an incredibly complex chain of events. At the time, the sea cucumber was being overfished. The smaller sea cucumber population allowed algae to grow more than usual. The algae overgrowth in turn negatively affected the urchin population. And what did land iguanas eat? Urchin, which led to a reduction in iguana population. As Cas describes it, it was a "domino effect," where one thing gets thrown off and an entire system goes out of balance. Counting the lessening iguana population on the Galapagos Islands led Cas to start thinking in systems:

In industrial design, I see myself as designing more than the product, but the whole system around it. With Rigamajig, I set up the whole manufacturing and distribution process. The plastic parts are injection molded from a factory that's run by wind turbines outside of Rochester, New York, and the wood parts are made outside of Providence, Rhode Island, so these logistical elements all need to be designed as well. The biodiversity I witnessed in Galapagos, even as it was thrown out of whack, influenced how I see systems in design and all my work today.

In addition to thinking systemically, the Galapagos experience helped her realize that despite her keen interest in the subject, she was a terrible scientist. Keeping data, doing things the same way twice, and the sheer detail orientation of the work were not in her wheelhouse. So she returned to the United States to continue her roundabout trajectory to toy designer. Stopovers as pastry chef, artist, student of feminist theory, and producer of playful resin toilet seats eventually brought Cas to graduate school at Cranbrook Academy of Art—the place where Geemo was born.

Cas's eclectic journey to toy design wove together a few key threads—systems thinking, feminist theory, and design—that all converged on a single goal. As Cas articulates it, "I'd like to think that I'm empowering children to change the world."[4] This singular mission drives Cas's design process to converge on play experiences that give children the power to imagine new possibilities with the toys, and in the long run, for themselves. As a design process, convergent thinking integrates knowledge gathered or gained from previous projects to inform the current one. Cas's business lessons from Geemo, her understanding of systems from her experiences on Galapagos, and her mission to empower children are integrated into the products she designs. Cas is not only a designer—she's also a small business owner, and because of that, must take into account the entire product ecosystem. This entails multiple forms of prototyping—sometimes focused on that all-important empowering of children, sometimes on materials and techniques, sometimes on business details like fabrication, profit margins, and retail considerations. And so Cas iteratively converges on a final design by moving from ideation to prototype to product testing to manufacturing to distribution. To most, this level of attention to many different things would sound daunting—but Cas makes it look fun.

Designing for Play

A strong sense of the value of play and optimism in the face of failure imbues Cas's career and the products she designs. As she says—and as is evident in her journey—"my entire career is a naively optimistic decision." That optimism is apparent in her primary goal: to enable empowering play. In many ways, making and play were the prelude to Cas's winding journey to toy designer. It just took her awhile to get back to her roots. Cas grew up in the Sierra foothills in northern California, raised by a Montessori educator and a tinkerer father.[5] She built everything, from treehouses to dune buggies, with nails, scrap wood, sticks, rocks, and anything else at hand. And while she may not have known it at the time, she was building the foundations for a play philosophy driven by unlimited possibilities, empowerment, problem solving, and becoming yourself.

Sticks and stones and mud are the perfect toys. At least, that's what the young Cas and millions of other kids have known. And with each new project, Cas returns to her scrappy, playful origins, messing around with sticks in the backyard. Tinkering is her design methodology. She solves problems with tinkering—using her hands to guide the process. Tinkering is also at the heart of her toys. Each of her projects converges on the empowering qualities of play and tinkering—the feeling that you can build anything. Playful tinkering is found in her debut toy, Geemo, and her work at the Rockwell Group on the award-winning Imagination Playground. Playful tinkering is also the basis of Rigamajig, a building product that evolved from a play set commissioned for the High Line park in New York City.

Cas is both a "toy designer" and a "play designer." Although toys are what Cas makes, what she really designs is the experience of playing with the toy. Toys are simply the means to a playful end. Playing with toys is a generative activity, reflecting the player's own exploration of the physical

Cas prototyping a chute with Rigamajig. Image: Megan Fischer for Heroes Will Rise.

properties of the toy, which gives rise to imagination and further discovery and play. In addition to discovering the properties of toys and how one might play with them, playing with toys is how children assert their own autonomy and discover themselves. As psychologist and play specialist Brian Sutton-Smith says, "Toys are the tools of self-assertion."[6] For children, part of that self-assertion is allowing oneself to try on different identities through free play. Cas's goal parallels Sutton-Smith's concept of self-assertion: empowering play through tinkering.

The benefits of play and tinkering are explored through her recent involvement in the Anji Play movement, a Chinese play-based educational philosophy. In action, it looks like a bunch of children performing somewhat dangerous feats with ladders and scrap building materials, but at its heart it is a deeply empowering learning experience. Ultimately, designing for play and for tinkering drives Cas's mission to empower young people, and to help them become equally empowered adults (as a professor at Rhode Island School of Design, Cas's design philosophy of empowerment at all ages is translated through her teaching). As she points out, "Child psychologists have known for decades that through play, children learn empathy, 'try on' identities, and experiment with their place in the world. Essentially, in childhood we play our way through discovering who we are."[7]

Let's take one of her best-known toys, Rigamajig, as an example. Rigamajig is like an oversized Erector set—"a collection of wooden planks, wheels, pulleys, nuts, bolts and rope."[8] With these parts, kids can make all kinds of structures, machines, and vehicles. Just as you can make anything with Rigamajig, you can be anything too. Tinkering with Rigamajig also involves tinkering with ideas and identities, enabling kids to imagine alternative worlds and their unique place within them. Cas's background in feminist studies, as well as her self-identification as queer, finds its way into her design sensibilities through her own ardent support of individuality and self-discovery. Her toys are building blocks—ready to be made into anything. Through their open-endedness, they embrace the individual as a self-determined being, one capable of forming fluid identities outside any fixed template. Toys like Rigamajig are decidedly non-gender-specific, a relief from the gendering of many mass-produced toys today. As she says, "In my mind what's important is that kids are creating identity with [Rigamajig]. That's queer." Picking up on these themes in Cas's work, curators recently featured Rigamajig in an exhibition entitled "Queering Space" at Yale.[9] At a Rigmajig workshop affiliated with the exhibition, participants created their own contraptions. When a discussion about the gender identity of the creations came up, one of the Rigamajig creations had the decidedly nonbinary gender of "40s Saxophone."

Human- (and Kid-)centric Design

We describe Cas's process as **convergent**: Through iteration, her work moves from a large possibility space to a singular design—a product. But the interesting twist in her work is that she uses convergent methods to create play experiences that allow for divergent, empowering experiences. In simpler terms, Cas designs for play. But how does one go about designing for such an elusive outcome?

The answer, in part, can be found in her human-centered design process, which takes inspiration from the industrial designer Henry Dreyfuss. Drefuss's foundational reimagining of industrial design, documented in the 1955 book *Designing for People*, ushered in a new era of human-centric design. Prior to Dreyfuss, design was mostly concerned with "window

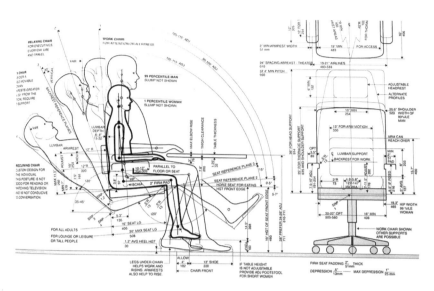

Chart from Henry Dreyfuss's *The Measure of Man and Woman.*

dressing," focusing on the visual aspects but not the functionality or experience of a project. Dreyfuss was one of the first designers to develop methodologies and models designed for human experience—by taking actual humans into account throughout the design process, Dreyfuss also encouraged designers to consider the ergonomics of a design: not just how the product functioned, but how it felt to the hand, fit the body, and took into account the variations in the human form.

Cas has a well-worn copy of Dreyfuss's other influential book *The Measure of Man and Woman: Human Factors in Design* in her studio, using it to reference the famous drawings Dreyfuss and his associates (at the aptly named Dreyfuss and Associates) made of human models to get the scale right for her prototypes and final designs. She marvels at how these drawings, done in the 1950s and 1960s, continue to be the gold standard in her field. These guide her prototyping process, helping her converge on a toy that is ergonomically scaled to its player. As Dreyfuss famously wrote, "if people are made safer, more comfortable, more eager to purchase, more efficient—or just plain happier—by contact with the product, then the designer has succeeded."[10]

Dreyfuss helped establish the human-centered design process many use to this day—a convergent design process aimed at an outcome suited to the user's needs. Cas's take on Dreyfuss's process is tuned to reaching convergent outcomes that deliver empowering play. To begin, she starts where Dreyfuss did—with humans.

Cas begins by talking with teachers, early education specialists, curriculum designers, play advocates, child psychologists, and children themselves. Throughout this process, she is listening, observing, and developing a design question. As she talked with educators who were helping her test Rigamajig, for instance, she found the need to design a storage solution for classrooms. So the design question became, "What would a good classroom storage solution look like?" At times, her questions are much more open, such as: "How can we increase opportunities for kids to learn and practice impulse control?" Design questions like this drive her explorations as she converges on a playful answer.

In addition to talking to people, Cas looks to her huge library of vintage toys for inspiration as she considers the playful affordances they provide. Dreyfuss wrote, "to look ahead one must learn to look back."[11] Cas's historic toy collection and personal history in tinkering are important ingredients in her initial research leading to a new toy system. Ultimately, her conversations with kids and educators and the inspiration she finds in historic toys help her converge on an idea of the toy she wants to make, and the kind of play it will enable.

Cas then moves on to sketching, but instead of starting with an idea and moving seamlessly to sketching from a mental image, her ideas start in her hand. She "tinkers" at drawing. As she describes it, her brain and hand work together to figure things out: "When I'm sketching a design, it's an incomplete idea, it's not like I have something in my head that just needs to be represented on paper … so my brain doesn't know what 'IT' is until my hand helps to figure it out."

From the sketches, she will build a model using whatever is available. She moves back and forth from sketching to building scale models, all the while referring back to Dreyfuss's ergonomic illustrations of human proportions. As she builds a model at scale, Cas uses a physical model of a child's hand to design at "kid scale." As she explains: "I go back and forth between sketching and building to scale. I have some very specific scales that I use—1:8 is a favorite—so I can model small and quickly with paper and glue, then compare [the model] to other familiar objects in that same scale."

Once she lands on something she thinks has promise, she will build it at full scale in true tinkerer fashion—with whatever she has lying around. This is what she calls a "works-like," a working model made up of spare parts:

I'll take something apart and be like, "oh well, I don't want to make a box, so I'll take this milk crate and hack it and put something on it." I call this kind of a proof of concept a "works-like"—a prototype—to figure out, is that going to be too heavy, or is that going to tip over?

From the tinkered-together "works-like" prototype, the model will be remade from scratch with materials like wood, and orthographic drawings will be made with all of the dimensions captured. The model might not look exactly the way she intends at this point, but it will work the way she intends, enough to be able to test it.

To test, Cas goes to the source: kids. How else to converge on play but to see how kids play? Cas finds the right children to test her designs through relationships she's developed with schools, nonprofits, and children's museums. Often, teachers will weigh in as well when they observe their students playtesting Cas's designs. The critique comes in a few different

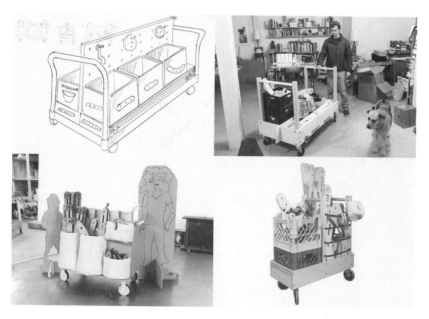

Clockwise from lower left: A paper scale model, a sketch, a "works-like," and the final Rigamajig storage cart. Images: Heroes Will Rise.

flavors. From the teachers, she hears feedback about how the toy connects to educational goals and the classroom context. The children's feedback gets expressed through their play. Do they understand how to play with the toy? Are they having fun? And most importantly, the litmus test for the success of a toy—do they make something unexpected? This is a true sign of empowerment—kids putting the pieces together in a unique way, imagining new forms, and expressing themselves through their unique creations. As Cas says, "when kids do something that I didn't imagine, then I know it's working."

As all of this is going on, Cas reaches the final point of convergence: ensuring that the toy can be made sustainably and affordably enough to get into the hands of as many children as possible. Cas will get the product priced with manufacturers to make sure they can hit the right balance of responsible sourcing and pricing. And once the playtests are over, and the final design changes made (typically after many iterations through these steps), she will send a final prototype for consumer product-safety testing. (Because of the high cost of safety tests, she won't begin this step until the design is complete.)

That is how Cas makes a toy: step by step, with many iterations along the convergent path to a market-viable and, most importantly, fun product. However, when the design is complete (aka fun), safety-approved, and ready for manufacturing, Cas is just getting started. This is where her experience with the Galapagos land iguanas proves relevant yet again. As Cas points out, "I design more than the product—I design the system around it."

As Cas is identifying final materials and rounding up manufacturers, she considers the ecosystem in which her toys are sourced and fabricated— the whole manufacturing system is set up to be sensitive to environmental systems. For Rigamajig, the plastic parts are injection-molded by a wind-turbine-powered plant outside of Rochester, New York, and the wood parts are fabricated in Smithfield, Rhode Island, near Cas's design studio, keeping production and design within a local distance.

Finally, Cas considers how her products are marketed and sold. Most public schools don't have budgets for products like Rigamajig, if indeed they have for basic books and supplies. So she has partnered with Kaboom!, a nonprofit play advocacy organization, as the marketing sales force and distributor. Kaboom! uses grants from large corporations to help schools acquire Rigamajig. This puts the empowering toy system into the hands of kids who wouldn't otherwise have a chance to play with it. By considering the ecosystem for Rigamajig, from how it's manufactured to how it gets into classrooms, Cas solved the problem Geemo had in the market. Failure, in the case of Rigamajig, didn't have to be an option.

At this point, Cas has converged on an outcome that meets Dreyfuss's measures for a successful design: safety, comfort, affordability, efficiency, and happiness. She begins with conversations with educators and kids, analyzing their needs and desires, which take form as a design question. She sketches and models possible solutions to the question by letting her hands lead the way—through her natural tinkering skills. She uses scale models to ensure her designs fit children's hands. She then tests her designs in the classroom, seeking the unexpected outcomes that are indicative of empowering play. She safety-tests her final designs. And finally, she considers the entire ecosystem for her products—where and how they are made as well as how they get into the hands of as many children as possible.

The Hands Lead, and the Head Follows

How do you design for play? How do you design to enable others to design? These are among the questions Cas is asking and answering through Rigamajig. So let's take a closer look at how she uses convergent design to answer a specific design question.

To the casual observer, Rigamajig is a collection of oversized plastic nuts, bolts, pulleys and wheels, wooden blocks and planks, and rope. To Cas, it's "a souped-up grandpa garage."[12] To a child, Rigamajig is everything. Like the Buddhist parable of the elephant and the blind men, it is something different for everyone, depending on their context. To educators, Rigamajig embeds twenty-first-century skills such as collaboration and problem solving through play-based learning. For kids, it's a chance to play with others to make towering, ambitious things. With Rigamajig, scale is important. The wooden pieces are often bigger than the children working with them, making it necessary to get others involved. Whether it's a structure to live in, a mechanical whale to ride on, or a thingamajig that moves sacks of potatoes from one end of the room to the other, the possibilities are endless.

Rigamajig. Image: Beth Flatley for Heroes Will Rise.

Rigamajig connects to the larger system of educational initiatives defined through the acronym STEAM: science, technology, engineering, art, and math. The "A" of "art" in STEAM is often left out, in favor of STEM, an effort to strengthen core competencies in technical fields. However, without creativity, much of the inventiveness enabled through the sciences, technology, engineering, and math would be lost. Rigamajig encourages that inventiveness and creativity through play, and STEAM comes along with it.

The instructions that come with Rigamajig aren't called instructions, they're called "play prompts." As the name suggests, they don't tell you what to build or how to build it. Instead, they provide prompts, or problems, to solve however you want. Teachers use these prompts to encourage their students to openly explore the vast possibility space Rigamajig provides. Cas sees these prompts as clues—not rules. They empower children to solve problems by tinkering in the ways that feel right to them. As she explains,

Rather than giving a kid a set of parts and saying "build a crane," the prompt would be, "build a machine that will get this bag of potatoes from here to there." So maybe that's a crane, maybe that's a conveyor, maybe it behaves the way a crane does, but the kids can figure out a completely different way to design it and rig it up.

One of the challenges of being a toy designer and CEO is that much of the time in the day is taken up by everything *but* design, from handling production logistics to the demands of running a business. Design often gets pushed either to the small hours of the night or to interns, who, as Cas says, often get to have all the fun. One of those projects that didn't find time in the day or an intern to design it was that cart to store Rigama-jig pieces, keeping classrooms across America clean and tidy. However one night, Cas found a solution, with the help of a little wine.

Cas has a standing "art date" with a friend, during which they drink wine while the friend paints and Cas draws. During one of these occasions, Cas warned her friend that she was going to have to work on their art date. Her friend didn't mind, so they turned it into a model-making date. As Cas describes it:

It was the first time that I actually sat down and focused. And this is a ridiculous thing to relearn, because it's what I already tell all my students, but the process from going from the sketch to making the model I totally changed everything on my sketch—I'm thinking through what's going to be too expensive, and instead of this joint, I can use this groove, and at the end of the night, I was like, oh—this is it. And literally I finished what I had been trying to figure out for a year and a half. And so as I am getting busier as a professor, I am trying to figure out how to keep the part of the design I love—sitting down and making the model—because in the process of making the model, I am designing it. Until I make it out of cardboard, there are things I won't have thought of. And that's the fun part.

Sitting down, and building a model—aka tinkering—provided the solution to a problem Cas was trying to solve for more than a year. She let her hands lead the process, and her head follow.

Interestingly enough, this small example—converging on the humble outcome of a cart for Rigamajig—returns to the lesson that Rigamajig instills through its slogan: "Make, play, do." Solve a problem by making, keep it playful (sometimes wine helps), and simply do what you are trying to do. Cas's process in designing the cart perfectly embodied this lesson. Her convergent outcomes derive from applying prior knowledge to a prob-lem, and keeping the process playful. It just so happens that knowledge can come as easily from the hands as it can from the head.

Connecting the Dots

Cas's convergent process finds it roots in tinkering, with a healthy dose of Dreyfuss-inspired "designing for people." Everything she designs takes

TINKERING   PLAYTESTING

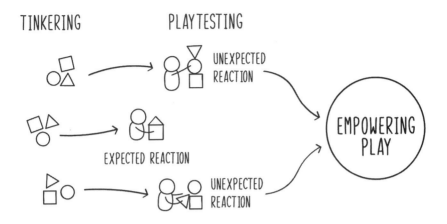

UNEXPECTED
REACTION

EXPECTED REACTION

UNEXPECTED
REACTION

EMPOWERING
PLAY

into account the educational and market ecosystem to enable her toys to reach as many children as possible. Her **process** is influenced by her early experiences building things in her backyard, her study of feminist and queer theory, her failed attempts as a scientist, and ultimately finding a career in toy design. One would imagine that such an eclectic array of experiences would lead to an adoption of divergent thinking in the design process—after all, divergence was the hallmark of her early career moves. But as educational psychologist Arthur Cropley notes, divergent and convergent thinking often work in tandem, with convergent processes translating prior experience and knowledge into tangible results.[13] It's certain that Cas's multiple experiences all created the unique knowledge she needed to develop empowering toys. The magic of Cas's process is that **convergent outcomes**—educational toys like Rigamajig—allow others to divergently explore their own way of thinking and making. So while she solves many of her design problems by converging on one solution, her toys enable all kinds of divergent outcomes (including that all-important tinkering, of course).

Cas's **intention** is guided by an ideal: empowering play. The process often begins with a question, such as "How might we enable twenty-first-century collaborative skills through play?" Or the more prosaic, "What would the perfect classroom Rigamajig storage cart be?" She might seek inspiration from historic toys or from her own experiences. When Cas begins making her way to a convergent outcome, she begins with tinkering—letting her hands come up with the ideas she'll further explore through prototypes. As Cas says, "my brain doesn't know what it is until my hand helps to figure it out." The outcomes are often considered as part of a larger **context**—a system—and how people (in our parlance, **actors**) will interact with that system. Whatever Cas designs impacts larger systems, whether they are environmental, political, or educational. So she asks, What are the systems at play in the production of this toy, and in its life in the world?

Cas **evaluates** the success of her prototypes based on the generative and empowering qualities of the play she sees enacted by her playtesters, and she knows the prototype is successful when she's surprised by what someone makes or does with it. Success in the market is measured on a continuum, however. With Geemo, Cas realized that failure is as relative as success. Rather than repeat past mistakes, she collaborates with other actors to help her connect her products to a sustainable ecosystem (educators, manufacturers, a salesforce, grants). Each project provides an opportunity to learn something. And in turn, her toys provide the opportunity for children to learn about themselves.

14 Divergent Outcomes: Miranda July, Artist

Miranda July is best known for her films *Me and You and Everyone We Know* and *The Future*. This isn't surprising, as both were critically acclaimed independent films. But to view Miranda as only a filmmaker is to miss the breadth of her practice. She is a conceptual artist working in a variety of mediums—performance, websites, film, literature, apps, even purses—at a variety of scales—short stories to novels, short films to feature films, tweets to full-scale websites, short solo performances to large-scale participatory performances. Across mediums and scales, she explores things like the hopelessness of connecting with others, whether or not we can really know someone, the impact of chance occurrence in our lives, and the impermanence of life. These are "big idea" topics, the kind that aren't resolved in a single work of art, if ever at all.

Framing all this is the exploration of the perimeters of emotional and social experiences of being a woman. Miranda's work is borne from a feminist perspective, but this is not in the foreground, even if it is quietly but confidently present. This point is both personal and political—from early in her career, she noticed the lack of opportunities for women in most creative disciplines—fine art, film, and performance art, to name a few. Inspired by the Riot Grrrl punk scene of 1990s Portland—a scene she was part of for a period—Miranda was inspired to do something about this imbalance. For example, her early project *Joanie 4 Jackie* was a do-it-yourself distribution system for women to share their films with one another.

We approach Miranda's practice as an example of **divergent outcomes**. Instead of the traditional conception of divergent thinking as a method to generate lots of ideas, Miranda uses divergence as a process of the continual exploration of mediums and themes. Her divergent practice prizes "unlearning," to use Leski's term (discussed in chapter 4), and the creative opportunities that arise from uncertainty on the path to the desired outcome. At the start of each project, Miranda knows the medium in which she will work, and has some ideas about the topics she wants to explore in that work. Her divergence is not one of medium or form, because she knows that from the outset—if she sets out to make a film, she'll make a film; if she sets out to write a novel, she'll produce a novel. Instead, hers is a divergence driven by uncertainty. How do you create and convey within a given medium? What can she learn about the medium and its expressive potential? How can understanding that potential help her explore the ideas under consideration? This approach to divergence—a process of unlearning driven by uncertainty—allows Miranda a vulnerability and openness that leads to a great range of projects across mediums.

Diverging through an Idea, One Medium at a Time

From early on, Miranda's work as an artist emerged from a do-it-yourself disposition. Her parents ran a small publishing company out of their home, which exposed Miranda to the sweat equity and attention to the boring but essential details that drive many small businesses. Later, when Miranda got to high school, she discovered the punk ethos of Berkeley, California, and the scene anchored by the community-run 924 Gilman venue. This all-ages space created a window of opportunity for young artists like Miranda, including her first public performance: a play that she wrote and directed as a high school project.

The get-it-done mindset of her parents' small business and her own affinities with the antiauthoritarian DIY Berkeley punk scene shaped Miranda's approach to creative practice. She remained fiercely self-reliant, and uninterested in traditional infrastructures that rejected or discouraged women's involvement. After a short stint at the University of California–Santa Cruz, she rejected formal education, instead developing a career deconstructed through learning by doing, and by prizing the value of the beginner's mindset by taking on projects in unfamiliar mediums. As Miranda explains:

I like that feeling of feeling like a novice. I create it in my life. Every time I make a movie, it has been years since I made a movie. Every time I write a book, it's been years. I always have this feeling of starting from scratch. I'm just not that person who gets off on bearing their craft, and years of wisdom. I think I probably actually have some by now, there are just some muscles that have gotten built up, and that's nice, but I don't present myself in that way, even to myself. I try to talk to myself like a kindly art teacher, very gently: "Well, let's just see what happens …" At the beginning of a project it's really important to feel like it's okay to not know, and to maintain a kind of lightness and curiosity.[1]

Miranda's embrace of uncertainty and a beginner's mindset led her to leave large gaps in time between works done in the same medium. For example, her two feature films are six years apart, and her collection of short stories and her first novel were eight years apart. These temporal gaps allow her to more easily approach each work from perhaps not a complete beginner's mindset, but certainly with a real need to again learn the particulars of the medium and form.

Miranda uses a divergent process in which the different mediums in her repertoire serve as a means of investigating a question or idea more fully, and through multiple creative processes. Instead of digging into a single mode of expression for an idea, she gives the question or idea multiple material forms. And instead of exploring what is known, she seeks to explore the less considered. To do this, she uses the beginner's mindset as a tool with the hope it will allow her to discover new potentials. This approach leads to what Miranda has described as "allowing uncertainty to take flight." By maintaining a sense of newness in a medium, she leaves herself open to difficult creative moments, but also to the potential of the unexpected that can emerge when an unfamiliar medium is used to engage with complex and underexamined aspects of the human experience. This all leads to a more divergent consideration of artistic outcomes. Miranda knows the medium of the work, but the means by which she will create within it, and what the final product will be and will come to mean—these are uncertainties unraveled through the process on the way to the desired outcome: a work of art.

One thread that runs through many of Miranda's works is the idea of human interaction:

Often, people say, "oh, connection is in all your work, the theme of people trying to connect." But actually I'm not that good at connecting; I don't think humans in general are really that good at it. Even in the best of circumstances, there's all these mistakes and misunderstandings, and most of the time you don't say exactly what you mean, and that's just kind of what we do. Everyone has their own unique way of doing that, and to me, *that's* what's interesting, people attempting to connect, and then doing kind of unique, almost creative things to sabotage that. In my stories there's often some basic, unresolved misunderstanding. That's where the art is and the beauty is.

Still from Miranda's 1996 film *Atlanta*, with Miranda in the role of the daughter.

As Miranda notes, this theme is less about the act of connection, and more about the beautiful mess that emerges when people attempt to interact with one another. This idea is present in almost all of her work, creating a near-continuous thread of divergent outcomes—films, performances, apps, stores, websites, books, short stories, purses—in which she continues to investigate the beauty of the wreckage created through human interaction.

Even early films like *Atlanta*, shot at the time of the 1996 Olympic Games held in Atlanta, Georgia, fit this idea. In the film, Miranda plays both a fictional young swimmer and her mother. On the surface, the film plays out like the unedited footage for an interview on a local newscast. But looking more closely, the separate interviews speak to the gaps between the mother and daughter, and the very different ways they think about the daughter's swimming. There is clearly love between the two, but also an obvious tension between what they both want and need from the swimming, and from one another, both informing how their relationship plays out.

The short stories in *No One Belongs Here More Than You* are a catalog of the ways people can fail in their attempts to be in the world, and the ways they connect with the people, places, and things around them. The stories include unspoken teen crushes, and the spirals of irrational behavior that uncoil when that love is unreturned; a person attending a romance workshop and accidentally making a fellow participant cry; a person who imagines everyone who they ever interacted with coming together to celebrate their love for them.

Regardless of the medium, Miranda is keen to create works that resonate with her audience and that elicit specific emotional and reflective responses. This is the site for another aspect of divergence in Miranda's work: the construction of audience participation. Throughout her career, she has relied on audience participation as part of the works themselves, and as a key ingredient in the audience experience. The best-known of these participatory works is *Learning to Love You More*, a collaboration with the social practice artist Harrell Fletcher.[2] Running from 2002 to 2009, the project took the form of a website with "assignments" for the public to enact, document, and submit to the online archive as "reports." These ranged from "reread your favorite book from fifth grade" (#45), to "make an encouraging banner" (#63), to "list five events from 1984" (#42), to "hang a wind chime on a tree in a parking lot" (#15). The seventy assignments posted between

Screenshot from *Learning to Love You More.*

2002 and 2009 resulted in a repository of nearly 10,000 reports created by more than 8,000 people. The submitted reports range in craft skill and conceptual sophistication from things that would easily pass for snapshots to serious works of art. What connects the reports are their sameness, but also the glimpses they provide into people's lives. Take assignment #50: "take a flash photo under your bed." The results are all quite similar—a floor, a hint of the bed frame, some stored stuff, maybe a bed leg—yet at the same time unique—shoes, packed boxes, backgammon sets, stacks of books and papers, pets, piles of clothes. Each of the reports becomes a document of that person's similarities to others and their unique qualities. As Miranda puts it,

I think in a way if everyone's doing the same thing what comes out is the difference. You stop thinking about what the assignment was and you're looking hungrily for the personal thing that's revealed. You also begin to notice a pattern, things that everyone has in common and that's sort of comforting.[3]

Miranda's collaboration with writer and programmer Paul Ford for Rhizome's and New Museum's 2016 Seven on Seven conference took participation and the Internet in a different direction. For their commission for the conference, Miranda and Paul decided to create a story based on information about the attending audience. Using the ticket holder list, Miranda, the radio producer Starlee Kine, and a researcher sifted through the publicly

Still from documentation of Miranda July and Paul Ford's collaboration.

available artifacts from the attendees' social media presences. Paul created a tool that used the attendees' Twitter handles to scrape their last 10,000 tweets and dumped them into a searchable database. Miranda took the material and wrote a performance script based on information, stories, images, videos, and sounds they had discovered in the audience's Twitter feed. Miranda and Paul then read the script, accompanied by a slideshow they created using photos and videos from the audience's social media archives.[4]

The audience, however, was not informed this was happening.[5] When the performance began, the audience likely assumed they were just hearing another one of Miranda's fictional tales:

You were born and raised in New York City. You were born in Korea. You were born in Hong Kong and raised in Toronto. You were born on Halloween. You were born and raised in Cairo. You were born in Beirut during the Civil War. You slept straight through the bombings. You were born in Brazil. You were born in Lima, Peru. You were born in Winnipeg, Manitoba, and were unschooled until age thirteen. You were born in Brooklyn to a Jamaican father and a Trinidadian mother. You were born in the town where David Bowie was arrested for smoking pot. You were born in Serbia. You were born in Guangzhou, China.

The story continued to weave through all facets of people's lives and the documentation thereof—addresses, birth dates, descriptions of personalities, purchases and activities, and lots of rainbows—all beginning with "You … ." The story is at once pure Miranda but also owned by everyone there that evening by virtue of their participation in its construction, knowingly or not.

Miranda took technology-enabled participation in completely different directions with the messaging app Somebody, a collaboration with designer Thea Lorentzen.[6] With Somebody, Miranda explores a different aspect of participation—the inherent awkwardness of person-to-person communication, made even more complicated by the inclusion of a third person to serve as the delivery mechanism. Instead of Miranda providing the prompts and structure, Somebody provided its users with a crowdsourced message delivery platform.[7] Typical messaging platforms deliver a message from a sender to a recipient. The Somebody app did this too, but in a much more human-scale manner. Instead of using the Internet to deliver the message directly, the app located another app user—the eponymous "somebody"— in the proximity of the intended recipient who would instead deliver the message. Let's say Toni wanted to send Jackie a message through Somebody. To do this, she would select Jackie as a recipient, and then type in her message. The app would then determine Jackie's location, and find another app user in his proximity—let's say Miranda. Miranda would

Screenshot from the promotional film for the Somebody app.

then look for Jackie so that she could deliver Toni's message by acting as a proxy—Miranda wouldn't just deliver the message *for* Toni, but *as* Toni. Somebody messages always begin with the deliverer saying the name of the recipient and letting them know who was sender: "Jackie, it's me, Toni" (Jackie is the recipient and Toni the sender). At that point, the contents of Toni's message would be delivered. Often, in addition to words to be read aloud, the messages included stage directions on what the deliverer should do—things like hug the recipient, make particular hand gestures, or strike specific poses. Once the message was successfully delivered, the deliverer and the recipient were supposed to take a selfie that was sent back to the sender. First released in 2014, and updated a year later, the app was used by ten thousand people a day, with about a quarter of all messages reaching the intended recipient. All sorts of messages were delivered before the app was shut down in late 2015—wedding proposals, long-distance hellos, olive branches between quarrelling friends, notes of concern and comfort, declarations of love.[8]

The final example of Miranda's divergent exploration of participation and communication is found in the participatory theater piece *New Society*. The show's title sets the premise—Miranda and the audience worked

Miranda and "citizens" in *New Society*. Photo by Rebecca Greenfield.

together to create a new society, right there in the theater space. The show began with Miranda on a minimally decorated stage where she seemingly stumbled through her lines, asking the audience for help. She regained her bearings and asked, "What if you just stayed? You didn't go home? Maybe this is it. Me. You. Us."[9] As the performance continued, Miranda invited audience members to join her in creating the trappings of their new nation: a national anthem, a flag, a medical staff in the case of emergency, and so on. Collectively, the citizens of New Society wrote a constitution, and generated the materials for a national currency. The play unfolded over a fictional twenty years, allowing Miranda and her fellow citizens of New Society to experience a full lifetime in their country; audience members were born, died, fell in love, made out, and otherwise conducted their lives in the theater. They reflected on the world they left behind, and reminisced about the people they missed. Miranda, who appointed herself leader of this new country, wove together songs, yoga classes, a swap meet, political speeches, and dramatic constitutional amendments that changed the fabric of life to create a sense of community and connection between the audience members.

Like most of her work, *New Society* comes back around to that question of the frailty of human interaction: "If there's something that interests me, about strangers engaging and connecting, it's how hard it is, how badly we do it, but each in our own unique way."[10] This topic is ultimately what connect *Atlanta*, *Learning to Love You More*, Somebody, the Paul Ford collaboration, and *New Society*. And it is what connects these participatory works to the feature film *Me and You and Everyone We Know*, her novel *The First Bad Man*, the book *It Chooses You*, the film *The Future*, and many of the characters occupying the short stories in *No One Belongs Here More Than You*. Miranda diverges from medium to medium to explore and celebrate the hopelessly broken ways in which we all engage. In these works, she does this through various technologies and mediums to see the beauty that emerges from our clumsiness. The film *Atlanta* shows the gulf between a mother and a daughter. The Somebody app creates an incredibly awkward, yet intimate form of communication mediated through a complete stranger. New Society asks an audience of strangers to band together to create and then maintain a community. The collaboration with Paul Ford builds a story from a room of strangers, leaving everyone wondering which life details came from whom. Ultimately, the medium becomes human interaction, regardless of the form it takes—film, performance, app, website, or literature. This, ultimately, is Miranda's divergent practice, the use of multiple mediums in service of her exploration of the beautiful frailties of human interaction.

Making Things with Monster Gloves and Tweezers

Throughout her career, Miranda has worked in a wide range of mediums—performance, short films, short stories, installation art, performance art, feature films, novels, participatory theater, mobile apps, websites, and music. Each has its own strengths and weaknesses as vehicles for self-expression, she feels:

> Writing is the finest medium, it's the one where you have the most control, like you are using tiny little precise tools, and they are like a hair paint brush. And then when you are making a movie, it's like big, clunky monster gloves. Performance is unique because the scale is so different. There isn't a market for it like the other things I do. With performance, it is purely creative. Being able to think this freely feeds my work in the more commercial mediums.

Performance provides the looseness and malleability to explore the potential shapes of an idea. Compared to printed words and film, the temporality and impermanence of performance gives Miranda the permission to try things she might not otherwise. Performance also has an inherent iterative quality—each performance is an opportunity to refine, try out new ideas, reorder things, and so on. Miranda usually begins with small, private audiences, and then once she is feeling comfortable with the scale and scope of the work, she moves to larger public workshops, and finally a run of performances.

Writing provides similar opportunities for iterative exploration; during the writing process of creating successive drafts, sometimes an edit pass will add substance, sometimes it will remove detail, sometimes it will refine and strengthen. All this happens in a more closed system, where the evaluative process is constrained to Miranda as the author, perhaps with an editor and a few additional people whose feedback she trusts. As Miranda notes, writing provides an artist fine-grain control of the medium. But beyond this, her divergent process opens things up in other ways. Particularly for someone like Miranda, who writes alone, writing affords opportunities to try things out, to change her mind, to be free to see where her work will take her. After all, the costs of revisions are minimal, at least up to the point that things start getting finalized.

In film, on the other hand, it is much harder to make on-the-fly changes, or to fill gaps when you realize they exist after the cameras are put away. The "big, clunky monster gloves" Miranda feels she's wearing when filmmaking are a metaphor for the complexities and collaborative nature of professional film production, even when practiced on a smaller scale. The filmmaking process is cautious, methodical, and not known for its embrace of spontaneity and last-minute changes, in large part due to the resource and schedule costs of large and small crew productions alike.

Situated somewhere between writing, performance, and film are Miranda's Internet-based works. These projects take aspects of all three of her typical mediums. From performance, particularly her more participatory works, Miranda takes her focus on the active engagement of her audiences. From writing, she takes the fine-grain approach to language, and her particular voice. As in film, she must engage with all manner of collaborators (cinematographers, producers, gaffers, actors, costume designers, and on and on) and the particular roles and craft skills they bring to the process. In apps and websites, the larger-scale, processual methods of software development require a more methodical approach to creation.

Particularly in mediums with which she is less familiar, Miranda pays close attention to the size of the project in order to be sure she can complete it. With filmmaking, she began making short ten-minute films, then worked her way up to thirty-minute films. From there, when she wanted to create a feature-length film, she approached it as three thirty-minute films, which gave her the security that she knew how to complete the project.

This methodical approach to scale and scope enables her divergent process—so long as she understands the contours of a project, Miranda feels comfortable allowing herself to embrace doubt and uncertainty: "What I'm trying to do is, in the process of making the things, I'm having to live with doubt. To me, that is so essential to the creative process. I mean, if you try to stamp that out or try to make everything tidy and doubtless, then you're done."

Doubt is another way to think about creative potential, and vice versa. Without doubt, there is no longer the potential for creativity. With doubt, there is still space for creativity. In this light, the presence of doubt is potential rather than negativity. Doubt plays a large role in divergent iterative practice—it is the presence of doubt, and not knowing the "right" answer or direction in which to take a project, that affords Miranda's divergence in the first place.

Take the *PennySaver* project Miranda started while working on the screenplay for her film *The Future*. Having hit a creative wall, she started looking at the *PennySaver*, a print-based circular for people selling things (a kind of print-based Craigslist). The project emerged from doubt, and a space it opened. Miranda began contacting people about the things they had for sale, and went to interview them.[11] She came to realize that it was better for her to get lost in the lives of the people from *PennySaver* than it was to remain lost in her own anxieties and fears around the then-unfinanced, incompletely scripted film.[12] At the time, she wasn't certain what form the *PennySaver* project would take—she brought along a videographer just in case she needed to shift the film to a documentary if she just couldn't get her script finished.[13] Miranda found solace in getting farther and farther away from her own experience and closer to the lives of the people she met and interviewed: "I was in a strung-out-enough place that I was kind of open. That's a good thing to remember: Sometimes when you are sort of not doing that well, you have sort of superpowers that you aren't going to have when your life gets better again."[14]

As she scoured the ads and conducted the interviews, she realized that she was venturing into new territory—nonfiction. Her fictional work took the first person most of the time, and even in her films she played the lead role. But with this project, Miranda wasn't playing one of her characters, she was just being herself, traveling around to interview people about the items they were selling. She came to explore the question, "What does it mean if 'I' really means 'me'?" as she thought about the ways she enacted fictional scenarios and moments that were far more brave and exploring than she herself lived, or was comfortable sharing about her own experiences.[15] While this didn't necessarily change the structure of the film, it did provide new ways for Miranda to approach the film, eventually allowing her to find her way to a script with which she was happy.

The *PennySaver* project ended up being part of three separate works—a series of interview videos, the book *It Chooses You*, and the film *The Future*. Within the film (the reason Miranda diverged into this project in the first place), the *PennySaver* project helped her reconsider the relationship between herself, her fictional work, and the experiences and thoughts she had. More importantly, it helped her think about the interplay between the three. More concretely, the interviews also led to formal and narrative experimentation. She considered folding the real moments from her interviews into *The Future*. This involved going back to the original people, with whom she attempted to reenact conversations, but this time, within the larger fictional story arc of the film. The first attempt at this didn't work out, leading Miranda to realize she was unreasonably asking her interviewee to transform from themselves into a fictional character of themselves. The artificiality of the film set, which differs in subtle but important ways from the more informal video interviews originally shot, didn't always work. As a result, Miranda stopped trying to shoehorn the interviews into *The Future*, and instead allowed the *PennySaver* project to become a separate project, the book *It Chooses You*.

As the *PennySaver* project neared completion, Miranda became increasingly panicked about *The Future*. The story she was working on was about a then-thirty-five-year-old woman's projections and fears of the future. One of the last *PennySaver* interviews was with Joe, a retired house painter nearing the end of his life. Listening to his stories, Miranda realized that his take on the future—one likely to end sooner than her own—helped her see there were other ways to approach time and its passing. She wanted to bring him and his stories into the film, but she felt uncomfortable just taking his stories, so she invited him to be in the film, playing himself. Joe did end up in the movie playing himself, though selling a hairdryer instead of greeting cards. He also ended up doing the voiceover for the character of the moon in the film.

The *PennySaver* interviews proved useful for her script-writing woes on *The Future*. The process enabled her to explore different ways to involve herself within her fictional works—she learned to be more comfortable thinking of herself as a character. She was the real-life character, Miranda July, who interacted with a host of other characters—the people she met through the *PennySaver*. As she noted, "you have to be a lot more honest, you can't just make up what happened or what the person is thinking or doing. It's the truth."[16]

Miranda pursued a single idea—imagining oneself in the future—through a divergent set of paths, eventually giving form to three separate projects, each connected to the original theme in unique ways, each shaping her thinking about the subject. In other words, though she initially set out to only create a film, she instead arrived at a divergent outcome composed of three separate works, each connected to the original theme.

Opening a Store without Retail Experience

In many ways, the clearest example of Miranda's divergent iterative process is her Interfaith Charity Shop at Selfridges.[17] Commissioned by the London-based arts organization Artangel, Miranda created a charity store pop-up shop inside Selfridges, a large London department store. This was no typical charity shop run by a single organization; instead, it was co-run by four religious charity organizations which shared the proceeds: Islamic Relief, Norwood Jewish Charity, London Buddhist Centre, and Spitalfields Crypt Trust. As with any other charity store stocked with secondhand goods, the Interfaith Charity Shop at Selfridges was full of clothes, toys, books, used electronics, jewelry, and all the other things one might imagine. The project picks up a number of threads from the *PennySaver* project and its publication, *It Chooses You*—the forced interaction of people from different walks of life, the role of commerce in human interaction, the peculiarity of money as a social instrument.

A shopper in the interfaith charity shop. Photo by Hugo Glendinning for ArtAngel.

An important facet of the project was Miranda's status as an outsider, and the extension of her beginner's mindset and the power of uncertainty and doubt. As an American, she was an outsider to London, and more importantly, to the deep-rooted British institution of charity shops. She was also an outsider to the four faiths and the ways each religion approached the idea of charity. She was an outsider to religious belief and practice in general, and the social and behavioral impacts religion can have in a person's life. She was an outsider in interacting with a larger corporation like Selfridges, particularly in the context of an art project. And finally, she was an outsider to the delicate work of bringing four organizations, each with its own values, together in collaboration.

The project also put Miranda's beginner's mindset into more direct artistic use: investigating the creative potential of using her cultural capital to help another organization (here, in conjunction with Artangel and Selfridges).[18] She first thought about reputation and cultural capital as an artistic medium while working on the app Somebody, which was a collaboration with the Italian luxury brand MiuMiu. The collaboration with an established brand caused some concern for Miranda, who still connects with her DIY Riot Grrrl roots. This led her to think about other ways she could leverage her cultural capital as an art medium—as she put it, "there must be some use for [the pop appeal] as a material, like paint or anything else."[19]

With the charity shop, Miranda was investigating what happens when she was more of an instigator than an author. Or as she more succinctly put it, "you don't need to geniusly 'author' something every time."[20] This was new territory for Miranda, putting her as much in the role of artist as in that of funder (bringing her cultural capital and artistic "brand" to the project) and project manager (working through the infrastructural and operational logistics of not only setting up the shop, but negotiating the interactions between the four faith-based groups). This was an unfamiliar place for Miranda, who was more accustomed to having a good deal of control over the development and content of her work.

Still, there were ways Miranda could draw upon previous practice that helped her make sense of the scale and scope of the project. She approached the design of the store's interior as she would the production design of a film set. Given the unusual setting for the shop—nested inside an existing department store—she knew it was important that shoppers would immediately understand they were looking at a charity shop. And so she brought her instincts from production design to the choices made in materials, floor plan, and even the ceiling tiles and product hang tags.

Making everyone feel welcome and comfortable in the shop was critical for Miranda. She thought of the shop as being like a film set, but instead of being a space occupied by actors performing fictional characters in a fictional scene, the charity shop was a place where real people would engage in real activities—commerce, conversation, browsing, and otherwise conducting their lives. Here, she drew on experiences from *New Society*, in which she created contexts within which her audience would perform, and Somebody, in which she facilitated interactions between strangers.

The Interfaith Charity Shop allowed her to divergently explore a new approach to artmaking while still drawing on experiences and skills in which she could anchor the project. Because the shop placed Miranda in a series of nested contexts in which she was an outsider, it gave her new opportunities to continue investigating the themes woven through her Riot Grrrl/DIY roots, the feature film *The Future*, the *PennySaver* project, the book *It Chooses You*, the Somebody app, and the *New Society* performance. Here, her divergence folds inward, using pieces of each other medium in which she has worked, which provide a foundation for her to work in a new medium with a beginner's mindset.

Connecting the Dots

The divergent outcomes of Miranda's work invert how one might usually think of divergence in creative practice. In the classic example of Alex Faickney Osborn's brainstorming techniques, a single process is used to tease out a multiplicity of ideas.[21] But in Miranda's divergent iteration, an idea or question remains consistent while the processes and products differ. In many ways, the question has remained constant throughout her twenty-plus years as an artist—Why are we so bad at communication? Permutations on this question, explored through different scenarios and contexts, can be identified throughout her body of work: Performance and participation are structured to give us new insights (the Somebody app; *It Chooses You*; *New Society*), or she creates fictional scenarios in which characters struggle to understand and be understood (*Me and You and Everyone We Know*; *The First Bad Man*; *Atlanta*). Each of the mediums Miranda

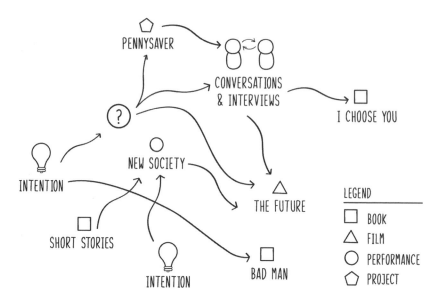

uses allows different emphasis and inflections as she explores the human foibles of being in a world filled with lots of other people struggling in their own right.

Miranda's work begins with an **intention**—create a work within a given medium. Her process to reach this intended **outcome** is left as open and exploratory as possible through her embrace of the beginner's mindset. This allows her to embrace the uncertainty that comes with the unfamiliarity of working in a new medium. The **context** of a given medium—the processes, tools, techniques, and **actors** typically involved—inform how Miranda proceeds in her creation of a new work. The more "bulky" mediums—film, for example—provide more friction in her exploration of ideas and her attempts at articulation within the form. Within each work, Miranda reaches a point where she understands the path forward. From there, the divergence comes to a close, and the focus is on formally completing the given work. When making a film, this is the period after the script is complete, and the larger team is assembled to shoot, edit, and score the work. For an app or website, this is the period after the functionality and design are established, and the team gets down to building out the finished software.

The **evaluation** component in Miranda's process is primarily an internal evaluation—her editing her own work, making decisions about what does and doesn't work. But when we spoke with Miranda, she had come to the realization that it was indeed okay to solicit the feedback of others. She puts it much better than we can: "I can go this far alone. But with just the right kind of help, I can go completely outside my own range. When I first started realizing that was even legal—that I'm allowed to get feedback—I was like, 'OMG, it's like free money! I'm better, and no one is upset.'"

Miranda's **process** then becomes more about the temporal gaps between projects that enable her to embody the beginner's mindset. This approach allows her to relearn the craft of a medium, which in turn creates the space for uncertainty and doubt. Around all of this is her particular approach to repetition—each new project is an iterative cycle exploring that same basic question about the frailties of human interactions.

Section III Failing Better

This book puts forward a simple proposition: Failure is the fuel of iterative creative practice. This is the real heart of creativity—the incremental movement through conceptualizing, making, and evaluating outcomes. The more we focus on achieving incremental successes one loop at a time, the less failure seems, well, like failure, and more like a part of a deliberate process. Success and failure simply become stops along the iterative cycle, inextricably linked.

In all kinds of contexts, from creativity to learning to solve society's most vexing problems, iteration is an antidote that can convert our fear of failure into a prepared openness for making the most of failure. In other words, the iterative mindset allows us to respect failure as an inevitable, even welcome, part of our lives. This is why we wrote this book. As we pondered our failure-riddled game design process, we wondered: Do other creative practices use iteration in a similar way? Through the process of talking to practitioners in a wildly diverse set of fields—art, cooking, comedy, animation, winemaking, architecture and game design, jazz, skateboarding, toy design, and radio—we found that, indeed, despite their extreme differences, iteration is one shared practice that connects them all.

15 Failing Better

Teaching a Bird about Its Practice

Barnett Newman famously quipped, "Aesthetics is for artists as ornithology is for the birds."[1] By this, he meant that theories about a practice aren't really helpful for those in the practice (not to mention that he found a pun to say what he thinks about the philosophy of art). Just as a bird doesn't really care what scientific name it is assigned, Newman makes clear that many artists live and work without any need for the conceptual scaffolding of art theory. This may well be true, but we do hope there is utility in the kind of observation and reflection on creative practice found in this book. Consider this book's alternative title "Ornithology for Self-Reflective Birds."

Denise Gonzales Crisp provides another perspective on the utility of describing practice, despite its seeming futility. In her essay "'Splainin' Craft: Bringing the Making into Writing," Gonzales Crisp reflects on the challenges of understanding, discussing, and transferring creative craft skills.[2] As an accomplished graphic designer and design educator, Crisp assumed she had mastered both the craft of graphic design and its transference to students. Her mastery, though, was challenged by her new interest, drumming. When Crisp tried to use the language and values of graphic design to discuss the craft of drumming, her teacher, Merritt, demurred, saying that wasn't how he thought about his practice. She realized drumming was a different world altogether, a community of practice with its own language and processes.

When Crisp struggled to develop an ear for isolating drum parts while listening to music, her teacher taught her to use "drumspeak," or the onomatopoeic conversion of the drum sounds into language: "BLdldldldldldl dat diggada cha chiggata dat diga doom gat." An hour and a half later, Crisp found herself on the other side of a deep conversation about the craft of drumming. Instead of talking directly, perhaps analytically about drumming, Merritt used stories, gestures, drumspeak, and playing itself to investigate the nuances of drumming as a craft.

A crystallizing moment for Crisp was watching drumming legend Bernard Purdie talk about the "Purdie shuffle,"[3] a drum pattern for which he is known. Unlike most tutorials, where the emphasis is purely on technique, Purdie exudes energy, laughing and musing as he introduces and then improvises on his drum patterns. Crisp recounts:

Purdie's delivery is brimming with exuberance, his movements constrained to near bursting. His knowledge and know-how is seeable, almost palpable. Most other videos I've watched, by contrast, offer little if any evocation of the process of playing, or the feeling of playing something well. Similar to Merritt's tales, the effectiveness of Purdie's "splainin" is rooted less in his breakdown of the eponymous shuffle and more in the demonstration of his own relationship with, first, the instrument and, second, the shuffle itself as he parses the beats and then plays them.[4]

The lesson, for Crisp, was that craft is enacted, and not always easily (or best) understood through lexical and logical parsing. This mirrors our own experiences in writing this book. Even more so, it reflects our experiences as design educators—more often than not, throwing words alone at students is ineffective. Instead, a mix of discussion, critique, storytelling, and above all, practice is essential to really understand a craft.

In each of our ten case studies, we delved into the idiosyncratic approach of a practitioner or team. Each of our case study subjects was part of their own community of practice, with distinct values that connected a group of practitioners to one another. Finding our footing and sorting out how to talk about their practice, and how they do or do not think about failure, was not always easy. When asked about when he first heard about iterative game design methods, Eric Zimmerman, for example, couldn't point to any particular example or individual. Instead, he remembers it being an intuitive and appropriate way to practice and teach the craft of game design.

Time and again, in talking with the practitioners in this book, we realized that something so essential and basic to our creative practice—iteration—was not necessarily an operative concept for everyone. Indeed, Miranda July noted that she hadn't really considered the idea until she began working with software developers on her app Somebody. Yet from our perspective, she was clearly iterating on ideas across mediums. Despite the variance in language, or even the absence of the concept, we found that iteration was indeed baked into everyone's practice, consciously or not. That's because creative practice is by nature iterative. One can't help drawing on the experiences of prior projects, on lessons learned, developing a set of personal or shared heuristics from which to strengthen one's process. This doesn't indicate that a practitioner's output is always better from one piece to the next, but it does suggest a certain amount of muscle memory is built up. From this perspective, each project is a single cycle in a career-long iterative process.

Putting the Pieces Together

Iteration is the unacknowledged secret behind the myth of creative genius, the myth in which a master effortlessly dashes off a perfect work every time. Even the master painter Bob Ross iterated on failures, transforming "happy accidents" into eye-pleasing details. The iterative mindset is the antidote to the "waterfall" approach to creation, in which a thing is conceived of, planned, built, then put into use—1, 2, 3, 4, done. In the waterfall approach, the process relies on the prior experience of the creator to anticipate every possible issue, and to come up with viable solutions in the abstract state of designing, planning, and production. Of course, few of us can fully predict every nuance, situation, and obstacle that our creations will face. The dean of failure studies, Henry Petroski, describes the basic problem:

The more complicated the design problem, naturally the more difficult the solution and hence the more likely that some details and features may be overlooked, only to have their absence come to the fore after the thing is manufactured or built and put to the test of use.[5]

To bring these ideas all together, let's revisit our core concepts of creativity, failure, and iteration. We've defined creativity as the **process** by which an **individual** or **group intentionally produces** an **outcome** that is **appropriate, aesthetic**, and **authentic** to its **context** and **community**. This is not an easy thing to do, let alone get right on the first try. Creative practitioners fail *a lot*. That's okay, even desirable, as long as the practitioner is able to detect, acknowledge, and analyze the failure so that they can learn from it.

From our perspective, the best way to negotiate the relationship between creative practice and failure is iteration. As we define it, an iterative project begins with an **intention**, from which emerges a **cyclical process** designed to reach a particular **outcome**, all happening within a **context** and carried out by **actors**. This outcome may or may not meet the intentions for the project. And so an **evaluation** must take place during the process *and* after the process is complete, to assess the outcomes.

In this light, iteration really is our best tool for turning what anthropologist and designer Jamer Hunt calls **predicted failures** into data that will inform the next loop in the cycle.[6] Whether it's a prototype for a vegetable peeler, a stress test on a scale model of a building, or a first attempt at a recipe, predicted failures are the kind of failure we expect to happen. In fact, learning from this kind of failure is a necessary part of the process. Hunt brings up another kind of failure that is common to most creative practitioners: **version failure**—an article submission sent back with editorial changes, alpha release software, a bad batch of cupcakes. These are the kind of failures that happen as part of incremental attempts to improve, revise, or otherwise change something.

Better Together

The craft of iteration is the heart of this book. Really, it is the *crafts* of iteration, as there is no one way to approach iteration. One thing that connects our case studies: The iterative approaches in each practitioner's work did not come from a "How to Iterate" book, and were not necessarily developed for their universality or generalizability. Instead, each was developed, consciously or not, as an approach for a given practitioner (or practitioners) to best meet the intentions and intended outcomes of their creative practice within the constraints of the context. In other words, iteration emerged organically for these practitioners as a way to learn from failure as they work within the constraints of their medium.

Though we wrote the case studies so that each would focus on a specific aspect of iterative practice, the truth is that we cannot easily isolate any one characteristic of iteration from the others. Indeed, each practitioner sets intentions, develops processes, generates outcomes, and evaluates their results—while also integrating all five of the approaches to iteration we've identified. For example, Amelia Brodka's skateboarding—while we focus on her internal evaluation—combines the material contexts of skating to achieve the divergent outcomes of new tricks. And while we emphasize how Matthew Maloney's filmmaking employs reflective contexts, it's in the service of his exploratory intentions, which often lead to convergent outcomes achieved through a methodological process anchored by internal evaluation. And Andy Milne listens to all forms of music as reflective iteration; and he equally employs internal and external evaluation depending on whether he's playing alone or with others, in front of an audience or in a recording studio.

Let's look at a couple of the case studies more closely to see how these multiplex approaches to iteration play out. The writer, comedian, and public commentator Baratunde Thurston's practice spans our five continua. Of course he makes use of external evaluation as an anchoring concern, but along with this comes a good deal of reflective iteration—his practice of externalizing his work, whether by printing out an in-progress piece of writing, listening to a stand-up set, or watching a recording of a live event. His emphasis on editing allows him to converge on a particular targeted outcome (a book, a stand-up routine, a tweet). This provides clarity on what he is seeking feedback on, and what he should look for in the responses to his work in order to get closer to his intentions. His work is guided by

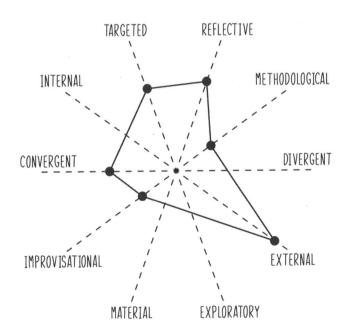

a methodological process, yet there is a good deal of improvisation in his path toward his intended outcomes, as the story of his sparsely attended stand-up night and resulting conversation with the audience shows.

Then there is winemaker Allison Tauziet, who served as the case study for material contexts. Her practice is guided by a targeted intention—making the best possible wine she can, given the weather, the environmental conditions, and the crop of grapes the vineyard yields. This requires a methodology open to improvisation—though she is working with strong external pressures, she is ultimately relying on her own internal evaluation to make decisions about how to care for the vines, when to pick the grapes, what ratios to use in the blending of her wines, and so on. In fact, much of her evaluation is based on her senses—a very internal and subjective process. And though her intentions are targeted, she allows for divergent outcomes—she focuses on making the best wine she can from the crops her vineyard yields, with each vintage telling its own story.

What becomes clear in these two examples is that there is no one way to approach iteration within creative practice—there are multiple approaches, combined in one practice. Each approach provides a different tool with which to engage in creative iteration—depending on where one is in the process (from intention to outcome) and on one's perspective—material

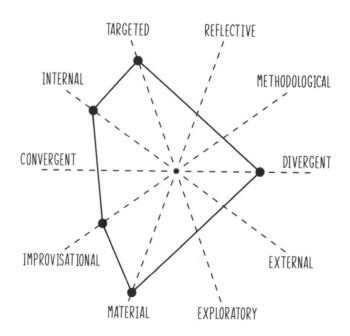

FIVE CONTINUA

MATERIAL & REFLECTIVE
ITERATION

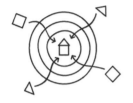 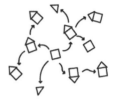

TARGETED & EXPLORATORY
INTENTIONS

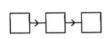 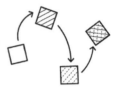

METHODOLOGICAL & IMPROVISATIONAL
PROCESSES

INTERNAL & EXTERNAL
EVALUATION

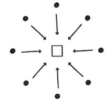 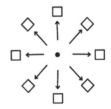

CONVERGENT & DIVERGENT
OUTCOMES

or reflective, targeted or exploratory, methodological or improvisational, etc. Our process in articulating these different approaches and perspectives is akin to looking at the stars and finding constellations. Through our case studies, we found patterns across different practices, but each pattern uniquely combines these iterative elements. To put it more simply: There is no one-size-fits-all method to iteration; approaches and perspectives are tailored to fit each individual.

Does It Take Ten Thousand Hours to Fail Better?

All of the case studies represent practitioners with many hours of experience in their fields—they have put in the time and energy to be reflective practitioners. So how does someone get to the point that they have these skills? A common answer is that it takes ten thousand hours of practice, an idea popularized by Malcolm Gladwell in his book *Outliers*.[7] Gladwell borrowed this idea from K. Anders Ericsson and Andreas C. Lehmann's 1996 article "Expert and Exceptional Performance: Evidence of Maximal Adaptation to Task Constraints"[8] and Ericsson, Ralf Th. Krampe, and Clemens Tesch-Römer's 1993 article "The Role of Deliberate Practice in the Acquisition of Expert Performance."[9] Years before Gladwell, or Ericsson and his collaborators, Herbert Simon and William Chase had started the quest to quantify the time it takes to become an expert in a field—in their case, the field was chess, which they estimated took ten thousand to fifty thousand hours. In the years since Gladwell's book, ten thousand hours has been interpreted as both a foolproof requirement for success and further evidence in support of cultural beliefs in the righteousness of hard work.

However, if you look back at Ericsson and Lehmann's research, their findings are much more subtle and nuanced. A key phrase in their research is "maximal adaptation and learning." First, take the word **adaptation**: For someone to master something, they need to adapt themselves to the demands of that craft. Imagine a runner training for a race. If they want to be able to run a six-minute mile, they will need to make the adaptations necessary to pull this off—develop the necessary musculature, strengthen their heart and lungs to provide the necessary resources, develop the discipline to run on a regular basis, and so on. In addition to these adaptations, the runner will need to **learn** how to run that fast: getting the right mechanics down so they run efficiently, learning how to mentally focus through the exhaustion and pain, and so on. And they must adapt and learn to the maximum of their potential.

These adaptations take time—thus the suspiciously specific ten thousand hours rule. However, as Ericsson and Lehmann point out, the fact that someone has put a lot of time into something has a weak correlation with expert performance.[10] The more important factor is what they have called **deliberate practice**: "the individualized training activities especially designed by a coach or teacher to improve specific aspects of an individual's performance through repetition and successive refinement."[11]

Our runner hoping to achieve a six-minute mile will therefore need to engage in deliberate practice in order to develop the necessary stride, to get into physical shape, and to prepare mentally for the challenge. "Practice," as used by Ericsson and his colleagues, is a more literal conception of practice than what we mean when we talk about creative practice. Deliberate practice is one of three kinds of core activities they see practitioners participating in alongside work and play. For them, **work** "includes public performance, competitions, services rendered for pay, and other activities directly motivated by external rewards."[12] **Play**, on the other hand, "includes activities that have no explicit goal and that are inherently enjoyable."[13]

This distinction is often lost in discussions of Ericsson and his colleagues' research. The **deliberate practice** they studied is literally practice: doing scales on a violin, shooting hundreds of shots in basketball practice, or studying chess moves.

For our purposes, deliberate practice is participating in a community of practice while someone skateboards, plays music, cooks, creates documentary radio or animated films, writes novels and short stories, designs toys or installations, makes wine, or performs comedy. The kinds of deliberate practice found in our case studies mostly don't involve coaching in the sense used by Ericsson and his colleagues, and instead involve a more self-directed kind of deliberateness.

In this light, the many hours of deliberate practice don't fully translate to all forms of practice. Yes, Amelia Brodka and Andy Milne participate in this sort of practice-that-isn't-work-or-play (and in a way, so does Matthew Maloney), but this idea doesn't really apply for the other creative practitioners we look at here. To look back at our humble cupcake baker from chapter 2, what would deliberate practice even look like if it wasn't the act of making cupcakes? And how could they possibly log ten thousand hours of cupcake practice without being a professional pastry chef?

It should be noted that more recent studies have not replicated Ericsson, Krampe, and Tesch-Römer's consistent results on deliberate practice, suggesting that practice isolated from other factors—even ten thousand hours' worth—isn't always going to create expertise.[14] And as Ericsson himself has pointed out, his research projects focused on individuals at the very highest end of expertise, and cannot be extrapolated to general application.[15]

So Gladwell's ten thousand hours aren't the silver bullet after all. Still, there are lessons we can glean from Ericsson and his colleagues' research that help us better understand the iterative mindset. For one, Ericsson's research is part of a stream of research investigating the age-old nature-or-nurture debate around expertise.[16] Efforts to quantify the time required suggest that one could earn excellence, rather than be born into it. This idea is related to Carol Dweck's observations of the fixed and incremental mindsets, explored in chapter 2.

Setting Goals to Fail

The creative practitioners in our case studies all share the iterative mindset, even if in radically different ways. They are all reflective practitioners, to use Donald Schön's term, putting into practice the important skills of reflection-in-action (being able to analyze one's performance while it happens) and reflection-on-action (being able to constructively critique one's performance after the fact), discussed in chapter 1. As Ericsson and others have pointed out, after a certain point, rote repetition of a task or exercise isn't going to advance someone's abilities or capacities. Instead, creative practice requires regular assessment of the practitioner's abilities and progress, paired with changes that will continue their development. For our runner, this means bringing variety to their training program. For anyone who's done a "couch to 5K" program, this approach will be familiar: The training starts out slowly with short run-walk intervals, and gradually ramps the runner from no experience up to a full 5-kilometer run.

The example of the runner points to another important aspect of developing a strong creative practice: having goals (or in our vocabulary, beginning with intentions to realize desired and defined outcomes). The point of origin for the mythical ten thousand hours was the achievement of, to use Ericsson, Krampe, and Tesch-Römer's term, "maximal performance."[17] Ericsson and his colleagues' research focused on elite performance by people who are literally the best in the world at whatever they do. This knowledge should temper our expectations and anxieties about what is required to become a reflective practitioner:

> The reason that you must put in ten thousand or more hours of practice to become one of the world's best violinists or chess players or golfers is that the people you are being compared to or competing with have themselves put in ten thousand or more hours of practice. There is no point at which performance maxes out and additional practice does not lead to further improvement. So, yes, if you wish to become one of the best in the world in one of these highly competitive fields, you will need to put in thousands and thousands of hours of hard, focused work just to have a chance of equaling all of those others who have chosen to put in the same sort of work.[18]

The creative practitioners we've discussed in this book are all amazingly talented individuals, no doubt. But to believe in the ten thousand hour rule is to focus on an outlandish intention: becoming the best in the world. While this works for some, setting one's sights on becoming not just a big-C creative (those impossibly genius practitioners discussed back in chapter 1) but *the* big-C creative in a field is to set oneself up for the wrong kind of failure.

Instead, each of the practitioners we interviewed were in process, iterating on themselves and their practice—and over time, learning from failure and success. This is the key to the whole business of iterative creative practices: always trying again, being open to learning from your failures so that you might be that much better when you start the process over. Let's end where we started, with Samuel Beckett's clear-eyed wisdom: "Ever tried. Ever failed. No matter. Try Again. Fail again. Fail better."

Beckett's prose encapsulates the iterative mindset better than anything else we've seen. We love his grim positivity—there's no shame in failure. Let's all keep failing until we see failure in a new light—as something we can always do better, not something to be avoided.

Fail better, indeed.

Postscript: Iterating on *Iterate*

After more than seven years of talking to a wide array of creative people—some of whom are included in this book—we learned something: Everyone iterates. Just as important, everyone iterates differently. In that spirit, we tried to find commonalities and distinctions in our case studies, and through the framework of our five approaches and ten perspectives.

Indeed, this book was an iterative project in itself.

The process began in 2011 with a conversation about iteration. We both had encountered a few different iterative methodologies in our own practices and through teaching, but they all seemed to be focused on problem solving, innovation, or mitigating complexities in software usage. We knew there had to be more iterative practices out there, but we hadn't really heard of many other fields that embrace the term. So we set about by identifying the different perspectives on iteration we knew about, or had an inkling must exist out there somewhere (material and reflective, targeted and exploratory, methodological and improvisational, internal and external, convergent and divergent). We would often start with one, say, "convergent," and then ask ourselves: What's a totally different angle on iteration from convergent? From that question we would come up with its opposite partner, "divergent." It was an odd strategy to identify the perspectives first—akin to mapping a territory we hadn't yet visited—but it helped us think about fields and practitioners we might not have thought of otherwise.

With our list of perspectives in hand, we made a list of creative practitioners whose processes felt in the least bit connected to iteration. We then organized these folks using our list of perspectives. From there, we began to talk to the practitioners to find out how they approached failure and iteration in their work. Many on our list at this stage were game designers.

We began to see a lot of similarity in the game designers' use of iteration, so we broadened our list to include a much wider assortment of practices. As we talked to practitioners, we returned to our lists, adding new people, moving people around from perspective to perspective—at times after an interview where we had discovered new perspectives we hadn't thought of before. We made revisions to the perspective to accommodate new things we discovered.

After a couple of years of slow but steady work on the project, we had homed in on our five approaches and ten perspectives on iteration. We eventually landed on a diverse range of fields that helped us tease out the broader uses of iterative processes: skateboarding, animation, radio journalism, comedy, the culinary arts, toy design, architecture and game design, contemporary art, winemaking, and jazz. By picking creative fields that haven't received as much attention from design studies, psychology, and engineering, we hoped we could discover a broader set of creative practices, and learn more about how other creative fields think about and address failure through iteration.

For each of our five approaches, we picked two creative practitioners, one for each perspective. For example, after speaking to architect Nathalie Pozzi and game designer Eric Zimmerman, we learned they used a very consistent methodology across their projects. Thus, methodological processes became a pole at one end of the process-focused approach. We hypothesized: If there are methodological processes, there must be an opposite perspective at the other end of the process approach. This led us to look around to see if there were creatives with improvisational processes. This search led us to jazz musician Andy Milne, and the solidification of methodological and improvisational processes as two different perspectives.

We began looking closely at what, exactly, goes on during creative practices approached with an iterative mindset. We started conducting the more formal interviews from which many of the quotes in this book are pulled, and that are available as videos on iterateproject.com. As we conducted these interviews, we continued to revisit our framework to integrate our findings. Toward the end of the interviewing process, we began to more fully scour the design, psychology, sociology, and education literature to see how these fields studied the phenomena of creativity, failure, and iteration. This research helped guide our construction of the five approaches, and helped shape the ideas explored in section I.

One unifying topic we asked creative practitioners about was their relationship to failure. Some were uncomfortable broaching the subject of failure. This isn't a surprise, considering the vulnerability required to really confront failure. Others were more open to thinking about it. A few had a hard time calling failure "failure"—viewing it instead as a natural occurrence without the negative connotations with which the concept is typically ascribed. The practitioners represented in the book were all definitely thinking about failure, even when they didn't use the "f word" themselves.

We've tried to use the clearest possible language to describe things, to locate the right points of emphasis, and so on. We spent long hours debating terminology, wrote each other excited texts about a new reference, and at times, worked alone in the wee hours to try to make sense of it all. It wasn't until pretty late in the process that we finalized our framework for iterative practice and its relationship to creativity and failure.

Our attempts to bring clarity to our investigations of nuanced material were not without their challenges. When we presented our framework at a conference several years before writing this book, we were met with a confusing mix of skepticism and excitement. Some of our peers loved the fact that we were exploding the one-size-fits-all approach to iterative design propagated in game design circles. Others were concerned that we were presenting too many varied approaches to iterative design, complicating the simplicity of the model they were used to teaching and practicing. And even more were worried that our framework came across as a comprehensive map of the entire territory of creative practice—which it most certainly is not.

Finally, as we began writing, we heard the same question arise from peers we talked with, and, as is the tradition with a book of this type, from anonymous reviewers who read the draft: Is this journalism or scholarship? People's opinions about this varied with their field—design researchers tended to think the book was journalism, while journalists and creative practitioners tended to view it as scholarship. We spent a lot of time trying to strike a balance between the two. We wanted to present these case studies as primary sources, individuals with their own unique perspectives on creativity. At the same time, we felt the need to ground our three primary concepts, creativity, failure and iteration, with the work of those who have studied these ideas closely. Indeed, the entire first section of the book is a response to feedback from scholars looking for more substantial research, while the "casual reader" tone of the case studies was honed to make sure the core of the book was as accessible as possible. Accessible, and academic—two characteristics that aren't always found in tandem, but we hope we struck a good balance between the two.

The diagrams and illustrations that populate the book were equally challenging. We spent literally years talking about approaches, even holding a "diagram jam" with students at Parsons. We wanted to find ways to visualize complex ideas in an approachable way. We experimented with different examples to illustrate our points, eventually landing on the cupcakes, business cards, yard sale poster, chairs, and toothbrushes created by Steven Davis and Yu Jen Chen. A similar process unfolded for the diagrams, with Carla Molins Pitarch and Tuba Ozkan going through many examples before landing on the simple building blocks and "meeples" approach. We're happy with where the imagery ended up, but if we had more time, we'd probably go through even more rounds of iteration to get it right!

All of this is to say, we wrote this book using an iterative process. It started out with a very targeted intention—to explore the breadth of iterative creative practices in order to develop a theory of iteration. Not unlike *Radiolab*'s targeted intention—make "something different" in the world of radio science journalism—we had only the vaguest notion of what form our theories of iteration would take. If we were to look back through the various drafts of this manuscript, we'd find all sorts of fits and starts around terminology, additions and subtractions of supporting arguments from the scholarly literature, rearrangements of the table of contents, and so on. But with each pass, we got closer to understanding our initial intention, and were able to more fully home in on our target.

Our process? Well, let's be charitable and call it improvisational after a methodological start. We'd written another book together,[1] but this project was very different in subject and form, so our instincts and expectations on the best process didn't always pan out. We talked a lot—among ourselves, with our research assistants at Parsons (who so charitably read early iterations of this book), with the creative practitioners in our case studies, with others who didn't end up in the book or on the website, with students in our classes.

More than anything, we wrote a lot, and then edited even more. This material iteration—words to paper—was really how we figured things out. One of us would write something—say, this chapter—and the other would then come back through to see if things were making sense or not. Pretty much every sentence in this book had no less than five edit passes *before* we handed the manuscript over to the editorial team at the MIT Press. Some passages have been revised dozens of times as we've worked through our ideas.

The accompanying video interviews found on the website were a whole other bundle of challenges. We had our basic framework in place, but were just getting into the work of carefully analyzing the ten practitioners. Though we left our questions out of the final versions, you can likely read between the lines to hear what we were asking. Often, our ideas about a given practitioner would change radically after talking to them. And then again after we drafted their case study. We also bit off more than we could comfortably chew with the videos—the short animations accompanying each topic proved to be too much within the constraints of the research grant that funded the series, causing things to move far more slowly than we had hoped.

One thing for certain: Our process was steeped in evaluation. Of course, there was an incredible amount of internal evaluation between the two of us, but also by each of us alone. (Perhaps someday we'll release a deep-cuts version with the twenty thousand words—roughly a quarter of this book—that ended up on the cutting room floor.) As we continued to work, we shared our framework with others to see if it was making sense, and to solicit ideas for iterative practices we had overlooked. In other words, we asked for a critique. Early in the project, we taught a course for Colleen's Parsons students and John's at Georgia Tech that workshopped our basic framework, and investigated the challenges of transposing one person's creative process onto another person's practice. We ran a couple of workshops and gave several talks that explored the in-progress material. The Parsons grad students who created the diagrams and illustrations were an incredibly important sounding board. If they couldn't make sense of the ideas, or struggled to find ways to visualize concepts and contexts, then we knew there was still work to do. And of course, this being a book published by a university press, we underwent two rounds of anonymous peer review— once for our proposal for the book, and another on a full draft manuscript (when the "journalism or scholarship?" question came to a head). We had the case study subjects review drafts, which yielded all sorts of helpful feedback on content and form.

All the forms of feedback we received during our research, writing, and teaching brought us back to our framework and our conceptions of creativity, failure, and iteration. We've revised our terminology more times than we care to remember as we strove to find clarity. We hope we've found the right balance between easily understood concepts and the nuanced realities of iterative practice.

This project was also divergent in its outcomes. Our intention from the outset was to write a book. But along the way, we ended up designing and running a course at two universities, using the framework to inform the curriculum in the program we teach, giving a number of talks, writing a book on game design, developing some workshops, releasing a video series, and finally writing this book. We hope we arrived at something that synthesizes observation, theory, and practice. It was challenging, but looking back through the process, we think we ended up failing better at describing the elusive and myriad things that are part of the creative process.

However, as we write this, the process is not over. It's up to you to integrate what you will into your own process. We hope this book provides an opportunity for reflection on your practice as a reflective practitioner. And ultimately, we hope you find it useful the next time you fail. Because it's only failure if you stop iterating.

Colleen and John, March 2018

Notes

Section I

1. From Samuel Beckett's novel *Worstward Ho*, in *Nohow On: Company, Ill Seen Ill Said, Worstward Ho* (New York: Grove Press, 1996), 89.

Preface

1. Nick Fortugno in conversation with the authors, May 2018.

2. Ben McAllister, "The 'Science' of Good Design: A Dangerous Idea," *Atlantic*, May 11, 2011, https://www.theatlantic.com/business/archive/2011/05/the-science -of-good-design-a-dangerous-idea/238750/.

3. Nigel Cross, "Designerly Ways of Knowing: Design Discipline versus Design Science," *Design Issues* 17, no. 3 (2001): 49–55.

Chapter 1

1. James Kaufman, *Creativity 101*, 2nd ed. (New York: Springer, 2016), Kindle location 493–547. Kaufman's discussion of the four C's draws on James C. Kaufman and Ronald A. Beghetto, "Beyond Big and Little: The Four C Model of Creativity," *Review of General Psychology* 13, no. 1 (2009): 1–12.

2. "Gnomes," *South Park*, season 2, episode 17 (1998), https://www.youtube.com/ watch?v=tO5sxLapAts.

3. Mark A. Runco, "Introduction to the Special Issue: Commemorating Guilford's 1950 Presidential Address," *Creativity Research Journal* 13, nos. 3–4 (2000–2001): 247.

4. Joy Paul Guilford, "Creativity," *American Psychologist* 5, no. 9 (1950): 444–454.

5. Kaufman, *Creativity 101*, Kindle locations 259–260.

6. David Cropley and Arthur Cropley, "A Psychological Taxonomy of Organizational Innovation: Resolving the Paradoxes," *Creativity Research Journal* 24, no. 1 (2012): 33.

7. Christoph Bartneck, "Notes on Design and Science in the HCI Community," *Design Issues* 25, no. 2 (Spring 2009): 52.

8. Robert Weisberg, "On the Usefulness of 'Value' in the Definition of Creativity," *Creativity Research Journal* 27, no. 2 (2015): 111–124.

9. Anatoliy V. Kharkhurin, "Creativity.4in1: Four-Criterion Construct of Creativity," *Creativity Research Journal* 26, no. 3 (2014): 338–352.

10. Teresa M. Amabile, *Creativity in Context: Update to The Social Psychology of Creativity* (Boulder, CO: Westview Press, 1996), 35.

11. Another concept we borrow from Teresa Amabile (*Creativity in Context*, 35).

12. Ibid., 3.

13. John B. Watson, *Behaviorism* (London: K. Paul, 1928), 198.

14. Graham Wallas, "Stages of Control," in *The Art of Thought* (New York: Harcourt, Brace, 1926).

15. Ibid., 38–39.

16. Pierre Bourdieu, *Pascalian Meditations*, trans. Richard Nice (New York: Polity Press, 2000), 138–141. A helpful overview of creative practice from a design research perspective is found in Lucy Kimbell, "Rethinking Design Thinking: Part II," *Design and Culture* 4, no. 2 (2012): 129–148.

17. Donald A. Schön, *The Reflective Practitioner: How Professionals Think in Action* (New York: Basic Books, 1983).

18. Scott McCloud, "The Six Steps," in *Understanding Comics: The Invisible Art* (New York: HarperPerennial, 1994), 162–184.

19. Jean Lave and Etienne Wenger, *Situated Learning: Legitimate Peripheral Participation* (Cambridge: Cambridge University Press, 1991).

20. Etienne Wenger, *Communities of Practice: Learning, Meaning, and Identity* (Cambridge: Cambridge University Press, 1998).

21. Gloria Dall'Alba, "Learning Professional Ways of Being: Ambiguities of Becoming," in Dall'Alba, ed., *Exploring Education through Phenomenology: Diverse Approaches* (Malden, MA: Wiley-Blackwell, 2009), 41–52.

22. Robin S. Adams, Shanna R. Daly, Llewellyn M. Mann, and Gloria Dall'Alba, "Being a Professional: Three Lenses into Design Thinking, Acting, and Being," *Design Studies* 32, no. 6 (2011): 590.

23. bell hooks, *Teaching Critical Thinking: Practical Wisdom* (New York: Routledge, 2010), 185.

Chapter 2

1. Jesper Juul, *The Art of Failure: An Essay on the Pain of Playing Video Games* (Cambridge, MA: MIT Press, 2013), 15.

2. Richard DeDomenici, "Embracing Failure," in Nicole Antebi, Colin Dickey, and Robby Herbst, eds., *Failure! Experiments in Aesthetic and Social Practices* (Los Angeles: Journal of Aesthetics and Protest Press, 2008), 83–84.

3. Judith [now Jack] Halberstam, *The Queer Art of Failure* (Durham: Duke University Press, 2011), 3.

4. "Failure Now an Option," *The Onion*, January 16, 2008.

5. Henry Petroski, *To Forgive Design: Understanding Failure* (Cambridge, MA: Belknap Press of Harvard University Press, 2012), 45. Petroski generally focuses on engineering in his work, thus the emphasis on technology.

6. Adrian Heathfield, "Introduction to the Launch of the Institute of Failure," transcript from a talk given at the launch event for the Institute of Failure (London), 2001, http://www.institute-of-failure.com/adrianIntro.html.

7. Kathryn Schulz, *Being Wrong: Adventures in the Margin of Error* (New York: Ecco Press, 2010).

8. Amy C. Edmondson, "Strategies for Learning from Failure," *Harvard Business Review*, April 2011, https://hbr.org/2011/04/strategies-for-learning-from-failure.

9. Ibid.

10. Mark D. Cannon and Amy C. Edmondson, "Learning from Failure," in Norbert M. Seel, ed., *Encyclopedia of the Sciences of Learning* (New York: Springer, 2012), 1859. A more detailed discussion is found in Cannon and Edmondson, "Failing to Learn and Learning to Fail (Intelligently): How Great Organizations Put Failure to Work to Improve and Innovate," *Long Range Planning* 38, no. 3 (June 2005): 299–319.

11. Christopher G. Myers, Bradley R. Staats, and Francesca Gino, "'My Bad!' How Internal Attribution and Ambiguity of Responsibility Affect Learning from Failure," working paper, Harvard Business School, April 18, 2014.

12. Carol S. Dweck, *Mindset: The New Psychology of Success* (New York: Random House, 2006), chapter 1: "The Mindsets."

13. Cannon and Edmondson, "Learning from Failure," 1859.

14. Matthew Sandler, "Gertrude Stein, Success Manuals, and Failure Studies," *Twentieth-Century Literature* 63, no. 2 (June 2017): 193–194.

15. Ibid., 194.

16. Ibid., 195.

17. Sidney Dekker, *Drift into Failure: From Hunting Broken Components to Understanding Complex Systems* (Farnham, UK: Ashgate, 2011), 2.

Chapter 3

1. Katie Salen-Tekinbas and Eric Zimmerman, *Rules of Play: Game Design Fundamentals* (Cambridge, MA: MIT Press, 2003), 168.

2. For a more complete look at game design as an iterative process, see Colleen Macklin and John Sharp, *Games, Design and Play: A Detailed Approach to Iterative Game Design* (Boston: Addison-Wesley, 2016).

3. Craig Larman and Victor R. Basili, "Iterative and Incremental Development: A Brief History," *Computer* 36, no. 5 (June 2003): 2–3.

4. Richard Feynman, introduction to lecture 2, "Basic Physics," in *The Feynman Lectures on Physics*, vol. 1 (New York: Basic Books, 2010).

5. Stephanie Houde and Charles Hill, "What Do Prototypes Prototype?," in Martin G. Helander et al., eds., *Handbook of Human-Computer Interaction* (Amsterdam: Elsevier, 1997), 367–382. A meta-overview of prototyping within the design literature is found in section 1 of Maria C. Yang, "A Study of Prototypes, Design Activity, and Design Outcome," *Design Studies* 26, no. 6 (October 2005): 649–669.

6. As in Malcolm Gladwell, "The Bakeoff: Competing to Create the Ultimate Cookie," *New Yorker*, September 5, 2005, 124–130.

7. We first encountered the term in Michael Mumford's "Creative Abilities: Divergent Thinking," in Mumford, ed., *Handbook of Organizational Creativity* (New York: Academic Press, 2012), 125–126. Mumford cites Guilford and Hoepfner, *The Analysis of Intelligence* (New York: McGraw-Hill, 1971), 149.

8. Mumford, "Creative Abilities: Divergent Thinking," 126.

9. Pradip N. Khandwalla, "An Exploratory Investigation of Divergent Thinking through Protocol Analysis," *Creativity Research Journal* 6 (1993): 241–259.

10. Gerard J. Puccio and John F. Cabra, "Idea Generation and Idea Evaluation: Cognitive Skills and Deliberate Practices," in Mumford, *Handbook of Organizational Creativity*, 207.

11. Alicia von Stamwitz, "If Only We Would Listen: Parker J. Palmer on What We Could Learn about Politics, Faith and Each Other," *The Sun*, no. 443 (November 2012), https://thesunmagazine.org/issues/443/if_only_we_would_listen.

12. Jamer Hunt, "Among Six Types of Failure, Only a Few Help You Innovate," *Fast Company*, June 27, 2011, https://www.fastcodesign.com/1664360/among-six-types -of-failure-only-a-few-help-you-innovate, accessed January 30, 2018.

Chapter 4

1. Unless otherwise noted, quotes relating to the case studies are from interviews with the authors.

2. John Maeda, "The Bermuda Quadrilateral (2006)," November 14, 2017, https:// maeda.pm/2017/11/14/the-bermuda-quadrilateral-2006/, accessed September 11, 2018.

3. Neri Oxman, "Age of Entanglement," *Journal of Design and Science*, January 13, 2016, https://jods.mitpress.mit.edu/pub/ageofentanglement, accessed September 11, 2018.

4. Ibid.

5. Ibid.

6. Lars Hallnäs, "The Design Research Text and the Poetics of Foundational Definitions," in "Art Text," special issue of *ArtMonitor* 8 (2010): 109.

7. Lucy A. Suchman, *Plans and Situated Actions: The Problem of Human-Machine Communication* (Palo Alto, CA: Xerox Corporation, 1985), 1.

8. Joy Paul Guilford, "The Structure of Intellect," *Psychological Bulletin* 53 (1956): 267–293.

9. Joy Paul Guilford, "Creative Abilities in the Arts," *Psychological Review* 6, no. 2 (1957): 110–118.

10. Guilford, "The Structure of Intellect."

11. Kyna Leski, "Unlearning," in *The Storm of Creativity* (Cambridge, MA: MIT Press, 2015), 11–34.

12. Ibid., 12.

13. Cited in ibid., 13–14.

14. Ibid., 13.

15. Arthur Cropley, "In Praise of Convergent Thinking," *Creativity Research Journal* 18, no. 3 (2006): 391–404.

Chapter 5

1. Carrie Coolidge, "Colgin Cellars: Superb Wines with an Excellent Return on Investment," *Forbes*, October 17, 2011, https://www.forbes.com/sites/carriecoolidge/

2011/10/17/colgin-cellars-superb-wines-with-an-excellent-return-on-investment/
#3a4d54ee6cb8.

2. Patrick E. McGovern, *Uncorking the Past: The Quest for Wine, Beer, and Other Alcoholic Beverages* (Berkeley: University of California Press, 2009), 9, 225.

3. Unless otherwise noted, quotes are from interviews with the authors.

4. Quoted in Coolidge, "Colgin Cellars."

5. Masanobu Fukuoka, *The One-Straw Revolution: An Introduction to Natural Farming* (New York: New York Review Books, 2010), 110–113.

6. "2011 Vintage Report: California," *Wine Spectator*, November 17, 2011, https://
www.winespectator.com/webfeature/show/id/46008

7. Quoted in ibid.

8. Donald A. Schön, *The Reflective Practitioner: How Professionals Think in Action* (New York: Basic Books, 1983).

9. Dan Ariely, "What Makes Us Feel Good about Our Work?," TEDxRiodelaPlata, recorded October 2012, https://www.ted.com/talks/dan_ariely_what_makes_us_feel
_good_about_our_work/transcript?language=en.

10. "2011 Vintage Report: California."

11. Robert Parker, "Colgin," *Robert Parker's Wine Advocate*, no. 209 (October 2013): 19–20.

12. Eric Asimov, "Napa Cabernets from a Cold, Wet Year," *New York Times*, April 14, 2014, https://www.nytimes.com/2014/04/16/dining/napa-cabernets-from-a-cold-wet
-year.html?mcubz=0.

Chapter 6

1. Unless otherwise noted, quotes are from interviews with the authors.

2. David Mamet, *On Directing Film* (New York: Penguin, 1992), 7.

3. Andrey Tarkovsky, *Sculpting in Time* (Austin: University of Texas Press, 1989), 40.

4. Joseph Campbell, *The Hero with a Thousand Faces* (New York: Pantheon Books, 1949).

5. Matthew Maloney, "Here Goes Nothing," *Angry Animation* blog, March 9, 2012, https://angry-animation.com/2012/03/09/hello-world/, accessed January 18, 2018.

Chapter 7

1. Quoted in "Sound and Science with Jad Abumrad," *Poptech*, December 1, 2010, https://www.youtube.com/watch?v=ILZYGrRlQkI, accessed January 31, 2018.

2. Robert Krulwich, "Speech to the Chamber Music Society of America," January 5, 2018, transcript provided by Krulwich.

3. Unless otherwise noted, quotes are from interviews with the authors.

4. Krulwich, "Speech to the Chamber Music Society of America."

5. "Sound and Science with Jad Abumrad."

6. Rebecca Solnit, *A Field Guide to Getting Lost* (New York: Viking, 2005), 5.

7. Krulwich, "Speech to the Chamber Music Society of America."

8. Maddie Oatman, "Radiolab's Jad Abumrad Tries Something Completely Nuts," *Mother Jones*, July/August 2012, https://www.motherjones.com/media/2012/05/jad-abumrad-radiolab-robert-krulwich-in-the-dark.

9. "Jad Abumrad," *Design and Failure*, December 3, 2015, http://www.designandfailure.com/jad-abumrad/.

10. "Jad and Robert: The Early Years," *Radiolab*, May 6, 2008, https://www.radiolab.org/story/91820-jad-and-robert-the-early-years/.

11. Ben Crandall, "Blinded by Science? Fear Not, Say the Creators of 'Radiolab.' You Don't Have to Know Anything, Because They Don't Know Anything," *South Florida Sun-Sentinel*, January 27, 2012.

12. "Radiolab (WNYC-FM)," Peabody Foundation website, 2010, http://www.peabodyawards.com/award-profile/radiolab, accessed March 3, 2018.

13. "Jad Abumrad, Radio Host and Producer," MacArthur Foundation website, September 20, 2011, https://www.macfound.org/fellows/1/, accessed March 3, 2018.

14. "Radiolab's Jad Abumrad on Creativity, Failure and the Virtues of Wonder," *Radiowaves* podcast, December 12, 2014, accessed September 3, 2018.

15. Ibid.

16. "Jad Abumrad: Embrace the 'Gut Churn' of the Creative Process," *99U* podcast, 2012, https://www.youtube.com/watch?v=8OH9p3hnWCY, accessed September 3, 2018.

17. Jad talks about this assignment in "Radiolab's Jad Abumrad on Creativity, Failure and the Virtues of Wonder," as well as in a talk: "These Are a Few of Jad Abumrad's Favorite Things," Third Coast Conference, 2012, https://soundcloud.com/thirdcoast/special-feature-jad-abumrad-at.

18. He has discussed this numerous times, including in his 2015 interview on *Radio-waves* and in his 2012 Third Coast Conference talk.

19. "These Are a Few of Jad Abumrad's Favorite Things," 2012 Third Coast Conference.

20. The story is recounted, and the segment played, in "Jad and Robert: The Early Years."

21. A great synthesis of this process is found in *American Hipster*'s video on *Radiolab*, "Radiolab: Audio Learning and Augmented Narrative," http://americanhipsterpresents.com/#radiolab, accessed March 3, 2018.

22. Typically, the hosts are Jad and Robert, but on occasion one of them is replaced by another staff member or, more rarely, by someone from outside *Radiolab*.

23. Originally broadcast February 4, 2005.

24. "Robert Krulwich," *Radiowaves* podcast, March 4, 2015, https://www.youtube.com/watch?v=4QkOZv2aJQs, accessed March 3, 2018.

25. Jad Abumrad, "How Radio Creates Empathy," *Big Think*, http://bigthink.com/videos/how-radio-creates-empathy, accessed March 3, 2018.

26. "Radiolab," *Charlie Rose*, January 2, 2013, https://charlierose.com/videos/17886, accessed March 3, 2018.

27. "Radiolab: Audio Learning and Augmented Narrative."

Chapter 8

1. William Grimes, "Chef's Second Course Is Food for Thought," *New York Times*, June 18, 2003.

2. Wylie Dufresne interviewed by Max Miller, "Better Cooking through Chemistry," Big Think video, August 6, 2010, http://bigthink.com/videos/better-cooking-through-chemistry, accessed July 25, 2018.

3. "Big Think Interview with Wylie Dufresne," Big Think, August 6, 2010, http://bigthink.com/videos/big-think-interview-with-wylie-dufresne, accessed March 3, 2018.

4. Rob Patronite and Robin Raisfeld, "Wylie Dufresne Debuts Egg Sandwich Like No Other at Du's Donuts," *Grubstreet*, June 12, 2017, http://www.grubstreet.com/2017/06/wylie-dufresne-debuts-egg-sandwich-at-dus-donuts-and-coffee.html, accessed March 3, 2018.

5. Robin Raisfeld and Rob Patronite, "He Is the Egg Man," *New York Magazine*, November 26, 2007, http://nymag.com/restaurants/features/30007/, accessed March 3, 2018.

6. Laura Neilson, "Plate Deconstruction: WD~50's Scrambled Egg Ravioli," *Food Republic*, August 16, 2012, http://www.foodrepublic.com/2012/08/16/plate -deconstruction-wd50s-scrambled-egg-ravioli/, accessed March 3, 2018.

7. Wylie Dufresne, interviewed by Max Miller, "Which Tastes Better: Peanut Butter or Caviar?," Big Think, August 6, 2010, http://bigthink.com/videos/which-tastes -better-caviar-or-peanut-butter, accessed March 3, 2018.

8. "Dufresne Prepares End of NYC Modernist Mecca," *New York Times*, September 30, 2014, https://www.nytimes.com/reuters/2014/09/30/us/30reuters-world-chefs -dufresne.html, accessed March 3, 2018.

9. All from the restaurant's tenth-anniversary menu from April 9, 2013, posted on the blog *Happy Noms* by Victor and Monte, https://happynoms.com/2013/04/10/ nyc-wd50-apr-2013-10th-anniversary-dinner/, accessed March 3, 2018.

10. Julia Moskin, "Time to Face the Music," *New York Times*, February 26, 2003, https://www.nytimes.com/2003/02/26/dining/time-to-face-the-music.html

11. Unless otherwise noted, quotes are from interviews with the authors.

12. At Alder, they used the cloud to store recipes, notes, and ideas.

13. Jocelyn Noveck, "Food World's 'Mad Scientist' Dufresne Ponders Next Steps," Willoughby, OH *News-Herald*, May 15, 2015, http://www.news-herald.com/article/ HR/20150515/NEWS/150519655, accessed March 3, 2018.

Chapter 9

1. Unless otherwise noted, quotes are from interviews with the authors.

2. Quoted in Michael Brown, "The Rules of the Playground Have Changed: Taking Time with Sissyfight Designer Eric Zimmerman," Polygon, May 28, 2013, https:// www.polygon.com/features/2013/5/28/4363458/eric-zimmerman-sissyfight-2000.

3. Katie Salen-Tekinbas and Eric Zimmerman, *Rules of Play: Game Design Fundamentals* (Cambridge, MA: MIT Press, 2003).

4. Mark Donald Gross, "Design as Exploring Constraints" (Ph.D. dissertation, Massachusetts Institute of Technology, 1986).

5. See Salen-Tekinbas and Zimmerman, *Rules of Play*.

6. Lara Sedbon, "Art, Architecture, and Gaming Meet in Interference: Q&A with Eric Zimmerman and Nathalie Pozzi," *Vice Creators Project*, July 19, 2012, https://creators .vice.com/en_us/article/4x4jgb/art-architecture-and-gaming-meet-in-iinterferencei -qa-with-eric-zimmerman-and-nathalie-pozzi.

7. Architectural historian Iain Borden provides a fascinating example of the relationships between play and architecture in *Skateboarding, Space and the City: Architecture and the Body* (Oxford, UK: Berg, 2001).

8. Colleen Macklin and John Sharp, *Games, Design and Play: A Detailed Approach to Iterative Game Design* (Boston, MA: Addison-Wesley Professional, 2016).

9. Jorge Luis Borges, "On Exactitude in Science," in *A Universal History of Infamy*, trans. Norman Thomas di Giovanni (Harmondsworth, UK: Penguin, 1985), 131.

Chapter 10

1. Steve Coleman, "What Is M-Base?," Steve Coleman, http://m-base.com/what-is-m-base/, accessed March 1, 2018.

2. Andy Milne, "About," Andy Milne, https://andymilne.com/about-2/, accessed February 26, 2018.

3. LaMont Hamilton, *"Five on the Black Hand Side*: Origins and Evolutions of the Dap," *Smithsonian Center for Folklife and Cultural Heritage Magazine*, September 22, 2014, https://www.folklife.si.edu/talkstory/2014/five-on-the-black-hand-sideorigins-and-evolutions-of-the-dap.

4. Unless otherwise noted, quotes are from interviews with the authors.

5. Wynton Marsalis, "Marsalis: Racism and Greed Put Blues at the Back of the Bus," *CNN* online, October 24, 2009, http://www.cnn.com/2009/OPINION/10/24/wynton.marsalis.blues.race/.

6. Christian Blauvelt, "The Mysterious Origins of Jazz," *BBC* website, February 24, 2017, http://www.bbc.com/culture/story/20170224-the-mysetrious-origins-of-jazz.

7. *MacGyver* "pilot," directed by Jerrold Freedman, written by Thackary Pallor, *ABC*, September 29, 1985.

8. Bryony Gordon, "Paul Merton: Why Tories Make the Best TV Presenters," *Telegraph*, May 23, 2011, https://www.telegraph.co.uk/culture/comedy/8526040/Paul-Merton-Why-Tories-make-the-best-TV-presenters.html.

9. Marsalis, "Marsalis: Racism and Greed Put Blues at the Back of the Bus."

10. Quoted in Calvin Wilson, "Roscoe Mitchell Is a True Jazz Great," *St. Louis Post-Dispatch*, December 5, 2014, https://www.stltoday.com/entertainment/music/roscoe-mitchell-is-a-true-jazz-great/article_62c7125b-c299-50b2-853c-b8000a0ba3c0.html.

11. Marsalis, "Marsalis: Racism and Greed Put Blues at the Back of the Bus."

12. "Andy Milne: Dreams and False Alarms," *Songlines*, http://songlines.com/release/dreams-and-false-alarms/, accessed February 26, 2018.

13. You can hear an excerpt on Andy's site (or listen to the full track via your favorite music streaming service): https://andymilne.com/music/dreams-and-false-alarms/track/message-in-a-bottle/.

14. Gary Sperrazza (paraphrasing Martin Mull), "Holding On: Original Soul Men," *Time Barrier Express: The Rock & Roll History Magazine,* September-October 1979.

Chapter 11

1. "Skating" is the shorthand term for skateboarding used by people in the skateboarding community.

2. Amelia Brodka, *Underexposed* documentary, https://ameliabrodka.com/underexposed-documentary/, accessed July 27, 2018.

3. Unless otherwise noted, quotes are from interviews with the authors.

4. Mihaly Csikszentmihalyi, *Flow: The Psychology of Optimal Experience* (New York: Harper Perennial, 2008).

5. Malcolm Gladwell, "The Physical Genius," *New Yorker,* August 2, 1999, https://www.newyorker.com/magazine/1999/08/02/the-physical-genius.

6. A very clear explanation of the trick can be found in Braille Skateboarding's "How to Frontside 5-0 the Easiest Way Tutorial," Youtube, March 16, 2013, https://www.youtube.com/watch?v=34QjuFBjYGc.

Chapter 12

1. Quoted in David Kaufman and the U.S. Digital Service, "The Unlikely Relationship between Comedy and Code: A Conversation with Baratunde Thurston," Medium, July 14, 2016, https://medium.com/the-u-s-digital-service/the-unlikely-relationship-between-comedy-and-code-a-conversation-with-baratunde-thurston-6253a38b81b.

2. Ibid.

3. Ryan and Tina Essmaker, "Baratunde Thurston: Comedian, Entrepreneur, Writer," *The Great Discontent,* December 3, 2013, http://thegreatdiscontent.com/interview/baratunde-thurston.

4. Baratunde Thurston, *How to Be Black* (New York: Harper, 2012), 12.

5. Baratunde Thurston, "Why Life Is a Scam," *Harvard Crimson,* April 6, 1999, https://www.thecrimson.com/article/1999/4/6/why-life-is-a-scam-ibaratunde/.

6. "Baratunde Thurston," *Medium,* June 28, 2017, https://noteworthy.medium.com/baratunde-thurston-e60e99d2966.

7. Ibid.

8. Will Rogers, quoted in Jonathan Schwartz, "Will Rogers, Populist Cowboy," review of *Will Rogers: A Political Life*, by Richard D. White Jr., *New York Times*, March 25, 2011, https://www.nytimes.com/2011/03/27/books/review/book-review -will-rogers-a-political-life-by-richard-d-white-jr.html.

9. Unless otherwise noted, quotes are from interviews with the authors.

10. M. P. Mulder, "Humour Research: State of the Art," Center for Telematics and Information Technology, TKI-Parlevink Research Group, University of Twente, The Netherlands, 2002, http://www.ub.utwente.nl/webdocs/ctit/1/0000009e.pdf, accessed March 1, 2018.

11. Baratunde Thurston, "In 1993, This Is What I Wrote about the Internet Coming to My High School," Medium, July 2, 2015, https://medium.com/@baratunde/in -1993-this-is-what-i-wrote-about-the-internet-coming-to-my-high-school -28be8bcfdaf8.

12. "Baratunde Thurston," Medium.

13. Baratunde Thurston, "About," Baratunde Thurston, http://baratunde.com/ about/, accessed February 26, 2018.

14. Baratunde Thurston, "Occupy Sparkle: The Full 'Box Set' of My Twilight #Livehatetweeting," Baratunde Thurston, November 16, 2012, http://baratunde .com/blog/2012/11/16/occupy-sparkle-the-full-box-set-of-my-twilight-livehatetweet .html.

15. Baratunde Thurston, "#Unplug: Baratunde Thurston Left the Internet for 25 Days, and You Should, Too," *Fast Company*, June 17, 2013.

16. We use the term "externalize" to describe the process Baratunde uses to externally evaluate his work through a transposition of the source or over a period of time. We don't mean "externalize" in the Freudian sense.

17. Chris Crawford, "Fundamentals of Interactivity," *Journal of Computer Game Design* 7 (1993–1994), http://www.erasmatazz.com/library/the-journal-of-computer/ jcgd-volume-7/fundamentals-of-interactivi.html, accessed February 26, 2018.

Chapter 13

1. "Failure Now an Option," *The Onion*, January 16, 2008, https://www.theonion .com/article/failure-now-an-option-2364.

2. Unless otherwise noted, quotes are from interviews with the authors.

3. As of the writing of this book.

4. Cas Holman, "Cas Holman; Identity in Play," video by Jason Greene, published January 23, 2015, https://www.youtube.com/watch?v=IL1n6LuUIcQ.

5. Shoham Arad, "Three Keys to Creative Kid Design, from the Creator of High Line Playground," *Fast Company*, August 16, 2011, https://www.fastcodesign.com/1664804/three-keys-to-creative-kid-design-from-the-creator-of-high-line-playground

6. Brian Sutton-Smith, *Toys as Culture* (New York: Gardner Press, 1986), 145.

7. Cas Holman, "The Case for Letting Kids Design Their Own Play," *Fast Company*, July 13, 2015, https://www.fastcodesign.com/3048508/the-case-for-letting-kids-design-their-own-play.

8. "Rigamajig," Kaboom!, https://kaboom.org/resources/rigamajig, accessed March 1, 2018.

9. "Queering Space," exhibition at Yale School of Art, October 2016, http://art.yale.edu/Queeringspace.

10. Henry Dreyfuss, *Designing for People* (New York: Simon and Schuster, 1955), 24.

11. Ibid., 20.

12. Arad, "Three Keys to Creative Kid Design."

13. Arthur Cropley, "In Praise of Convergent Thinking," *Creativity Research Journal* 18, no. 3 (2006): 391–404.

Chapter 14

1. Unless otherwise noted, quotes are from interviews with the authors.

2. "Learning to Love You More," http://www.learningtoloveyoumore.com, accessed January 31, 2018. As of 2010, this work is in the collection of the San Francisco Museum of Modern Art, where it exists as an archive.

3. Quoted in Ruby Russell, "Learning to Love You More: Spread a Little Love," *Telegraph*, January 14, 2009, https://www.telegraph.co.uk/culture/art/4238338/Learning-to-Love-You-More-spread-a-little-love.html, accessed March 3, 2018.

4. Video of the reading and subsequent Q&A is at Rhizome, "Seven on Seven 2016: Miranda July and Paul Ford," Vimeo, May 18, 2016, https://vimeo.com/167171454, accessed August 2, 2018.

5. A description of the experience from an audience member's perspective: Whitney Mallett, "Miranda July and Paul Ford Cyberstalked Me," Vice Motherboard, May 18, 2016, http://motherboard.vice.com/en_us/article/miranda-july-and-paul-ford-cyberstalked-me.

6. Somebody: A Messaging App by Miranda July, August 28, 2014–October 31, 2015, http://somebodyapp.com, accessed August 2, 2018.

7. A useful discussion of the design and implementation challenges for an app like this are touched upon in Joe Berkowitz's "Why Miranda July Created 'Somebody'— An App That Sends Strangers to Deliver Messages," *Fast Company*, August 29, 2014.

8. July set up a Tumblr to capture stories about Somebody usage: http://somebodyapp.tumblr.com.

9. Don Aucoin, "Discovering the Possibilities of 'Society,'" *Boston Globe*, October 6, 2013, https://www.bostonglobe.com/arts/theater-art/2013/10/06/discovering -possibilities-society-with-miranda-july/M3KMpTh73A15c230duxkIO/story.html.

10. "Miranda July's New Society," *Frieze*, https://frieze.com/media/miranda-julys -new-society.

11. Yes, she paid for the items, but she didn't take them (mentioned in "Miranda July: It Chooses You," interview with Joshuah Bearman, Library Foundation of Los Angeles's *ALOUDla* series, Q&A, November 29, 2011, https://vimeo.com/ 33785017).

12. Ibid.

13. Ibid.

14. Ibid.

15. Also discussed in ibid.

16. Ibid.

17. The project's full name is: Artangel and Miranda July present Norwood Jewish Charity Shop, London Buddhist Centre Charity Shop & Spitalfields Crypt Trust Charity Shop in solidarity with Islamic Relief Charity Shop at Selfridges.

18. Discussed in "Miranda July in conversation with Jeremy Deller," *Vimeo* video, October 20, 2017, https://vimeo.com/239133702.

19. Ibid.

20. Ibid.

21. Alex F. Osborne, *Applied Imagination: Principles and Procedures of Creative Problem Solving*, rev. ed. (New York: Charles Scribner's Sons, 1979).

Chapter 15

1. Originally stated at the 1952 Woodstock Arts Conference in slightly different phrasing, later polished into this gem.

2. Denise Gonzales Crisp, "'Splainin' Craft: Bringing the Making into Writing," *Design and Culture* 6, no. 3 (2014): 413–422.

3. Purdie explains the "Purdie Shuffle" in this video: https://www.youtube.com/watch?v=T1j1_aeK6WA.

4. Gonzales Crisp, "'Splainin' Craft," 416.

5. Henry Petroski, *Success through Failure: The Paradox of Design* (Princeton, NJ: Princeton University Press, 2006), 4–5.

6. Jamer Hunt, "Among Six Types of Failure, Only a Few Help You Innovate," *Fast Company*, June 27, 2011, https://www.fastcodesign.com/1664360/among-six-types -of-failure-only-a-few-help-you-innovate, accessed January 30, 2018.

7. Malcolm Gladwell, *Outliers: The Story of Success* (New York: Back Bay Books, 2011), 35–68.

8. Anders Ericsson and Andreas C. Lehmann, "Expert and Exceptional Performance: Evidence of Maximal Adaptation to Task Constraints," *Annual Review of Psychology* 47 (February 1996): 273–305.

9. Anders Ericsson, Ralf Th. Krampe, and Clemens Tesch-Römer, "The Role of Deliberate Practice in the Acquisition of Expert Performance," *Psychological Review* 100, no. 3 (1993): 363–403.

10. Ericsson and Lehmann, "Expert and Exceptional Performance," 278.

11. Ibid., 278–279.

12. Ericsson, Krampe, and Tesch-Römer, "The Role of Deliberate Practice," 368.

13. Ibid.

14. Brooke N. Macnamara, David Z. Hambrick, and Frederick L. Oswald, "Deliberate Practice and Performance in Music, Games, Sports, Education, and Professions: A Meta-Analysis," *Psychological Science* 25, no. 8 (2014): 1608–1618; David Z. Hambrick, Frederick L. Oswald, Erik M. Altmann, Elizabeth J. Meinz, Fernand Gobet, and Guillermo Campitelli, "Deliberate Practice: Is That All It Takes to Become an Expert?," *Intelligence* 45 (2014): 34–45; Phillip L. Ackerman, "Facts Are Stubborn Things," *Intelligence* 45 (2014): 104–106; Anique B. H. de Bruin, Ellen M. Kok, Jimmie Leppink, and Gino Camp, "It Might Happen in the Very Beginning: Reply to Ericsson," *Intelligence* 45 (2014): 107–108.

15. Anders Ericsson, "Why Expert Performance Is Special and Cannot Be Extrapolated from Studies of Performance in the General Population: A Response to Criticisms," *Intelligence* 45 (2014): 81–103.

16. Hambrick et al., "Deliberate Practice: Is That All It Takes," 34–35.

17. Ericsson, Krampe, and Tesch-Römer, "The Role of Deliberate Practice," 365.

18. Anders Ericsson and Robert Pool, "Malcolm Gladwell Got Us Wrong: Our Research Was Key to the 10,000-Hour Rule, but Here's What Got Oversimplified," *Salon*, April 10, 2016, https://www.salon.com/2016/04/10/malcolm_gladwell_got_us _wrong_our_research_was_key_to_the_10000_hour_rule_but_heres_what_got _oversimplified/.

Postscript

1. Actually, we wrote that book in the middle of our research process for this book, but don't tell our editor.

Bibliography

Abumrad, Jad. "How Radio Creates Empathy." Big Think. Accessed March 3, 2018. http://bigthink.com/videos/how-radio-creates-empathy.

Abumrad, Jad. "These Are a Few of Jad Abumrad's Favorite Things." Third Coast Conference. 2012. https://soundcloud.com/thirdcoast/special-feature-jad-abumrad-at.

Ackerman, Phillip L. "Facts Are Stubborn Things." *Intelligence* 45 (2014): 104–106.

Adams, Robin S., Shanna R. Daly, Llewellyn M. Mann, and Gloria Dall'Alba. "Being a Professional: Three Lenses into Design Thinking, Acting, and Being." *Design Studies* 32 (6) (2011): 588–607.

ALOUDla. "Miranda July: It Chooses You." Interview with Joshuah Beaman. Vimeo video, November 29, 2011. Accessed January 30, 2018. https://vimeo.com/33785017.

Amabile, Teresa M. Creativity in Context: Update to The Social Psychology of Creativity. Boulder, CO: Westview Press, 1996.

"Andy Milne: Dreams and False Alarms." *Songlines*. Accessed February 26, 2018. http://songlines.com/release/dreams-and-false-alarms/.

Arad, Shoham. "Three Keys to Creative Kid Design, from the Creator of High Line Playground." *Fast Company*, August 16, 2011. https://www.fastcodesign.com/1664804/three-keys-to-creative-kid-design-from-the-creator-of-high-line-playground.

Ariely, Dan. "What Makes Us Feel Good about Our Work?" TEDxRiodelaPlata. Recorded October 2012. https://www.ted.com/talks/dan_ariely_what_makes_us_feel_good_about_our_work/transcript?language=en.

Asimov, Eric. "Napa Cabernets from a Cold, Wet Year." *New York Times*, April 14, 2014. https://www.nytimes.com/2014/04/16/dining/napa-cabernets-from-a-cold-wet-year.html?mcubz=0.

Aucoin, Don. "Discovering the Possibilities of 'Society.'" *Boston Globe*, October 6, 2013. https://www.bostonglobe.com/arts/theater-art/2013/10/06/discovering-possibilities -society-with-miranda-july/M3KMpTh73A15c230duxkIO/story.html.

"Baratunde Thurston." Medium, June 28, 2017. https://noteworthy.medium.com/ baratunde-thurston-e60e99d2966.

Bartneck, Christoph. "Notes on Design and Science in the HCI Community." *Design Issues* 25 (2) (Spring 2009): 46–61.

Beckett, Samuel. Nohow On: Company, Ill See Ill Said, Worstward Ho. New York: Grove Press, 1996.

Berkowitz, Joe. "Why Miranda July Created 'Somebody'—An App That Sends Strangers to Deliver Messages." *Fast Company*, August 29, 2014. https://www.fastcompany .com/3035077/why-miranda-july-created-somebody-an-app-that-sends-strangers -to-deliver-messages.

"Big Think Interview with Wylie Dufresne." Interview by Max Miller. Big Think video, August 6, 2010. Accessed March 3, 2018. http://bigthink.com/videos/big-think -interview-with-wylie-dufresne.

Blauvelt, Christian. "The Mysterious Origins of Jazz." *BBC* website, February 24, 2017. http://www.bbc.com/culture/story/20170224-the-mysetrious-origins-of-jazz.

Borden, Iain. Skateboarding, Space and the City: Architecture and the Body. Oxford, UK: Berg Publishers, 2001.

Borges, Jorge Luis. "On Exactitude in Science." In *A Universal History of Infamy*, trans. Norman Thomas di Giovanni. Harmondsworth, UK: Penguin Books, 1985.

Bourdieu, Pierre. *Pascalian Meditations*. Trans. Richard Nice. New York: Polity Press, 2000.

Braille Skateboarding. "How to Frontside 5-0 the Easiest Way Tutorial." YouTube, March 16, 2013. https://www.youtube.com/watch?v=34QjuFBjYGc.

Brown, Michael. "The Rules of the Playground Have Changed: Taking Time with Sissyfight Designer Eric Zimmerman." *Polygon*, May 28, 2013. https://www.polygon .com/features/2013/5/28/4363458/eric-zimmerman-sissyfight-2000.

Campbell, Joseph. *The Hero with a Thousand Faces*. New York: Pantheon Books, 1949.

Cannon, Mark D., and Amy C. Edmondson. "Failing to Learn and Learning to Fail (Intelligently): How Great Organizations Put Failure to Work to Improve and Innovate." *Long Range Planning* 38 (3) (June 2005): 299–319.

Cannon, Mark D., and Amy C. Edmondson. "Learning from Failure." In *Encyclopedia of the Sciences of Learning*, ed. Norbert M. Seel, 1859–1863. New York: Springer, 2012.

Coleman, Steve. "What Is M-Base?" Steve Coleman website. Accessed March 1, 2018. http://m-base.com/what-is-m-base/.

Coolidge, Carrie. "Colgin Cellars: Superb Wines with an Excellent Return on Investment." *Forbes*, October 10, 2011. https://www.forbes.com/sites/carriecoolidge/2011/10/17/colgin-cellars-superb-wines-with-an-excellent-return-on-investment/#3a4d54ee6cb8.

Crandall, Ben. "Blinded By Science? Fear Not, Say the Creators of 'Radiolab.' You Don't Have to Know Anything, Because They Don't Know Anything." *South Florida Sun-Sentinel*, January 27, 2012.

Crawford, Chris. "Fundamentals of Interactivity." *Journal of Computer Game Design* 7 (1993–1994). Accessed February 26, 2018. http://www.erasmatazz.com/library/the-journal-of-computer/jcgd-volume-7/fundamentals-of-interactivi.html.

Cropley, Arthur. "In Praise of Convergent Thinking." *Creativity Research Journal* 18 (3) (2006): 391–404.

Cropley, David, and Arthur Cropley. "A Psychological Taxonomy of Organizational Innovation: Resolving the Paradoxes." *Creativity Research Journal* 24 (1) (2012): 29–41.

Cross, Nigel. "Designerly Ways of Knowing: Design Discipline versus Design Science." *Design Issues* 17 (3) (2001): 49–55.

Csikszentmihalyi, Mihalyi. *Flow: The Psychology of Optimal Experience*. New York: Harper Perennial, 2008.

Dall'Alba, Gloria. "Learning Professional Ways of Being: Ambiguities of Becoming." In *Exploring Education through Phenomenology: Diverse Approaches*, ed. Gloria Dall'Alba, 41–52. Malden, MA: Wiley-Blackwell, 2009.

de Bruin, Anique B. H., Ellen M. Kok, Jimmie Leppink, and Gino Camp. "It Might Happen in the Very Beginning: Reply to Ericsson." *Intelligence* 45 (2014): 107–108.

DeDomenici, Richard. "Embracing Failure." In *Failure! Experiments in Aesthetic and Social Practices*, ed. Nicole Antebi, Colin Dickey, and Robby Herbst, 83–94. Los Angeles: Journal of Aesthetics and Protest Press, 2008.

Dekker, Sidney. Drift into Failure: From Hunting Broken Components to Understanding Complex Systems. Farnham, UK: Ashgate, 2011.

Dreyfuss, Henry. *Designing for People*. New York: Simon and Schuster, 1955.

"Dufresne Prepares End of NYC Modernist Mecca." *New York Times*, September 30, 2014. https://www.nytimes.com/reuters/2014/09/30/us/30reuters-world-chefs-dufresne.html.

Dweck, Carol. *Mindset: The New Psychology of Success.* New York: Random House, 2006.

Edmondson, Amy C. "Strategies for Learning from Failure." *Harvard Business Review,* April 2011. https://hbr.org/2011/04/strategies-for-learning-from-failure.

Ericsson, K. Anders. "Why Expert Performance Is Special and Cannot Be Extrapolated from Studies of Performance in the General Population: A Response to Criticisms." *Intelligence* 45 (2014): 81–103.

Ericsson, K. Anders, Ralf Th. Krampe, and Clemens Tesch-Römer. "The Role of Deliberate Practice in the Acquisition of Expert Performance." *Psychological Review* 100 (3) (1993): 363–403.

Ericsson, K. Anders, and Andreas C. Lehmann. "Expert and Exceptional Performance: Evidence of Maximal Adaptation to Task Constraints." *Annual Review of Psychology* 47 (February 1996): 273–305.

Ericsson, Anders, and Robert Pool. "Malcolm Gladwell Got Us Wrong: Our Research Was Key to the 10,000-Hour Rule, but Here's What Got Oversimplified." *Salon,* April 10, 2016. https://www.salon.com/2016/04/10/malcolm_gladwell_got_us_wrong _our_research_was_key_to_the_10000_hour_rule_but_heres_what_got _oversimplified/.

Essmaker, Ryan, and Tina Essmaker. "Baratunde Thurston: Comedian, Entrepreneur, Writer." *The Great Discontent,* December 3, 2013. http://thegreatdiscontent.com/ interview/baratunde-thurston.

"Failure Now an Option." *The Onion,* January 16, 2008. https://www.theonion.com/ article/failure-now-an-option-2364.

Feynman, Richard. *The Feynman Lectures on Physics.* Vol. I. New York: Basic Books, 2010.

Fukuoka, Masanobu. The One-Straw Revolution: An Introduction to Natural Farming. New York: New York Review Books, 2010.

Gladwell, Malcolm. "The Bakeoff: Competing to Create the Ultimate Cookie." *New Yorker,* September 5, 2005, 124–130.

Gladwell, Malcolm. *Outliers: The Story of Success.* New York: Back Bay Books, 2011.

Gladwell, Malcolm. "The Physical Genius." *New Yorker,* August 2, 1999. https:// www.newyorker.com/magazine/1999/08/02/the-physical-genius.

Gonzales Crisp, Denise. "'Splainin' Craft: Bringing the Making into Writing." *Design and Culture* 6 (3) (2014): 413–422.

Gordon, Bryony. "Paul Merton: Why Tories Make the Best TV Presenters." *Telegraph*, May 23, 2011. https://www.telegraph.co.uk/culture/comedy/8526040/Paul-Merton -Why-Tories-make-the-best-TV-presenters.html.

Grimes, William. "Chef's Second Course Is Food for Thought." *New York Times*, June 18, 2003.

Gross, Mark Donald. "Design as Exploring Constraints." Ph.D. diss., Massachusetts Institute of Technology, 1986.

Guilford, Joy Paul. "Creative Abilities in the Arts." *Psychological Review* 6 (2) (1957): 110–118.

Guilford, Joy Paul. "Creativity." *American Psychologist* 5 (9) (1950): 444–454.

Guilford, Joy Paul. "The Structure of Intellect." *Psychological Bulletin* 53 (1956): 267–293.

Halberstam, Judith. *The Queer Art of Failure*. Durham: Duke University Press, 2011.

Hallnäs, Lars. "The Design Research Text and the Poetics of Foundational Definitions." In "Art Text." Special issue, *Art Monitor* 8xt (2010): 109–117.

Hambrick, David Z., Frederick L. Oswald, Erik M. Altmann, Elizabeth J. Meinz, Fernand Gobet, and Guillermo Campitelli. "Deliberate Practice: Is That All It Takes to Become an Expert?" *Intelligence* 45 (2014): 34–45.

Hamilton, LaMont. "Five on the Black Hand Side: Origins and Evolutions of the Dap." *Smithsonian Center for Folklife and Cultural Heritage Magazine*, September 22, 2014. https://www.folklife.si.edu/talkstory/2014/five-on-the-black-hand-sideorigins -and-evolutions-of-the-dap.

Heathfield, Adrian. "Introduction to the Launch of the Institute of Failure." Transcript from a talk given at the launch event for the Institute of Failure. London, 2001.

Holman, Cas. "The Case for Letting Kids Design Their Own Play." *Fast Company*, July 13, 2015. https://www.fastcodesign.com/3048508/the-case-for-letting-kids -design-their-own-play.

Holman, Cas. "Cas Holman: Identity in Play." YouTube video, January 23, 2015. https://www.youtube.com/watch?v=IL1n6LuUIcQ.

hooks, bell. Teaching Critical Thinking: Practical Wisdom. New York: Routledge, 2010

Houde, Stephanie, and Charles Hill. "What Do Prototypes Prototype?" In *Handbook of Human-Computer Interaction*, ed. Martin G. Helander et al., 367–382. Amsterdam: Elsevier, 1997.

Hunt, Jamer. "Among Six Types of Failure, Only a Few Help You Innovate." *Fast Company*, June 27, 2011. Accessed January 30, 2018. https://www.fastcodesign.com/1664360/among-six-types-of-failure-only-a-few-help-you-innovate.

"Jad Abumrad: Embrace the 'Gut Churn' of the Creative Process." *99U* podcast. 2012. Accessed March 3, 2018. https://www.youtube.com/watch?v=8OH9p3hnWCY.

"Jad Abumrad, Radio Host and Producer." MacArthur Foundation website, September 20, 2011. https://www.macfound.org/fellows/1/.

"Jad and Robert: The Early Years." *Radiolab* podcast, May 6, 2008. https://www.radiolab.org/story/91820-jad-and-robert-the-early-years/.

July, Miranda. *The First Bad Man: A Novel*. New York: Scribner, 2015.

July, Miranda. *It Chooses You*. New York: McSweeney's, 2012.

July, Miranda. *No One Belongs Here More Than You: Stories*. New York: Scribner, 2008.

Juul, Jesper. The Art of Failure: An Essay on the Pain of Playing Video Games. Cambridge, MA: MIT Press, 2013.

Kaufman, David, and the U.S. Digital Service. "The Unlikely Relationship between Comedy and Code: A Conversation with Baratunde Thurston." Medium, July 14, 2016. https://medium.com/the-u-s-digital-service/the-unlikely-relationship-between-comedy-and-code-a-conversation-with-baratunde-thurston-6253a38b81b.

Kaufman, James C. *Creativity 101*. 2nd ed. New York: Springer, 2016. Kindle.

Kaufman, James C., and Ronald A. Beghetto. "Beyond Big and Little: The Four C Model of Creativity." In *Review of General Psychology* 13 (1) (2009): 1–12.

Khandwalla, Pradip N. "An Exploratory Investigation of Divergent Thinking through Protocol Analysis." *Creativity Research Journal* 6 (1993): 241–259.

Kharkhurin, Anatoliy V. "Creativity.4in1: Four-Criterion Construct of Creativity." *Creativity Research Journal* 26 (3) (2014): 338–352.

Kimbell, Lucy. "Rethinking Design Thinking: Part I." *Design and Culture* 3 (3) (2011): 285–306.

Kimbell, Lucy. "Rethinking Design Thinking: Part II." *Design and Culture* 4 (2) (2012): 129–148.

Krulwich, Robert. "Speech to the Chamber Music Society of America." January 5, 2018.

Larman, Craig, and Victor R. Basili. "Iterative and Incremental Development: A Brief History." *Computer* 36 (5) (June 2003): 2–11.

Lave, Jean, and Etienne Wenger. *Situated Learning: Legitimate Peripheral Participation*. Cambridge, UK: Cambridge University Press, 1991.

Leski, Kyna. *The Storm of Creativity*. Cambridge, MA: MIT Press, 2015.

Macklin, Colleen, and John Sharp. *Iterate Project*. Accessed January 30, 2018. http://www.iterateproject.com.

Macklin, Colleen, and John Sharp. *Games, Design and Play: A Detailed Approach to Iterative Game Design*. Boston: Addison-Wesley Professional, 2016.

Macnamara, Brooke N., David Z. Hambrick, and Frederick L. Oswald. "Deliberate Practice and Performance in Music, Games, Sports, Education, and Professions: A Meta-Analysis." *Psychological Science* 25 (8) (2014): 1608–1618.

Mallett, Whitney. "Miranda July and Paul Ford Cyberstalked Me." Motherboard, *Vice*, May 18, 2016. http://motherboard.vice.com/en_us/article/miranda-july-and-paul-ford-cyberstalked-me.

Maloney, Matthew. "Here Goes Nothing." *Angry Animation* blog, March 9, 2012. https://angry-animation.com/2012/03/09/hello-world/.

Mamet, David. *On Directing Film*. New York: Penguin, 1992.

Marsalis, Wynton. "Marsalis: Racism and Greed Put Blues at the Back of the Bus." *CNN* online, October 24, 2009. http://www.cnn.com/2009/OPINION/10/24/wynton.marsalis.blues.race/.

McAllister, Ben. "The 'Science' of Good Design: A Dangerous Idea." *Atlantic*, May 11, 2011. https://www.theatlantic.com/business/archive/2011/05/the-science-of-good-design-a-dangerous-idea/238750/.

McCloud, Scott. *Understanding Comics: The Invisible Art*. New York: HarperPerennial, 1994.

McGovern, Patrick E. Uncorking the Past: The Quest for Wine, Beer, and Other Alcoholic Beverages. Berkeley: University of California Press, 2009.

Meadows, Donella H. *Thinking in Systems: A Primer*. White River Junction, VT: Chelsea Green Publishing, 2008.

Milne, Andy. "About." Andy Milne website. Accessed February 26, 2018, https://andymilne.com/about-2/.

"Miranda July in Conversation with Jeremy Deller." Vimeo video, October 20, 2017. https://vimeo.com/239133702.

"Miranda July's New Society." Frieze video, December 18, 2015. https://frieze.com/media/miranda-julys-new-society.

Moskin, Julia. "Time to Face the Music." *New York Times*, February 26, 2003. https://www.nytimes.com/2003/02/26/dining/time-to-face-the-music.html.

Mulder, M. P. "Humour Research: State of the Art." Center for Telematics and Information Technology, TKI-Parlevink Research Group, University of Twente, The Netherlands. 2002. Accessed March 1, 2018. http://www.ub.utwente.nl/webdocs/ctit/1/0000009e.pdf.

Mumford, Michael. "Creative Abilities: Divergent Thinking." In *Handbook of Organizational Creativity*, ed. Michael Mumford, 115–139. New York: Academic Press, 2012.

Myers, Christopher G., Bradley R. Staats, and Francesca Gino. "'My Bad!' How Internal Attribution and Ambiguity of Responsibility Affect Learning from Failure." Working paper, Harvard Business School, April 18, 2014.

Neilson, Laura. "Plate Deconstruction: WD~50's Scrambled Egg Ravioli." Food Republic, August 16, 2012. http://www.foodrepublic.com/2012/08/16/plate-deconstruction -wd50s-scrambled-egg-ravioli/.

Noveck, Jocelyn. "Food World's 'Mad Scientist' Dufresne Ponders Next Steps." Willoughby, OH *News-Herald*, May 15, 2015.

Oatman, Maddie. "Radiolab's Jad Abumrad Tries Something Completely Nuts." *Mother Jones*, July/August 2012. https://www.motherjones.com/media/2012/05/jad -abumrad-radiolab-robert-krulwich-in-the-dark.

Osborn, Alex F. Applied Imagination: Principles and Procedures of Creative Problem-Solving. Rev. ed. New York: Charles Scribner's Sons, 1979.

Parker, Robert. "Colgin." *Robert Parker's Wine Advocate*, no. 209, October 2013.

Parker, Trey, and Matt Stone. "Gnomes." *South Park*. Episode 17 (December 16, 1998).

Patronite, Rob, and Robin Raisfeld. "Wylie Dufresne Debuts Egg Sandwich Like No Other at Du's Donuts." *Grubstreet*, June 12, 2017. http://www.grubstreet.com/2017/06/ wylie-dufresne-debuts-egg-sandwich-at-dus-donuts-and-coffee.html.

Petroski, Henry. *Success through Failure: The Paradox of Design*. Princeton, NJ: Princeton University Press, 2006.

Petroski, Henry. *To Forgive Design: Understanding Failure*. Cambridge, MA: Belknap Press of Harvard University Press, 2012.

Plucker, Jonathan A. "Introduction to the Special Issue: Commemorating Guilford's 1950 Presidential Address." *Creativity Research Journal* 13 (3–4) (2000–2001): 247.

Puccio, Gerard J., and John F. Cabra. "Idea Generation and Idea Evaluation: Cognitive Skills and Deliberate Practices." In *Handbook of Organizational Creativity*, ed. Michael Mumford, 189–215. New York: Academic Press, 2012.

"Radiolab." *Charlie Rose* TV program, January 2, 2013. https://charlierose.com/videos/17886.

"Radiolab: Audio Learning and Augmented Narrative." *American Hipster Presents.* Accessed March 3, 2018. http://americanhipsterpresents.com/#radiolab.

"Radiolab's Jad Abumrad on Creativity, Failure and the Virtues of Wonder." *Radiowaves* podcast, December 12, 2014. Accessed March 3, 2018. https://www.youtube.com/watch?v=T5jtFzn5-n0.

"Radiolab (WNYC-FM)." Peabody Foundation website, 2010. http://www.peabodyawards.com/award-profile/radiolab.

Raisfeld, Robin, and Rob Patronite. "He Is the Egg Man." *New York*, November 26, 2007. http://nymag.com/restaurants/features/30007/.

Rhizome, "Seven on Seven 2016: Miranda July & Paul Ford." Vimeo video, May 18, 2016. https://vimeo.com/167171454.

"Rigamajig." Kaboom! Accessed March 1, 2018, https://kaboom.org/resources/rigamajig.

"Robert Krulwich." *Radiowaves* podcast, March 4, 2015. Accessed January 30, 2018. https://www.youtube.com/watch?v=4QkOZv2aJQs.

Runco, Mark A. "Introduction to the Special Issue: Commemorating Guilford's 1950 Presidential Address." *Creativity Research Journal* 13 (3–4) (2000–2001): 247.

Russell, Ruby. "Learning to Love You More: Spread a Little Love." *Telegraph*, January 14, 2009. https://www.telegraph.co.uk/culture/art/4238338/Learning-to-Love-You-More-spread-a-little-love.html.

Salen-Tekinbas, Katie, and Eric Zimmerman. *Rules of Play: Game Design Fundamentals.* Cambridge, MA: MIT Press, 2003.

Sandler, Matthew. "Gertrude Stein, Success Manuals, and Failure Studies." *Twentieth-Century Literature* 63 (2) (June 2017): 191–212.

Schön, Donald A. The Reflective Practitioner: How Professionals Think in Action. New York: Basic Books, 1983.

Schulz, Kathryn. *Being Wrong: Adventures in the Margin of Error.* New York: Ecco Press, 2010.

Schwartz, Jonathan. "Will Rogers, Populist Cowboy." Review of *Will Rogers: A Political Life*, by Richard D. White Jr. *New York Times*, March 25, 2011. https://www.nytimes.com/2011/03/27/books/review/book-review-will-rogers-a-political-life-by-richard-d-white-jr.html.

Sedbon, Lara. "Art, Architecture, and Gaming Meet in Interference: Q&A with Eric Zimmerman and Nathalie Pozzi." Creators Project, *Vice*, July 19, 2012. https://

creators.vice.com/en_us/article/4x4jgb/art-architecture-and-gaming-meet-in
-iinterferencei-qa-with-eric-zimmerman-and-nathalie-pozzi.

Solnit, Rebecca. *A Field Guide to Getting Lost.* New York: Viking, 2005.

"Sound and Science with Jad Abumrad." *Poptech*, December 1, 2010. Accessed January 31, 2018. https://www.youtube.com/watch?v=ILZYGrRlQkI.

Sperrazza, Gary. "Holding On: Original Soul Men." *Time Barrier Express: The Rock & Roll History Magazine*, September-October 1979.

Stamwitz, Alicia von. "If Only We Would Listen: Parker J. Palmer on What We Could Learn about Politics, Faith and Each Other." *The Sun*, no. 443 (November 2012). https://www.thesunmagazine.org/issues/443/if_only_we_would_listen

Suchman, Lucy A. Plans and Situated Actions: The Problem of Human-Machine Communication. Palo Alto, CA: Xerox Corporation, 1985.

Sutton-Smith, Brian. *Toys as Culture.* New York: Gardner Press, 1986.

Tarkovsky, Andrey. *Sculpting in Time.* Austin: University of Texas Press, 1989.

Thurston, Baratunde. "#Unplug: Baratunde Thurston Left the Internet for 25 Days, and You Should, Too." *Fast Company*, June 17, 2013. https://www.fastcompany.com/3012521/baratunde-thurston-leaves-the-internet.

Thurston, Baratunde. *How to Be Black.* New York: Harper, 2012.

Thurston, Baratunde. "In 1993, This Is What I Wrote about the Internet Coming to My High School." Medium, July 2, 2015. https://medium.com/@baratunde/in-1993-this-is-what-i-wrote-about-the-internet-coming-to-my-high-school-28be8bcfdaf8.

Thurston, Baratunde. "Occupy Sparkle: The Full 'Box Set' of My Twilight #Livehatetweeting." Baratunde Thurston, November 16, 2012. http://baratunde.com/blog/2012/11/16/occupy-sparkle-the-full-box-set-of-my-twilight-livehatetweet.html.

Thurston, Baratunde. "Why Life Is a Scam." *Harvard Crimson*, April 6, 1999. https://www.thecrimson.com/article/1999/4/6/why-life-is-a-scam-ibaratunde/.

Tilley, Alvin R., and Henry Dreyfuss. *The Measure of Man and Woman: Human Factors in Design.* Rev. ed. New York: Wiley, 2001.

Wallas, Graham. *The Art of Thought.* New York: Harcourt, Brace, 1926.

Watson, John. *Behaviorism.* London: K. Paul, 1928.

Weisberg, Robert W. "On the Usefulness of 'Value' in the Definition of Creativity." *Creativity Research Journal* 27 (2) (2015): 111–124.

Wenger, Etienne. *Communities of Practice: Learning, Meaning, and Identity.* Cambridge: Cambridge University Press, 1998.

Wilson, Calvin. "Roscoe Mitchell Is a True Jazz Great." *St. Louis Post-Dispatch*, December 5, 2014. https://www.stltoday.com/entertainment/music/roscoe-mitchell -is-a-true-jazz-great/article_62c7125b-c299-50b2-853c-b8000a0ba3c0.html.

Wine Spectator. "2011 Vintage Report: California." *Wine Spectator*, November 17, 2011 https://www.winespectator.com/webfeature/show/id/46008

Yang, Maria C. "A Study of Prototypes, Design Activity, and Design Outcome." *Design Studies* 26 (6) (October 2005): 649–669.

Index

Page numbers followed by f indicate figures.